SAYINGS OF
SRI RAMAKRISHNA

SAYINGS OF
SRI RAMAKRISHNA

BY
SRI RAMAKRISHNA

GYAN

Published by

GYAN

Gyan Publishing House
5, Ansari Road
Daryaganj, New Delhi-110002
Phone: 011-47034999, 9811692060
E-mail: books@gyanbooks.com

Distribution Network
gyanbooks.com
India, USA, Canada, UK, Australia

ISBN: 978-93-6433-360-3 (PB)
First Published, 1920

2nd Impression 2024

Printed at: Gyan Press, Delhi.

SAYINGS OF SRI RAMAKRISHNA
Author: SRI RAMAKRISHNA

SRI RAMAKRISHNA IN A HIGH STATE OF YOGA

SAYINGS OF

SRI RAMAKRISHNA

THE MOST EXHAUSTIVE COLLECTION OF THEM,
THEIR NUMBER BEING 1120

SRI RAMAKRISHNA MATH
MYLAPORE, MADRAS, INDIA
1949

Published by
THE PRESIDENT
SRI RAMAKRISHNA MATH
MYLAPORE, MADRAS

Seventh Revised Edition

Printed by
C. SUBBARAYUDU
AT THE VASANTA PRESS
THE THEOSOPHICAL SOCIETY
ADYAR, MADRAS

CONTENTS

BOOK III

MAN AND THE DIVINE

BOOK IV

MAXIMS AND PARABLES

INTRODUCTION

I

THE sayings and parables of Sri Ramakrishna included in this volume speak for themselves as far as their spiritual value and philosophic depth are concerned. The stamp of genius they bear cannot escape the notice of even a casual reader. But wise maxims and admirable reflections on life have been given also by great intellectuals and first-rate literary men. The sayings embodied in this volume should, however, be distinguished from the productions of such men. For with all their artistic beauty and sublimity of thought, the writings of one, who is merely an academic philosopher or a man of letters, lack authority in matters relating to God and spiritual life, since their author is only groping in the dark, just like any plain man, as far as these subjects of transcendental significance are concerned. The sayings of Sri Ramakrishna stand on quite a different footing in this respect, because Sri Ramakrishna possessed not only a great intellect and an artistic mind, but had the additional qualification that he had 'seen God face to face', 'talked with Him' and shared the Divine life. Hence his words on these transcendental themes come with a weight of authority derived from the Supreme Being Himself. Our excuse for writing the following brief life-sketch of his as an Introduction to this edition of his sayings, is that there may be, among its readers, persons who have had no occasion to study any detailed biography of his and to be acquainted with this unique aspect of his life and teachings.

II

Sri Ramakrishna was born in a poor Brahmin family of the village called Kamarpukur in Bengal, on the 17th February, 1836. His father Khudiram Chatterjee was a man of great piety and uprightness of character. His adherence to truth was so great that he would not break this cherished principle of his life even when he found that its observance meant utter ruin to himself and his family. Once when bidden by the landlord of the village to bear false witness in his favour, Khudiram refused to do so, and in his wrath at the defiance of this virtuous Brahmin, the big man of the village despoiled him of all his earthly possessions. His mother Chandramani Devi too was a paragon of womanly virtues. And tradition has it that this pious couple had many Divine visions and experiences before the birth of Sri Ramakrishna, indicative of the divinity of their Gadadhar, as they called their son in his early days.

From his infancy Sri Ramakrishna showed signs of the great power of personality that became a distinguishing feature of his in later life. As a boy he could easily fascinate people, and become the darling of his elders and the beloved leader of his own playmates. He had the soul of an artist that revelled in Nature's beauties, and caught the subtle shades of difference in sounds and images as well as in the formation of the faces and muscles of men. The favourite pastimes of his boyhood therefore consisted in mimicry, portraiture, clay-modelling, dramatic performances, devotional music and contemplation of epic heroes and heroines. And it was perhaps the artist in him that led him to revolt against the dull routine of the school and its curriculum of stereotyped studies, and show special dislike for exact sciences like mathematics. But his keen intellectual powers and prodigious memory more than compensated for this dislike of academic study. He educated himself in a higher sense by mastering the Hindu epics embodying the great spiritual ideals of India through listening to their recital and exposition by scholars, and above all by going direct to Nature to study men and things through observation.

Among the boys of his age he was noted for his courage and stubborn spirit of independence. Even from infancy he knew no shyness or timidity. Full of health and vigour, he would never allow himself to be bullied or put down by elders when he considered himself in the right. In the face of some of the influential elders of the village he defied the rules of Purdah (the system of secluding women) which he considered in themselves to be of no use in educating women in high ideals of character. He must have been considered a revolutionary by many in that conservative village when, on the occasion of his Upanayana ceremony (investiture with sacred thread), he insisted, in the face of much opposition, on receiving his first Bhiksha or alms from a blacksmith woman, according to the promise he had made to her previously.

But the young rebel was not without the quality of reverence. For love of God was ingrained in him from childhood, and both in the worship of the Deity in his own house as well as in the religious activities of the village in general, he took a leading part. From early life he had a fancy for wandering ascetics, and he mixed and conversed with them freely whenever he got an opportunity. With the advance of years his devotional inclinations took a more definite form. Enwrapped in Divine contemplation, he was often seen to pass into high spiritual moods that culminated in ecstasy. The most noteworthy occasions of such occurrences in his early days were mainly three—once while observing a flight of snow-white cranes against a dark sky overcast with sombre thunderclouds, next in the course of enacting the part of Siva in a village drama, and again while singing songs in praise of the Deity during a pilgrimage. And it was this devotional strain that ultimately dominated over the leader, the artist and the rebel in him, and organised the diverse qualities of his personality in the service of the supreme spiritual ideal, the achievement of which made him one of the noted figures in modern times.

III

The proper environment for the full development of Sri Ramakrishna's personality was provided by the Kali temple of Dakshineswar in Calcutta, founded by the Rani Rasmani in 1855. The daily round of pious duties as the chief priest in the Divine Mother's temple fanned the fire of devotion in him. He was observed to spend hours in deep meditation and in singing devotional songs. It was also found that he was spending a large part of his nights in contemplation in the jungly regions of the garden, quite bereft of all clothing and even the sacred thread. In his method of worship the rigid observance of rituals was noticed to give place gradually to an informality of procedure born of a sense of intimacy with the object of worship.

All this was only the sign of the storm that was raging in his soul—the passionate longing to know whether the Mother whom he worshipped was real or not. As days passed, this longing became so great that one day he was about to put an end to his own life in despair. Suddenly the screens that hid the Truth from his soul's eyes disappeared, and passing into a state of ecstasy, he had a vision of the Divinity as 'a boundless, effulgent Ocean of Intelligence'. The solace and the sense of Divine presence accompanying this experience did not, however, last for many days. He found that it gave him only a glimpse of the higher life, but did not enrich his consciousness with a perpetual experience of the Divinity. Hence this first flight of the soul only went to whet his appetite for the Divine, and in the period of dryness that soon followed, he was filled with a longing, even more powerful than the previous, to feel the presence of God everywhere and at all times. The intensity of the urge was so great that he practically lost all sense of reality for the external world. Without any thought of even food or sleep, he began to spend his whole time in praying to the Divine Mother in the agony of his soul. It became impossible for him to perform the daily worship of the Deity in the temple any longer. Therefore Mathuranath, the manager of the temple and son-in-law of Rani Rasmani, who had by this time contracted great affection and respect for Sri Ramakrishna, relieved him of his duties in the temple, and gave him every facility to pursue his spiritual inclinations. And Sri Ramakrishna utilised this opportunity to plunge himself into prayer, meditation and ascetic practices with an intensity of spiritual aspiration that has seldom been witnessed in the world. Often, seized with a desperate longing, he was seen to rub his face on the ground until it bled.

Describing this insatiable longing of his soul for God, he said to his disciples in later days that it was something like the organic craving that a man kept under water felt for a breath of air. Again he used to say that one could have a hazy idea of that craving for God if one could imagine a concentration of these three types of attachments —a miser's fondness for his hoarded wealth, a noble lady's love of her husband, and a parent's affection for an only child.

About this time he went on a visit to his village at Kamarpukar. His mother thought that if he married, his madness for God and supreme unconcern for the world would be checked, and that he would naturally come back to normal ways of living in course of time. Accordingly in 1859 he was wedded to Saradamani Devi, a little girl of five, daughter of Ramachandra Mukhopadhyaya of a neighbouring village. Though this marriage was destined to have important consequences in his later days, it did not have the intended effect of abating his zeal for God. For immediately after his return to Dakshineswar in 1860, his soul was again caught in the same cyclonic passion of God-love.

Till now his spiritual strivings may be described as a solitary and unaided quest. From this time onwards many great spiritual teachers went to him, as if sent by Divine Providence, to help him in his search after God, and with their guidance he began to practise various spiritual disciplines as enjoined in the scriptures.

There are two outstanding features that distinguish Sri Ramakrishna from other spiritual aspirants in this aspect of his life. One is the rapidity with which he attained success in each Sadhana (spiritual practice), which may be explained as due to the intensity of his quest. The other is the variety of Sadhanas he underwent, which is unprecedented in the spiritual history of mankind.

The first of his teachers to arrive was Bhairavi, the Brahmani, who met Sri Ramakrishna in 1861. She was a middle-aged Brahmin woman of great learning and high spiritual attainments; and under her guidance he successfully underwent all the principal spiritual practices mentioned in the sixty-four Tantras of the Sakta cult. All these practices relate to the worship of the Deity as the Divine Mother of the universe, and several of them are so difficult to follow that none but those who are perfect masters of the senses, and are capable of seeing the Divinity in everything, can practise them with advantage or safety. His successful pursuit of them gives one a fair idea of the great purity of his mind and his innate spiritual genius. Besides bestowing on him the realisation of the Divine Mother in Her diverse aspects, this discipline of Mother-worship established him in the conviction that every woman is a manifestation and a symbol of the Divine Mother in a special sense.

The Vaishnava form of Sadhana was another type of spiritual discipline that Sri Ramakrishna practised. The Vaishnavas worship the Deity by cultivating various forms of personal relationship with Him, known as Bhavas or attitudes, as those of the servant towards the Master (Dasya), of the friend towards a friend (Sakhya), of the parent towards the child (Vatsalya), and of the beloved towards her sweet-heart (Madhura). Sri Ramakrishna adopted all these attitudes one after another, and while doing so, he used to identify himself with the classical personalities with whom a particular attitude has been traditionally associated—with Mahavir for Dasyabhava, with Radha for Madhura-bhava, and so on. During such periods of identification, he used to live like those very personalities and express in himself their consciousness and behaviour. Thus for many months he lived like a woman, in the company of women, while practising the Sakhya and Madhura forms of Sadhana; and neither he nor the ladies in whose company he lived felt any sense of strangeness or artificiality in this. So radical was the transformation he could effect at will on his consciousness and even on his physical life.

Next in 1864 he came into contact with a great Vedantin of the non-dualistic school, an itinerant monk named Totapuri. Sri Ramakrishna was initiated by him into the life of Sannyasa. Till now he was worshipping the Deity as the Divine Personality endowed with attributes.

From Totapuri he learnt the method of contemplating on Him in His attributeless and impersonal aspect. So ripe was his mind for this highest form of spiritual discipline that within a period of three days after his initiation, he attained the Nirvikalpa-samadhi or the state of unconditioned consciousness, which the Advaita scriptures speak of as the goal of all the spiritual endeavours of man. And after Totapuri had left Dakshineswar at the close of nearly an year's stay in the temple, Sri Ramakrishna remained in the non-dual state of Nirvikalpa-samadhi continuously for six months.

In 1866 he received initiation in Islamic spiritual practices from a Sufi ascetic named Govinda, and discovered that that path also ultimately led to the same spiritual realisation which the Hindu systems of spiritual discipline had given him. Some time later he meditated on Christ and his ideals, and found the goal of that path also to be identical with that of the other religions.

The long period of Sri Ramakrishna's spiritual practices came to a close in 1872 with the inspiring rite known as the Shodasi Pooja when he worshipped his own wedded wife as the symbol of the Deity. His girl wife, Saradamani Devi, had by this time grown up into a young woman. During these years she had seen her husband only on two or three occasions. In 1872 she went to Dakshineswar, anxious as she was to serve her husband whom the village gossip described as mad. Quite unlike an ordinary ascetic, Sri Ramakrishna received her kindly, and did everything to educate her in secular and spiritual matters. Her presence at Dakshineswar also helped him to test his own realisation and sense-control, but in every form of crucial test, he found that he was above all bodily cravings, and that he could view every woman, including his own wife, as a manifestation of the Divine Mother. In token of this attainment, he placed his own wife before him as the Deity, offered her worship with all the proper rituals, surrendered all the fruits of his spiritual practices at the feet of the Deity manifest as the pure virgin, and at the close of the worship entered into deep Samadhi.

IV

The Shodasi Pooja is supposed to mark the close of Sri Ramakrishna's life as an aspirant (Sadhakabhava), and herald the period of his spiritual ministration as the world-teacher (Gurubhava). After this time his insatiable craving for practising spiritual disciplines abated. In place of it he felt the unshakable conviction of truth within himself. What was more, he began to have a vivid consciousness of the mighty spiritual power and wisdom that the Divine Mother was manifesting through his body and mind, and he felt an intense longing to minister unto the spiritual needs of men.

Indeed, a detailed study of his life-incidents would show that from his boyhood onwards there was present in him the inborn quality of a teacher, and that gleams of spiritual wisdom emanating from him used to enlighten the hearts of men every now and then. This became more and more prominent in the course of his spiritual practices. His attitude towards Rani Rasmani and Mathuranath, the proprietors of Dakshineswar temple, was not that of an employee, but that of an intimate friend at ordinary times, and that of their lord and saviour in his exalted spiritual moods. Persons who came to teach him often learned from him more than what they taught him. By his contact Bhairavi, the Brahmani, had the defects of her character rectified and came to be endowed with supreme renunciation. From him, Totapuri, his spiritual preceptor in the path of Advaita, learned the secret of the love of the Personal God, to which he was a stranger before. Besides, when he went on pilgrimage with Mathuranath in 1870, many an aspirant in the holy places he visited drew inspiration from his company. And what was more, from time to time innumerable ascetics of various orders were flocking to Dakshineswar, and most of the sincere aspirants among them received spiritual help from him. Among these aspirants were also some of the scholarly Pandits of those days like Vaishnavacharan, Padmalochan, Gauri and Narayan Sastri, who were so filled with inspiration in his company that they looked upon him as an Incarnation of Godhead.

Thus from his early days the mood of the teacher was present in him. But it was, however, occasional, the dominant attitude of his till now being that of a Sadhaka or spiritual aspirant. But after the Shodasi Pooja the ardour of the spiritual aspirant got transformed into the intensity of the redeeming love of the world-teacher.

Sri Ramakrishna was now a Divya, a divine man. His awareness of God had become perpetual, and did not depend on any particular state of mind like ecstasy, although the phenomenon of ecstasy continued to be a frequent occurrence with him till the last. The state of mind that he had gained may be described in terms of Christian mysticism as theopathetic, or in his own words as Bhava-mukha—a state in which the mind could ever dwell in the Divine both in His absolute and relative aspects, and yet, without the least distraction to this union, apply itself actively to everyday concerns of life. That his experience of God was not an imaginary state or a degenerate sub-normal condition, we know from its effect on his character, which, in its power and purity, stands in striking contrast with that of the so-called great and mighty men of the world. Unlike even the best and greatest of them, he was established in a state of peace, poise and radiant joy, which could not in the least be affected by any change of worldly fortune. He was absolutely free from carnality, and in all women, whether noble or fallen, he saw the expression of the Divine Mother. Nor had he any selfish attachment to possessions, —a trait of character which he expressed by developing in himself a spontaneous inability to possess anything or even to touch any metal. For in the period of Sadhana he used to take mud and precious metal in hand and throw them both into the Ganges, discriminating within himself that, though their value differed in point of purchasing worldly goods, they were both alike, and to an equal degree worthless, in gaining for oneself the realisation of God. This idea went so deep into him that in course of time he began to feel even physical pain at the touch of any metal, and a violent shock in body and mind when anybody offered him money or property. He was also devoid of all worldly snobbery and discrimination against men placed in low positions of life, and this he symbolised by cleaning the dirty places in the huts of scavengers with his own long matted hair. His adherence to truth was something phenomenal. Not only did his habit of truthfulness extend to the major issues of life, but even to petty matters like an agreement to visit a place on a particular day, or to take a medicine from a particular person and not another. Even if his conscious mind happened to forget a promise or an agreement, his body reminded him of it by refusing to act in any way that would be contrary to his words. Indeed, he said that when he surrendered everything to the Divine Mother, he could not surrender the virtue of truthfulness: for, if that was done, the very truth of his self-surrender would be falsified. And withal, he possessed such wonderful powers of personality, of which we shall say more in the succeeding sections.

V

Although this phase of his life as the world-teacher might be said to have begun from 1872, his spiritual ministry reached its climax only after 1875 when he got acquainted with great Brahmo leader Keshub Chandra Sen. Keshub's public utterances and writings about him attracted the notice of the educated men of Calcutta to him, and a constant stream of them, both young and old, began to visit him, attracted by the power of his love and holiness. Among those who met him and held him in great respect may be mentioned the names of many of India's best thinkers, writers and leaders of those days, like Keshub Chandra Sen, Pratap Chandra Mazumdar, Sivanath Sastri, Vijay Krishna Goswami, Devendra Nath Tagore, Iswar Chandra Vidyasagar, Bankim Chandra Chatterjee, Michael Madhusudan Dutt, Aswini Kumar Dutt and Girish Chandra Ghosh.

From among the many earnest souls who went to him, a good many became very intimate with him, and formed into the group of his devotees through whom his message was destined to be transmitted to the world at large in later days. This group was formed of two sets of people —one, of elderly, married gentlemen settled down in life, and the other, of young school and college boys who had not yet taken upon themselves the responsibilities of life. It was this second group that took to the life of Sannyasa afterwards, and formed into the Ramakrishna Order of monks under the leadership of Swami Vivekananda, then known as Narendranath Datta. The Swami was the special object of Sri Ramakrishna's love and grace, and in later life spread his Master's message far and wide, and made a lasting impression on the consciousness of his countrymen as the great patriot-saint of modern India.

The rest of Sri Ramakrishna's life was spent in teaching these devotees and in moulding their lives in the light of the highest spiritual ideal. The manner and method of his teaching, as well as his relationship with his disciples, were in many respects unique. He never undertook the work of teaching in an egoistic sense. He was the humblest of men, without any sense of ego in him, and he attributed all that he achieved to the Divine Mother of the universe. And it was because of this very fact of his having surrendered his ego completely to the Divine that the Guru Sakti (the redeeming power of the Lord) manifested itself through his body and mind in so remarkable a degree, sanctifying and enlightening all that came within their influence.

Before he accepted people as disciples, he subjected them to very minute tests and got a thorough understanding of their character. He would study their nature by observing their physical features—an art in which he was a past master. He would watch carefully the little actions of their daily life at unguarded moments, and besides gauge their worth by putting them questions and observing their reactions towards his teachings and ideals. In addition to these methods he would also sometimes use his Yogic powers to see into the hearts of men, or to put them into a sort of trance in which they revealed the innermost contents of their minds.

As for those whom he accepted as disciples, he made them his own by the power of his love, the like of which they never received even from their parents. He spared no pains in instructing them, and in seeing that they carried out his instructions into practice. Often by a touch or an act of will, he would obliterate any undesirable tendency he found in them, and bestow on them the highest experiences of spiritual life. The very contact with his dynamic personality, radiant with the flame of holiness and Divine love, imported strength and steadiness to their aspiration for the Divine life. He never entered into arguments with people or delivered academic discourses to them, but just stated his settled convictions on spiritual matters in all humility, and left each person to understand and accept according to his capacity. He never forced his views on any one. Those of his disciples who were critically minded were free to criticise his teachings, and also to test him just as he himself tested them. Such conduct on their part only brought his praise, never his displeasure.

He had the strange capacity to make himself interesting and intelligible to people of diverse temperaments and stages of intellectual development. He could astound learned Pandits like Sasadhar and Iswar Candra Vidyasagar by the profundity of his wisdom, and he could also bring himself to the intellectual level of the ignorant village woman who went to him to get the wounds of her heart healed, or to have her simple doubts cleared. Himself an orthodox Hindu in his life and thought, and quite innocent of modern scientific and social ideas, he could yet have appreciation and sympathy for the ideals and aspirations of champions of reform and rationalism. In his room could therefore meet on friendly terms a Viswanath Upadhyaya and a Keshub Chandra, a Narendranath and a Nag Mahashay, a Dr Mahendra Lal Sircar and a Girish Chandra Ghosh. As in the practice of diverse religions with mutually conflicting traditions, here too the unparalleled catholicity of his mind and heart could alone account for this wide range of his sympathy and his appeal as a teacher to men of diverse temperaments and outlooks. Truly he was the most universal yet most individual of men.

There was with him none of the formal features usually characteristic of the relationship between Guru and disciple, nor did he demand any cringing reverence or any attitude of awful expectancy from those whom he taught. His disciples were more intimate with him than the members of a loving family, and he was to them dearer than their earthly parents. He preached no particular dogma, creed or philosophy. What he did was to convey to people a spirit that transformed their outlook on life and gave them an insight into the ultimate nature of the world and of human personality. In doing this, he relied not on formal sermons and discourses, but on loving contacts, illustrations drawn from Nature, a life of purity and self-control, and above all the practice of silent Japa and meditation. He never failed to impress on his disciples that the scrupulous observance of truth and absolute continence was the unavoidable condition for the realisation of spiritual ideals.

Another remarkable feature of his method was its unconventionality, and its intermingling of the serious and the funny, the sublime and the ridiculous. Almost every day, centering round him, were enacted in his room scenes that by turn inspired, entertained, instructed and consoled those who were present. He would sing devotional songs with an ecstatic abandon, and dance with the joy of the Mother's name. This might be followed by simple and luminous exposition of abstruse metaphysical and ethical problems like the relation between the Impersonal and the Personal God, or the compatibility of God's goodness with the existence of evil in the world. From these thoughts on transcendental wisdom, he could, with the utmost ease, come to sound practical instruction on conduct in the world. He taught the simple-minded Yogen about the ways of bargaining in the market; checked the impetuous Niranjan in his rash actions; taught Hari, the disciple who hated women, to be considerate towards the fair sex; consoled old Mani Mallick in the bereavement of his only son; and reprimanded the brother of S. for neglecting his duty towards wife and children. His instructions, whether on philosophy, devotion or conduct, would take the form of witty sayings, striking analogies and illuminating parables couched in his rustic conversational Bengali of a highly expressive type, and delivered in his sonorous voice with a 'slight though delightful stammer' in it. Often these talks were punctuated with humorous remarks that created side-splitting laughter among his hearers and with masterly caricatures of men and things—of the Kirtani (professional singer of religious songs) receiving rich visitors, of the idle talks of pilgrims going for bath in the Ganges, of hypocritical devotees bargaining with fish-mongers, of domineering widows asserting authority in their brothers' houses, of hen-pecked husbands submissive only to their wives, and of several other features of daily life which revealed great powers of observation and of healthy criticism. In the midst of all this fun and frolic, a slight suggestion would set his mind to a high spiritual pitch, and he would lose himself in devotional fervour, or in deep Samadhi, radiating the influence of his powerful thought on all who were around.

But with all his ecstasy and Divine intoxication, few men could excel him in attention to the minute details of life. He was very particular about personal cleanliness and about the orderliness of the things kept in his room. He disliked to see people going about with torn clothes and shoes, or keeping their houses insufficiently lighted. Whenever he went anywhere on a visit, he always carried the few things required for his personal use, and he advised his disciples never to go to a place at a time or in a manner calculated to cause inconvenience to their host. It is also remarkable that never in his life he came away from a place leaving behind any of his things in forgetfulness, be it shoe, umbrella or cloth. And in spite of all his Samadhi and self-forgetfulness in the thought of God, the powers of his senses were so very keen that when he entered a room, his eagle eyes would at a glance observe all objects present there, and he could, even long after, give exact descriptions of the shape and position of even such of those things as were hardly noticed by others accompanying him.

Thus this great teacher of men spent his life, holding forth before the world the ideal of a perfect man, and actively ministering to the spiritual needs of those who flocked to him, until his delicate frame broke down under the strain of constant teaching. In 1885 he had an attack of cancer of the throat. About a few months later, his devotees took him to Calcutta and put him under the treatment of the famous doctor Mahendra Lal Sircar. With the passing of days, the disease got only aggravated in spite of the best medical aid. But even the prolonged tortures of this excruciating disease could not in the least affect the joy and serenity of his mind, or disturb his perpetual consciousness of the Divine Presence everywhere.

Moreover, this period of physical suffering formed also the most active part of his ministry. For the Divine Power that was working through his body and mind found

Its fullest expression during this period. ,By 1884 his name had already become widely known in Calcutta, and therefore his presence in the city for treatment attracted large crowds to him. Though he was prohibited by doctors from speaking, his great love of men made him go against medical restrictions and give himself up entirely to the service of his visitors, quite regardless of its fatal effect on his own health.

The period of his illness was also the occasion for the spiritual advancement of his intimate devotees, and for the formation of a spirit of brotherhood among them, which later on fructified into the Ramakrishna order of monks. For while the expenses of his stay and treatment were defrayed by the householder devotees, his young disciples under the leadership of Narendranath (Swami Vivekananda) undertook to stay with him and nurse him in his illness. Thus at the bed-side of their sick Master the disciples formed themselves into a community, unified by their common devotion to him and their earnestness to realise the spiritual ideal.

In spite of his physical illness, Sri Ramakrishna was like a living spiritual dynamo during this period. He blessed many of his devotees with higher experiences. Especially on the 1st of January, 1886, he was in a highly exalted mood, and by an act of will he roused the latent spiritual powers of all the devotees who went to him for blessings. A few days after, he imparted the experience of Nirvikalpa Samadhi to Swami Vivekananda.

After a period of nearly one year's illness, he gave up the body in the early hours of Monday, the 16th of August,

1886, leaving behind him a new spirit to be broadcast in this world by his disciples, especially by the young men who took to the life of renunciation, following in his footsteps.

VI

What did Sri Ramakrishna teach? Evidently he taught more by his life than by words. He never wrote or lectured, but imparted all his teachings in the shape of informal conversations, some of which have been faithfully recorded by his disciples. By their very nature, even these original sources of information cannot claim to exhaust his teachings. Whatever he taught by words, and whatever of it has been recorded by his direct disciples —of that the present book is a faithful and fairly comprehensive summary, consisting as it does of all the precious instructions lying scattered in a voluminous literature. Being a collection of extracts from various contexts, the subject-matter of the present book is bound to appear fragmentary in spite of all attempts to give it a logical sequence by devices of arrangement. While no effort has been spared to arrange the sayings logically, we trust the general reader would find it easier to follow their trend of thought if we give below a summary of the fundamental principles embodied in them. The following brief summary should not, however, be taken as the statement of a creed—for the Master taught no special creed or dogma—or as an exhaustive exposition of his teachings, but only as a guide to their detailed study.

Reality is in essence a principle of Intelligence. It is this one Intelligent Principle that is variously known as God, Allah, Buddha, Siva, Vishnu, Brahman, etc., in the different religions of the world. It is both personal and impersonal, with attributes and without attributes. Impersonal does not mean less than personal, but without the limitations of personality.

While Reality transcends every form of relation in its absolute nature, it is, in its cosmic aspect, intimately related to the world of living and non-living beings as their cause, support and substratum. In this aspect the Intelligent Principle is spoken of as He or She, as Father or Mother of the universe. Both the Jivas (living beings) and the Jagat (non-living beings) are the manifestations of this Father-Mother Divinity. He is the source alike of what is pleasing and terrific in Nature.

For the devotee, however, He is the God of Love, the pains and terrors of life being only the devices He employs to draw His careless and forgetful children to His feet. He is present in every being, but is very near to a devoted heart in a special sense. He hears the sincere prayers that well up from the heart of man, and responds to them in His infinite mercy.

As the Impersonal, He can be approached through Knowledge, and as the Personal, through Love. But the path of Love and self-surrender is easier and more natural, and on one who treads this path He confers also the fruit of Knowledge—the sense of identity with the Absolute. In the path of Love He may be looked upon as Father, Mother, Friend, Child, Lover or in any other intimate form of human relationship. According to the devotee's attitude He manifests Himself in various forms of beauty and holiness to his purified vision.

A special form of Divine mercy is the Incarnation. From time to time He embodies Himself as a human being of great holiness and spiritual power in order to show mankind the way of holy and righteous living. The founders of all the great religions, who have opened new paths of spiritual life to men of different ages and climes, are either such special Divine manifestations, or are souls specially commissioned by Him. To worship them and to meditate on their life and doings form one of the most effective forms of spiritual upliftment.

The human personality is intimately related to the Cosmic Intelligence; for it is a manifestation of that Intelligence through the limitations of matter. Every soul is therefore potentially Divine, and the goal of life is to manifest this indwelling Divinity by controlling Nature within and without. All forms of righteous activity in life can aid this process, provided the proper attitude of mind is brought to bear on it. Religion embodies the methods evolved by mankind for the attainment of life's goal, and does not consist in mere intellectual assent to dogmas or creeds, or performance of rituals. Religion, in a vital sense, means the realisation or the actualisation of the great spiritual truths in our consciousness and daily activities. We shall have to do this through work, worship, psychic control, or philosophy—through one or all of these.

Strength is one of the most essential requirements of spiritual life. For strength is virtue and weakness is sin.

Faith is the source of all strength—faith in God and faith in oneself. Self-depreciation, or morbidly dwelling upon one's essential sinfulness, is no part of true religion, and should, by all means, be avoided; for sin is not overcome by dwelling on thoughts of sin but by contemplating the inherent Divinity of the soul. Man is no sinner but a child of God. An abiding consciousness of this is the true faith, the source of all strength and therefore of all virtue.

Spiritual life is impossible without a sound moral basis. The underlying principle of all morality is unselfishness. A man cannot be unselfish unless he is imbued with the spirit of renunciation. Renunciation means the giving up of Kama and Kanchana, i.e., lust and greed. The spirit of renunciation manifests in life as purity of character, as devoted service to fellow-beings, and as a strong and steady aspiration for the Divine. The vision of God dawns in a heart in which the spirit of renunciation and the intensity of aspiration have reached their maturity. If a man does not reach this goal, or at least make some progress towards its realisation, his life on earth, as a man, has surely been in vain.

BOOK I

MAN AND THE WORLD

An eternal portion of Myself, having become a living soul in the world of life, draws to itself the mind and the five senses that rest in Nature.

Three are the gates of this hell leading to the ruin of the soul—lust, wrath aud greed. Therefore let man renounce these three.

The man who has escaped these three gates of darkness, O Arjuna, works out his own good and reaches the highest state.

—Bhagavadgita

CHAPTER I

MAN

[*The destiny of man—Real nature of man—Man in bondage—Death and reincarnation*]

THE DESTINY OF MAN

1. You see many stars in the sky at night, but not when the sun rises. Can you therefore say that there are no stars in the heavens during the day? O man, because you cannot find God in the days of your ignorance, say not that there is no God.

2. He is born in vain, who, having attained the human birth, so difficult to get, does not attempt to realise God in this very life.

3. A man is rewarded according to his thoughts and motives. The Lord is like Kalpataru. the wish-yielding tree of heaven. Everyone gets from Him whatever he seeks. A poor man's son, having received education and become a judge of the High Court by hard work, is apt to think, "Now I am happy. I have reached the highest rung of the ladder. It is all right now." To him the Lord says, "Do thou remain so." But when the judge of the High Court retires on pension and reviews his past, he understands that he wasted his life, and exclaims, "Alas!

What real work have I done in this life!" To him the Lord also says, "Alas! What hast thou done!"

4. Man is born in this world with two tendencies—Vidya, the tendency to pursue the path of liberation, and Avidya, the leaning towards worldliness and bondage. At his birth, both these tendencies are, as it were, in equilibrium like the two scales of a balance. The world soon places its enjoyments and pleasures in one scale, and the Spirit, its attractions in the other. If the mind chooses the world, the scale of Avidya becomes heavy, and man gravitates towards the earth; but if it chooses the Spirit, the scale of Vidya becomes heavier and pulls him towards God.

5. Know the One, and you will know the all. Ciphers placed after the figure one gets the value of hundreds and of thousands, but they become valueless if you wipe out that figure. The many have value only because of the One. First the One and then the many. First God, and then the Jivas and the Jagat (creatures and the world).

6. First gain God, and then gain wealth; but do not try to do the contrary. If, after acquiring spirituality, you lead a worldly life, you will never lose your peace of mind.

7.* Do you talk of social reform? Well, you may do so after realising God. Remember, the Rishis of old gave up the world in order to attain God. This is the one thing needful. All other things shall be added to you, if indeed you care to have them. First see God, and then talk of lectures and social reforms.

8. A new-comer to a city should first secure a comfortable room for his rest at night, and after keeping his luggage there, he may freely go about the city for sight-seeing. Otherwise he may have to suffer much in the darkness of night to get a place for rest. Similarly, after securing his eternal resting place in God, a new-comer to this world can fearlessly move about doing his daily work. Otherwise, when the dark and dreadful night of death comes over him, he will have to encounter great difficulties and sufferings.

9. At the doors of large granaries are placed traps containing fried rice (Moori) to catch mice. The mice, attracted by the flavour of the fried rice, forget the more solid pleasure of tasting the rice inside the granary, and fall into the trap. They are caught therein and killed. Just so is the case with the soul. It stands on the threshold of Divine bliss, which is like millions of the highest worldly pleasures solidified into one; but instead of striving for that bliss, it allows itself to be enticed by the petty pleasures of the world and falls into the trap of Maya, the great illusion, and dies therein.

10. A Pandit: The Theosophists say that there are 'Mahatmas'. They also say that there are different planes and spheres like astral plane, Devchanic plane, solar sphere, lunar sphere, etc., and that man's subtle body can go to all these places. They say many other such things. Well, Sir, what is your opinion on Theosophy?

The Master: Bhakti alone is supreme—Bhakti or devotion to God. Do they care for Bhakti? If they do, that is well. It is well if they have God-realisation for their aim and goal. But remember, to be engrossed in such trivial things as solar sphere, lunar sphere, astral sphere, etc., is not genuine search after God. One has to do Sadhanas (spiritual practices) in order to get devotion to His lotus feet; one has to weep for Him with the intense longing of the heart. The mind should be gathered up from the different objects and concentrated exclusively on Him. He is not in the Vedas or Vedanta or in any scripture. Nothing will be achieved unless one's heart yearns for Him. One has to pray to Him with intense devotion, and practice Sadhanas. God cannot be realised so easily. Sadhanas are necessary.

11. Will all men see God? No man will have to fast for the whole day; some get their food at 9 a.m., some at noon, others at 2 p.m., and others again in the evening or at sunset. Similarly, one time or other, in this very life or after many more lives, all will, and must, see God.

12. Little children play with dolls in the outer room just as they like, without any care or fear or restraint; but as soon as their mother comes in, they throw aside their dolls and run to her crying, "Mamma mamma". You too, O man, are now playing in this material world, infatuated with the dolls of wealth, honour, fame, etc., and do not feel any fear or anxiety. If, however, you once see your Divine Mother, you will not afterwards find pleasure in all these. Throwing them all aside, you will run to Her.

13. There are pearls in the deep sea, but you must hazard all perils to get them. If you fail to get at them by a single dive, do not conclude that the sea is without them. Dive again and again, and you are sure to be

rewarded in the end. So also in the quest for the Lord, if your first attempt to see Him proves fruitless, do not lose heart. Persevere in the attempt, and you are sure to realise Him at last.

14. Meditate upon the Knowledge and the Bliss Eternal, and you will have bliss. The Bliss is indeed eternal, only it is covered and obscured by ignorance. The less your attachment to the sense-objects, the more will be your love for God.

15.* Mere possession of wealth does not make a man rich. The sign of a rich man's house is that a light burns in each room. The poor cannot afford the oil; therefore they do not arrange for many lights.

This temple of the body should not be kept in darkness; the lamp of Knowledge must be lighted in it. "Light the lamp of Knowledge in your room, and look at the face of the Mother Divine." Everyone can attain Knowledge. There is the individualised self and there is the higher Self. Every individual is connected with the higher Self. There is a gas connection in every house, and gas can be had from the Gas Company. Only apply to the proper authorities, and the supply will be arranged. Then you will have gas-light in your room.

REAL NATURE OF MAN

16. The digit one may be raised to a figure of any value by adding zeroes after it; but if that one is omitted, zeroes by themselves have no value. Similarly so long as the Jiva (individual soul) does not cling to God, Who is the One, he has no value, for all things here get their value

from their connection with God. So long as the Jiva clings to God, Who is the value-giving figure behind the world, and does all his work for Him, he gains more and more thereby: on the contrary, if he overlooks God and adds to his work many grand achievements, all done for his own glorification, he will gain nothing therefrom.

17. As a lamp does not burn without oil, so a man cannot live without God.

18. God is to man what a magnet is to iron. Why does He not then attract man? As iron thickly imbedded in mud is not moved by the attraction of the magnet, so the soul thickly imbedded in Maya does not feel the attraction of the Lord. But when the mud is washed away with water, the iron is free to move. Even so, when, by the constant tears of prayer and repentance, the soul washes away the mud of Maya that compels it to stick to the earth, it is soon attracted by the Lord to Himself.

19. The union of the Jivatman with the Paramatman is like the union of the hour and the minute hands of a watch once in every hour. They are inter-related and interdependent, and though usually separate, they may become united as often as favourable opportunities occur.

20. The soul enchained is man, but when free from the chain (Maya), it is the Lord.

21. What is the relation between the Jivatman and the Paramatman? As a current of water seems to be divided into two when a plank of wood is placed against it edgewise, so the Indivisible appears divided into two, the Jivatman and the Paramatman, due to the limitation of Maya.

22. Water and a bubble on it are one and the same. The bubble has its birth in the water, floats on it, and is ultimately resolved into it. So also the Jivatman and the Paramatman are one and the same, the difference between them being only one of degree. For one is finite and limited while the other is infinite; one is dependent while the other is independent.

23*. The idea of an individual ego is just like enclosing a portion of the water of the Ganges and calling the enclosed portion one's own Ganges.

24. As a piece of lead thrown into a basin of mercury soon becomes an amalgam with it, so an individual soul loses its limited existence when it falls into the ocean of Brahman.

25. God is the infinite Being, while Jiva is only a finite being. How then can the finite grasp the Infinite? It is like a doll made of salt trying to fathom the depth of the ocean. In doing so the salt doll is dissolved into the sea and lost. Similarly the Jiva, in trying to measure God and know Him, loses, its separateness and becomes one with Him.

26. The Lord Himself is playing in the form of man. He is the great juggler and this phantasmagoria of Jiva and Jagat is His great jugglery. The Juggler alone is true, the jugglery is false.

27. The human body is like a pot, and the mind, the intellect and the senses are like water, rice and potato. When you place a pot containing water, rice and potato on fire, they get heated, and if any one touches them, his finger is burnt, even though the heat does not really

belong to the pot, or the water, or the potato, or the rice. Similarly it is the power of Brahman in man that causes the mind and the intellect and the senses to perform their functions; and when that power ceases to act, these also stop work.

MAN IN BONDAGE

28. The true nature of the Jiva is eternal Existence-Knowledge-Bliss. It is due to egotism that he is limited by so many Upadhis (limiting adjuncts), and has forgotten his real nature.

29. The nature of the Jiva changes with the addition of each Upadhi. When a man dresses like a fop, wearing the fine black-bordered muslin, the love songs of Nidhu Babu spring to his lips. A pair of English boots inflates even a languid man with the delight of vanity; he begins to whistle immediately, and if he has to ascend a flight of stairs, he leaps up from one step to another like a Saheb. If a man holds a pen in his hand, he will go on scratching carelessly on any paper he happens to get.

30. As the snake is separate from its slough, even so is the Spirit separate from the body.

31. The Self is not attached to anything. Pleasure, pain, sinfulness, righteousness, etc., can never affect the Self in any way; but they can affect those who identify themselves with the body, as smoke can blacken only the wall but not the space enclosed within it.

32. The Vedantins say that the Atman is completely unattached. Sin or virtue, pain or pleasure, cannot affect it; but they can inflict sufferings on those who have

attachment to the body. The smoke can soil the walls, but can do nothing to the sky.

33. Men are of different natures according to the preponderance of Sattva, Rajas, or Tamas in them.

34. Though all souls are one and the same in their ultimate nature, they are of four classes according to their respective conditions. They are Baddha or bound, Mumukshu or struggling for liberation, Mukta or emancipated, and Nityamukta or ever-free.

35. A fisherman cast his net into the river and had a large haul. Some fish lay in the net calm and motionless, not exerting in the least to go out of it. Others struggled and jumped but could not extricate themselves, while a third class of fish somehow managed to force their way out of the net. In the world men too are thus of three kinds—those who are bound and never strive to be free, those who are bound but struggle for freedom, and those who have already attained freedom.

36. There are three dolls—the first made of salt, the second made of cloth, and the third of stone. If these dolls are immersed in water, the first will become dissolved and lose its form, the second will absorb a large quantity of water but retain its form, and the third will remain impervious to water. The first doll represents the man who merges his self in the universal and all-pervading Self and becomes one with It; he is the liberated man. The second represents the Bhakta or the true lover of God, who is full of Divine bliss and knowledge. And the third represents the worldly man who will not admit even a particle of true knowledge into his heart.

37. Men are like pillow-cases. The colour of one may be red, that of another blue, and that of a third black; but all contain the same cotton within. So it is with man; one is beautiful, another is black, a third holy, and a fourth wicked; but the Divine Being dwells in them all.

38. The outer layers of cakes are made of rice flour, but inside they are stuffed with different ingredients. The cake is good or bad according to the quality of its stuffing. So all human bodies are made of one and the same material, yet men are different in quality according to the purity of their hearts.

39. A Brahmin's son is no doubt a Brahmin by birth; but some of these born Brahmins grow up into great scholars, some become priests, others turn out cooks, and still others roll themselves in the dust before courtesans' doors.

40. It is true that God is even in the tiger; but we must not therefore go and face that animal. It is true that God dwells even in the most wicked beings, but it is not proper that we should associate with them.

41. The Deity Narayana (God) broods over the water, but every kind of water is not fit for drinking. Similarly, though it is true that God dwells in every place, yet every place is not fit to be visited by man. One kind of water may be used for washing our feet, another for purposes of ablution, and a third for drinking, while there are still others which are unfit even to be touched. Similarly there are different places, of which some may be approached and others visited, while there are still others which should only be saluted from a distance and bidden good-bye.

42. Beware of the following: the garrulous man; the man who is not open-hearted; the man who makes a parade of his devotion by sticking sacred Tulsi leaves on his ears; the woman who wears a long veil; and the cold water of the stagnant pool overgrown with rank vegetation, which is very injurious to health.

DEATH AND REINCARNATION

43. Even at the time of death the 'bound souls' speak of worldly matters only. There is no use in visiting places of pilgrimage, or bathing in the holy Ganges, or counting beads; if there are worldly attachments in the heart, they are sure to manifest themselves at the dying moment. Hence 'bound souls' indulge in random talks even at that time. A parrot may ordinarily sing the holy name of Radha-Krishna, but when it is attacked by a cat, it cries out 'Kang', 'Kang'—its natural cry.

44. Man suffers so much simply for want of devotion to God. One should therefore adopt such means as would help the thought of God to arise in the mind at the last moment of one's life. The means is practice of devotion to God. If this is done during one's life-time, the thought of God is sure to occur to one's mind even at the last hour.

45. A man's rebirth is determined by what he has been thinking about just before death. Devotional practices are therefore very necessary. If, by constant practice, one's mind is freed from all worldly ideas, then the thought of God, which fills the mind in their place, will not leave it even at the time of death.

46. When an unbaked pot is broken, the potter can use the mud to make a new one; but when a baked one is broken, he cannot do the same any longer. So when a person dies in a state of ignorance, he is born again; but when he becomes well baked in the fire of true knowledge and dies a perfect man, he is not born again.

47. A grain of boiled paddy does not sprout again when sown. Only unboiled paddy sends forth the shoot. Similarly when one dies after becoming a Siddha, a perfect man, he has not to be born again, but an Asiddha, an imperfect man, has to be born again and again until he becomes a Siddha.

CHAPTER II

MAYA

[Maya as the Cosmic Power of the Lord—Maya as the deluding power (Avidya)—Maya as the liberating power (Vidya)]

MAYA AS THE COSMIC POWER OF THE LORD

48. Maya is to Brahman what the snake in motion is to the snake at rest. Force in action is Maya, force in potency is Brahman.

49. As the water of the ocean is now calm and next agitated into waves, so are Brahman and Maya. The ocean in the tranquil state is Brahman, and in the turbulent state, Maya.

50. The relation of Brahman to Sakti is that of fire to its burning property.

51. Siva and Sakti (Intelligence and Energy) are both necessary for creation. With dry clay no potter can make a pot ; water also is necessary. So Siva alone cannot create without the help of Sakti.

52. Desirous of seeing Maya I had one day a vision : A small drop slowly expanded and formed itself into a girl ;

the girl became a woman and gave birth to a child; and as soon as the child was born, she took it up and swallowed it. In this way, many children were born to her and were devoured by her. Then I knew that she was Maya.

53. The snake itself is not affected by the poison in its fangs; but when it bites, the poison kills the creature bitten. Likewise Maya is in the Lord but does not affect Him, while the same Maya deludes the whole world.

MAYA AS THE DELUDING POWER (AVIDYA)

54. A certain Sadhu lived for sometime in a room in the temple of Dakshineswar. He did not speak to anybody and spent his whole time in meditation on God. One day, all of a sudden, a cloud darkened the sky, and shortly afterwards, a light wind blew away the cloud. The holy man now came out of his room and began to laugh and dance. Upon this the Master asked him, "How is it that you, who spend your days so quietly in your room, are dancing in joy and feeling so jolly today?" The holy man replied, "Such is Maya that envelops this life! No trace of it was there before; but suddenly it appears in the serene sky of Brahman, creating the whole universe, and is dispersed by the breath of Brahman."

55. Rama, Sita and Lakshmana went to the forest as exiles. Rama walked in front, Sita in the middle, Lakshmana behind her. Lakshmana was very anxious to have always a full view of Rama; but as Sita was in the middle, he could not have it. Then he prayed to Sita to move aside a little; and as soon as she did so, Lakshmana's wish

was fulfilled, and he saw Rama. Such is the arrangement of Brahman, Maya and Jiva in this world. So long as the illusion of Maya does not move aside, the creature cannot see the Creator—man cannot see God.

56. A holy man used to look and smile at the chandelier prism day and night. The reason for his doing so was that he saw various colours through the prism—red, yellow, blue, etc. Knowing these colours to be false, he realised with a smile that the world also was equally false.

57. Hari, wearing the mask of a lion's head, looks indeed very terrible. He goes where his little sister is playing, and yells hideously. She is shocked and terrified, and shrieks out in pain to escape from the frightful creature. But when Hari puts off the mask, the frightened girl at once recognises her loving brother and runs up to him, exclaiming, "Oh, it is my dear brother after all!" Such is the case with all men. They are deluded and frightened and made to do all sorts of things by the inscrutable power of Maya or nescience, behind which Brahman hides Himself. But when the veil of Maya is removed from the face of Brahman, one does not see in Him a terrible and uncompromising Master, but one's own most beloved inner Self.

58. If God is ommipresent, why do we not see Him? Observing from the bank of a pool thickly covered with scum and weeds, you will not see the water in it. If you desire to see the water, remove the scum from the surface of the pond. With eyes covered with the film of Maya, you complain that you cannot see God. If you wish to see Him, remove the film of Maya from your eyes.

59. As the cloud covers the sun, so Maya hides the Deity. When the cloud moves away, the sun is seen again; when Maya is removed, God becomes manifest.

60. The mythical swan can separate milk from the water with which it is diluted, and drink only the milk, leaving the the water behind. Other birds cannot do this. God is intimately mixed up with Maya. Ordinary men cannot see Him apart from Maya. Only the Paramahamsa can reject Maya, and reach God in His purity.

61. If you can find out the nature of Maya, the universal illusion, it will leave you just as a thief runs away when detected.

MAYA AS THE LIBERATING POWER (VIDYA)

62. In God there are both Vidya Maya and Avidya Maya. The Vidya Maya takes man towards God, whereas the Avidya Maya leads him astray. Knowledge, devotion, dispassion, compassion—all these are expressions of Vidya Maya; only with their help can one reach God.

63. It is Maya which reveals Brahman. Without Maya, who could have known Brahman? Without knowing Sakti, the manifested power of God, there is no means of knowing Him.

64. It is only due to Maya that the attainment of supreme knowledge and final beatitude becomes possible for us. Otherwise who could even dream of all this? From Maya alone spring duality and relativity; beyond Maya there is neither the enjoyer nor the object of enjoyment.

65. The cat catches her kitten with her teeth and they are not hurt; but when a mouse is so caught, it dies. Thus Maya never kills the devotee, though it destroys others.

CHAPTER III

MAYA AS 'WOMAN AND GOLD'[1]

[The bondage of sex—Sex and spiritual progress—How to conquer sex?—Riches and the spiritual aspirant]

THE BONDAGE OF SEX

66. What is Maya? It is lust which forms an obstacle to spiritual progress.

67. Is it Maya or Meye (woman, sex) which has devoured everything?

68. Souls enmeshed in worldliness cannot resist the temptation of 'woman and gold' and direct their minds to God, even though these things bring upon them a thousand humiliations.

69. Be careful, O householders! Put not too much confidence in women; they establish their mastery over you very insidiously!

70. You cannot live in a sooty room, and at the same time escape being somewhat blackened in spite of all your caution. So also, if a man lives in the company of women, some carnality, however little, is bound to arise in him,

[1] In reading the sayings contained in this chapter and others, where reference is made to Kamini-Kanchana, 'woman and gold', one must specially bear in mind that the Master is propounding no cult of woman-hatred. The study of his sayings in their entirety, as well as perusal of the Introduction to

even though he may be very circumspect and has his senses under control.

71. If pitchers of ice-cold water and bottles of savoury sauces are placed near a man who is suffering from very high fever and is semi-delirious, do you think that it is possible for him, thirsty and restless that he is, to resist the temptation of drinking the water or tasting the sauces? Similarly the worldly man who suffers from the high fever of lust, and is thirsty for sensual pleasures, cannot resist temptations when he is placed between the charms of beauty on one side, and those of wealth on the other. He is sure to deviate from the path of devotion.

72. Once a Marwari gentleman approached Sri Ramakrishna and said, "How is it, Sir, that I do not see God although I have renounced everything?"

The Master: Well, haven't you seen leather jars for keeping oil? If one of them is emptied of its contents, still it retains something of the oil as well as its smell.

this Volume, will show that his attitude towards womankind was one of profound respect bordering on worship. For he saw in them a symbol of the Divine Mother of the universe in a special sense. It was in this light that he himself viewed all women, and he wanted his devotees also to cultivate the same attitude. But at the same time he impressed on his disciples that when viewed with a sensual eye, 'woman' was the greatest danger to the spiritual aspirant. Of course, by 'woman' he meant 'sex' or 'carnality'; but the great teacher that he was, with deep insight into the workings of the human mind, he preferred to use the concrete for the abstract, and always spoke of the bondage of 'woman' and not of 'sex'. His motive must have been purely psychological; for speaking on the same subject to his women devotees, he used to warn them against the dangers from 'man'. Since his teachings were all recorded by men devotees, we naturally get warnings against dangers from 'woman' only, and not from 'man'. Just as 'woman' stands for sex, 'gold' stands for the acquisitive instinct, and is a concrete representation of all the material things that men value and like to possess. The correct English expression for it is 'wealth' or 'riches'.

In the same way there is still some worldliness left in you, and its odour persists.

73. 'Woman and gold', remember, keep men immersed in worldliness and away from God. It is strange that no one has anything but praise for his own wife, be she good, bad or indifferent.

74. As the monkey sacrifices his life at the feet of the hunter, so does a man at the feet of a beautiful woman.

SEX AND SPIRITUAL PROGRESS·

75. Those who wish to attain God or make progress in their devotional practices should particularly guard themselves against the snares of lust and wealth. Otherwise they will never attain perfection.

76. Nityananda asked Sri Chaitanya, "Why is it that all my teaching of Divine love produces no tangible result on the minds of men?" Sri Chaitanya replied, "Because, due to their association with women, they cannot retain the higher teachings. Listen, Brother Nityananda, there is no salvation for the worldly-minded."

77. When does the indicator of a balance move away from the pointed needle attached to the top? When one of the scales becomes heavier than the other. Similarly the mind runs away from God and gets unbalanced when the pressure of woman and wealth is placed upon it.

78. If there is a small hole at the bottom of a jar of water, the whole water will leak out. Similarly, if there is the smallest tinge of worldliness in the aspirant, all his exertions will come to naught.

79. Try to gain absolute mastery over the sexual instinct. If one succeeds in doing this, a physiological change is produced in the body by the development of a hitherto rudimentary nerve known as Medha (the function of which is to transmute the lower energies into the higher). The knowledge of the higher Self is gained after the development of this Medha nerve.

80. The mind steeped in affection for 'woman and gold' is like the green betel-nut. So long as the betel-nut is green, its kernel remains adhering to its shell, but when it dries up shell and nut are separated, and the nut moves within, if shaken. So when the affection for 'woman and gold' dries up, the soul is perceived as quite different from the body.

81. When the mind is free from attachment to sense-objects, it turns to God and is fixed on Him. The bound soul becomes free in this way. That soul is bound which takes the path leading away from God.

82. When attachment for wealth and sex is wiped out from the mind, what else is left in the soul? Only the bliss of Brahman.

HOW TO CONQUER SEX?

83. As persons living in a house infested with venomous snakes are always alert, so should men living in the world be always vigilant against the allurement of lust and greed.

84. On coming across a snake usually we say, "Mother Manasa, please move away showing your tail and hiding your head." So also it is wise to hold aloof from such

influences as have a tendency to excite sensuality. It is far better not to come in contact with them than to gain experience by a fall.

85. A disciple once asked Sri Ramakrishna how he was to conquer lust; for, though he was passing his days in religious contemplation, evil thoughts were arising in his mind from time to time. To him the Master said: "There was a man who had a pet dog. He used to caress it, carry it inabout his arms, play with it and kiss it. A wise man, seeing this foolish behaviour of his, warned him not to lavish such affection on a dog. For it was, after all, an irrational brute, and might bite him one day. The owner took the warning to heart and putting away the dog from his arms, resolved never again to fondle or caress it. But the animal could not at first understand the change in his master, and would run to him frequently to be taken up and caressed. Beaten several times, the dog at last ceased to trouble his master any more. Such indeed is your condition. The dog that you have been cherishing so long in your bosom will not easily leave you, though you may wish to be rid of it. However, there is no harm in it. Do not caress the dog any more, but give it a good beating whenever it approaches you to be fondled, and in course of time you will be altogether free from its importunities."

86. 'Woman and gold' have drowned the whole world in sin. Woman is disarmed when you view her as the manifestation of the Divine Mother. God cannot be seen so long as one's passion for 'woman and gold' is not extinguished.

87. Once a man attains God through intense Vairagya (freedom from worldly passions), temptations of sex disappear, and he finds himself in no danger even from his own wife. If there are two unequal magnets at an equal distance from a piece of iron, which of them will draw it with greater force? Certainly the larger one. Verily, God is the larger magnet. What can the smaller magnet, woman, do against it?

88. Snakes are venomous reptiles. If you try to catch them, you are sure to be bitten. But to the man who has learnt the art of snake-charming by the use of magnetised dust, it is not a very difficult affair to catch them. He can play even with seven of them twisted together and coiled round his neck. (Similarly a man of realisation is immune from the dangers of worldly life.)

89. One day a Marwari gentleman went to Sri Ramakrishna and asked him for permission to present him with some thousands of rupees. But the Master had nothing but a stern refusal for this well-meant offer. He said, "I shall have nothing to do with your money; for if I accept it, my mind would always be dwelling on it." The gentleman then proposed to invest the amount in the name of one of Sri Ramakrishna's relatives to be used by him for the Master's service. To this the Master replied, "No, it would be double-dealing. Moreover, it would always be in my mind that I am keeping my money with so-and-so."

But the Marwari still persisted in his proposal, quoting one of Sri Ramakrishna's own sayings, "If the mind is like oil, it will float even upon an ocean of 'woman and gold'.

At this the Master retorted: "That is true indeed; but if the oil floats on water for a considerable length of time, it becomes putrefied. In the same way, even if the mind were only to float over the ocean of 'woman and gold,' the continuous contact of the latter for a long period would surely tend to vitiate the mind and make it give out an evil odour."

RICHES AND THE SPIRITUAL ASPIRANT

90. Referring to the fact that the pursuit of wealth diverts an aspirant from the path of God, the Master once said to a young disciple: "Like a man of the world you have accepted a paid appointment. But you are working for your mother. Otherwise I should have said, 'For shame! For shame!'" He repeated this several times and then said, "Serve the Lord alone."

91. Referring to the degradation that service undertaken for the sake of money brings about, the Master said to a young disciple: "A change for the worse has come over his face. A dark shadowy film seems to have spread over it. All this is due to office work. There are the accounts and a hundred other matters to attend to.'

92. Money is an Upadhi (a deceptive influence) of a very strong nature. As soon as a man becomes rich, he is thoroughly changed. A Brahmin who was very meek and humble used to come here (Dakshineswar) every now and then. After some time he stopped his visits, and we knew nothing of what happened to him. One day we went to Konnagore in a boat. As we were getting

down from the boat, we saw him sitting on the bank of the Ganges, where, in the fashion of big folk, he was enjoying the pure breeze of the river. On seeing me, he accosted me in a patronising tone with the words, "Hallo, Thakkur! How do you do now?" At once I noticed the change in his tone and said to Hriday who was with me, "I tell you, Hriday, this man must have come by some riches. See what a great change has come over him!" And Hriday burst into laughter.

93. Money can fetch you bread alone. Do not consider it as your sole end and aim.

94. There are some who boast of their wealth and power, of their name and fame, and high status in society; but all these are for a few days only. None of these will follow them after death.

95. On two occasions the Lord smiles: First when the doctor comes to the bed-side of a patient who is seriously taken ill and is about to die, and says to his mother, "Why, madam, there is no cause for anxiety at all. I take upon myself the responsibility of saving your son's life." Next He smiles when two brothers, who are busy partitioning their land, take a measuring tape, put it across the land and say, "This side is mine, that side is yours."

96. There is nothing to be proud of in money. If you say you are rich, there are richer and richer men than you, in comparison with whom you are a mere beggar. After dusk when the glow-worms make their appearance, they think, "We are giving light to the world." But when the stars begin to twinkle, the pride of the glow-worms is

humbled. Now the stars begin to think, "We are illumining the universe." But after a while the moon ascends the sky, and her silvery light humiliates the stars and they pale away in sadness. Again, the moon grows proud and thinks that by her light the world is lighted and bathed in beauty. But presently the dawn proclaims the ascent of the sun on the eastern horizon. And where is the moon now!

If they who think themselves rich ponder over these facts of Nature, they would never, never boast of their riches and power.

97. Water always flows out under a bridge but never stagnates; so money passes through the hands of the free, and is never hoarded by them.

98. He is truly a man to whom money is only a servant; but, on the other hand, those who do not know how to make proper use of it, hardly deserve to be called men.

CHAPTER IV

MAYA AS AHAMKARA OR EGOTISM[1]

[*Evils of egotism—The difficulty of conquering egotism—'Ripe' ego and 'unripe' ego—How to conquer the ego—Ego in the man of realisation*]

EVILS OF EGOTISM

99. The sun can give heat and light to the whole world, but he cannot do so when the clouds shut out his rays. Similarly as long as egotism veils the heart, God cannot shine upon it.

100. Egotism is like a cloud which keeps God hidden from our sight. If it vanishes by the mercy of the Guru, God is perceived in all His glory. For instance, you see in the picture that Sri Ramachandra, Who is God, is only two or three steps ahead of Lakshmana (the Jiva), but Sita (Maya), coming in between the two, prevents Lakshmana from having a view of Rama.

[1] *Ahamkara and Aham*—These two words have been variously translated here, accordingly to context, as egotism, the sense of 'I', the 'I', the ego, the 'I-ness' and so on. None of these is perhaps an exact equivalent. Indian philosophy and system of spiritual discipline understand by it the basic principle of individuation giving rise to the sense of 'I', the concomitant feeling of separation from God and other individuals, and all other psychical and physical developments following from it. The aim of spiritual life is to root out this prime source of all worldliness, and realise the unity of all existence.

101. *Q.* Sir, why are we in bondage like this? Why do we not see God?

A. Man's ego itself is Maya. It is the veil that shuts out the Light. Verily, with the death of the 'I' all troubles cease. If by the grace of the Lord a man once gains the knowledge that he is not the doer, then he assuredly becomes a Jivanmukta, one freed in this very life, and transcends all fear.

102. If I hold this cloth before me, you cannot see me any more, though I am still as near you as ever. So also though God is nearer to you than anything else, because of the screen of egotism you cannot see Him.

103. As long as there is egotism, neither Self-knowledge (Jnana) nor liberation (Mukti) is possible; and there is no cessation of birth and death.

104. Rice, pulse, potatoes and other things put in cold water in an earthen vessel can be touched with hand until they are heated on a fire. The same statement applies to the Jiva. This body is the earthen vessel; wealth and learning, caste and lineage, power and position are like rice, pulse and potatoes. Egotism is the heat. The Jiva is made hot (haughty) by egotism.

105. Rain-water never stands on high ground, but runs down to the lowest level. So also the mercy of God remains in the hearts of the lowly, but drains off from those of the vain and the proud.

106. Egotism is so injurious to man that as long as it is not eradicated there is no salvation for him. Look at the young calf and the troubles that come upon it through egotism. As soon as it is born, it cries,

'Ham hai'—'I am', 'I am'. The result of its egotism is that, when it grows up, if it is an ox, it is yoked to the plough, to drag carts full of heavy load; if a cow, it is kept tied to its post and is sometimes even killed and eaten. But still, in spite of all this punishment, the animal does not lose its egotism; for drums that are made of its hide produce the same sound of 'Ham', I. The creature does not learn humility until the cotton-carder makes bow-strings out of its entrails; for it is then that the animal's intestines sing out 'Tu hai'—'Thou art'. The 'I' must go and give place to the 'Thou'; and this is not achieved until man becomes spiritually awakened.

107. Freedom will come when your 'I-hood' (egotism) vanishes and you yourself are merged in the Divinity.

108. When does a man attain salvation? Only when his egotism dies.

109. Q. When shall I be free?

A. When that 'I' vanishes from you. 'I' and 'mine'—this is ignorance; 'Thou' and 'Thine'—that is, true knowledge. The true devotee always says, "O Lord, Thou art the doer (Karta). Thou doest everything. I am a mere instrument in Thy hands. I do whatever Thou makest me do. All this is Thy glory. This home and this family are Thine, not mine; I have only the right to serve as Thou ordainest."

THE DIFFICULTY OF CONQUERING EGOTISM

110. The vanities of all others may gradually die out. but the vanity of a saint regarding his sainthood is hard indeed to wear away.

111. The cup in which garlic juice is kept retains the odour, though washed several times. Egotism is such an obstinate aspect of ignorance that it never disappears completely, however hard you may try to get rid of it.

112. The dyspeptic knows only too well that sour things are injurious to him, but such is the force of association that the sight of them is enough to make his mouth water. So, even if one tries hard to suppress the idea of 'I-ness' and 'mine-ness', yet when one begins to act, the 'unripe' ego asserts itself.

113. There are few who can attain Samadhi and get rid of the Aham—the feeling of 'I' within. Generally it does not go. You may reason and discriminate without end, yet this 'I' comes back again and again. Today you may cut down the Pepul tree, but tomorrow you will see it sprouting again.

114. Those who seek name and fame are under a delusion. They forget that everything is ordained by the Great Dispenser of all things and that all is due to the Lord and the Lord alone. The wise man says always, "It is Thou, O Lord, It is Thou"; but the ignorant and the deluded say, "It is I, it is I."

'RIPE' EGO AND 'UNRIPE' EGO

115. There are two types of egoes, one 'ripe' and the other 'unripe'. "Nothing is mine, whatever I see, or feel, or hear, nay, even this body itself, is not mine; I am always eternal, free and all-knowing,"—such ideas arise from the 'ripe' ego. "This is my house, this is my child, this is my

wife, this is my body,"—thoughts of this kind are the manifestation of the 'unripe' ego.

116. The ego that asserts "I am the servant of God" is characteristic of the true devotee. It is the ego of Vidya (Knowledge), and is called the 'ripe' ego.

117. What is the 'mischievous I'? The 'I' which says, "What! Don't they know me? I have so much money! Who is so wealthy as myself? Who dares to surpass me?"

118. The 'I' which makes a man worldly and attached to lust and wealth is mischievous. The individual soul and the Universal Being are separated because this 'I' comes in between them. If a stick is placed on the surface of water, the water will appear to be divided into two sections. The stick is the Aham—the 'I'. Take that away, and the water becomes again undivided.

HOW TO CONQUER THE EGO

119. If one ponders over this word 'I', trying to track it down, one sees that it is only a word which denotes egotism. But it is extremely difficult to shake it off. So one must say, "You wicked 'I', if you will not go by any means, remain as the servant of God." The ego that feels itself to be the servant of God is called the 'ripe I'.

120. Sankaracharya had a disciple who had been serving him for a long time but was not still given any instruction by him. Once, while seated alone, Sankara heard the footsteps of someone coming behind. So he called out, "Who is there?" The disciple answered, "It is I." The

Acharya thereupon said, "If this 'I' is so dear to you, then either expand it to infinity (*i.e.*, know the universe as yourself), or renounce it altogether."

121. If you find that you cannot drive off this feeling of 'I', then let it remain as the 'servant I'. There is not much to fear from the ego which is centered in the thought, "I am the servant of God; I am His devotee." Sweets cause dyspepsia, but not sugar candy which is an exception. The 'servant I', the 'I' of a devotee, the 'I' of a child—each of these is like a line drawn with a stick on the surface of water. 'I' does not last long.

122. Just as sugar candy has no unwholesome effect like other sweets, so also the 'ripe' ego which considers itself to be the servant or worshipper of God causes none of those evil consequences characteristic of the 'unripe' ego. On the other hand it leads to God, and signifies that one has progressed in Bhakti Yoga or the path of devotion.

123. What is the nature of the feelings and impulses of one who has the attitude of the 'servant I'? If his conviction is true and sincere, then there remains only the forms, the appearance, of his former feelings and impulses. Even if the 'ego of the servant' or the 'ego of the devotee' remains, one who has realised God can hurt none. The whole sting of individuality vanishes from him. The sword becomes gold by a touch of the philosopher's stone. It retains its former shape, but can no longer hurt any one.

124. If you feel proud, let it be in the thought that you are the servant of God, the son of God. Great men have the nature of children. They are always children before Him; so they are free from pride. All their strength

is of God, and not their own. It belongs to Him and comes from Him.

125. A person who is convinced that everything is done by the will of God, feels himself to be a mere tool in His hands. He is then free from all bondage even in this very life. "Thou doest Thy work, Lord; but man says, 'I do it'!"

126. As long as one says, "I know" or "I do not know", one looks upon oneself as a person. My Divine Mother says: "It is only when I have effaced the whole of this Aham (I-ness) in you, that the Undifferentiated Absolute (My impersonal aspect) can be realised in Samadhi." Till then there is the 'I' in me and before me.

127. After a process of severe struggle with one's lower nature and the assiduous practice of spiritual discipline leading to Self-knowledge, one attains the state of Samadhi. Then the ego with all its train vanishes. But it is very difficult to attain Samadhi; the ego is very persistent. That is why we are born again and again in this world.

128. So long as one is not blessed with the vision Divine, so long as the touch of the philosopher's stone has not transmuted the base metal in one into gold, there will be the illusive feeling: 'I am the doer'. And until this illusion ceases, there will persist the idea that gives the sense of distinction between 'I have done this good work', and 'I have done that bad work'. Maya means this sense of distinction, and it is because of it that the world continues. One reaches Him if one takes refuge in Vidya Maya —that aspect of Divine Power having the preponderance

of Sattva—which leads one by the right path. He alone crosses the ocean of Maya, who comes face to face with God—realises Him. A man is truly free, even here in this embodied state, if he knows that God is the true agent and he by himself is powerless to do anything.

THE EGO OF THE MAN OF REALISATION

129. Will the sense of 'I' never die away completely? The petals of the lily drop off in time, but they leave their mark behind. So the ego of man entirely disappears (when he realises God), but traces of its former existence remain; this, however, does not produce any evil effect.

130. The truly wise man is he who has seen the Lord. He becomes like a child. The child, no doubt, seems to have an individuality, a separateness, of its own. But that individuality is a mere appearance, not a reality. The self of the child is nothing like the self of the grown-up man.

131. Some great souls who have reached the seventh or the highest plane of Samadhi, and have thus become merged in God-consciousness, are pleased to come down from that spiritual height for the good of mankind. They keep the ego of Knowledge (the Aham of Vidya), which is the same as the higher Self. But this ego is a mere appearance. It is like a line drawn across water.

132. As a piece of rope, when burnt, retains its form, but cannot serve to bind, so is the ego which is burnt by the fire of supreme Knowledge.

133. A man dreams that someone is coming to cut him to pieces. Frightened, he awakens with a groan and sees

that the door of his room is closed from within and that no one is inside it. Even then, his heart continues to beat fast for some minutes. So does our Abhimana, or sense of 'I', leave behind it some momentum even when it has departed.

134. After the attainment of Samadhi some still retain the ego—the 'I' of the servant or worshipper of God. Sankaracharya kept the ego of Vidya (knowledge) for the teaching of others.

135. Hanuman was blessed with the vision of God both with form and without it (Sakara and Nirakara). But he retained the ego of a servant of God. Such was also the case with Narada, Sanaka, Sananda and Sanatkumara.

A devotee. Were Narada and others only Bhaktas, or were they Jnanis also?

The Master: Narada and others had attained the highest Knowledge (Brahmajnana). But still they went on like the murmuring water of the rivulet, talking and singing the praise of God. This shows that they too kept this ego of Knowledge, a slight trace of individuality, to mark their separate existence from the Deity, for the purpose of teaching others the saving truths of religion.

136. Once the Master asked a disciple of his in a playful mood, "Well, do you notice in me any Abhimana (pride arising from the sense of 'I')? Have I any Abhimana?

The Disciple: Yes, Sir, a little; but that little has been kept for the following purposes: firstly for the preservation of the body; secondly, for the practice of devotion to God, thirdly, for mixing with the company of devotees; and fourthly, for giving instruction to others. At the same time, it must be said that you have retained it only after a good deal of prayer. I mean, the natural state of your soul is capable of being described only by the word Samadhi. Hence I say that the Abhimana or egoism which you possess is the result of your prayer.

The Master: Yes, but it has been retained not by me but by my Divine Mother. It lies with my Divine Mother to grant the prayer.

CHAPTER V

BONDAGE OF BOOK-LEARNING

[Barrenness of mere book-learning—Vanity of disputation—The true end of learning]

BARRENNESS OF MERE BOOK-LEARNING

137. One day the late Keshab Chandra Sen came to Sri Ramakrishna in the temple of Dakshineswar and asked him, "How is it that even learned people remain so profoundly ignorant of things that truly matter in spiritual life, although they have read a whole library of religious books?" The Master replied, "The kite and the vulture soar high up in the air, but all the time their eyes remain fixed on charnel-houses in search of putrid carcasses; similarly the minds of the so-called learned men are attached to the things of the world, to lust and wealth, in spite of their erudition in sacred lore, and hence they cannot attain true Knowledge."

138. That knowledge which purifies the mind and heart alone is true Knowledge, all else is only a negation of Knowledge.

139. What is the use of mere book-learning? The Pandits may be familiar with plenty of sacred texts and couplets. But what is the good of repeating them? One must realise in one's life the truths embodied in the

scriptures. Mere reading will not bring Knowledge or salvation as long as one is attached to the world, as long as one is fond of 'woman and gold'.

140. Our so-called Pandits will talk big. They will talk of Brahman, of God, of the Absolute, of Jnana Yoga, of philosophy, of ontology, and the rest. But there are very few who have realised what they talk about. They are dry and hard, and good for nothing.

141. It is easy to utter 'do, re, mi, la, si, do' with the mouth, but it is difficult to play them on an instrument. So it is easy to talk on religion, but difficult to practise it.

142. A parrot repeats by rote the holy name of Radha-Krishna, but as soon as it is caught by a cat it screams 'kang, kang', betraying its natural cry. Worldly-wise men sometimes repeat the name of Hari (God) and perform various pious and charitable deeds with the hope of worldly gains, but when misfortune, sorrow, poverty and death overtake them, they forget Him and all such deeds.

143. Can love of God be acquired by reading holy books? In the Hindu almanac it is mentioned that on a particular day there will be twenty Adas (a unit of measure) of rain-water. But you will not be able to squeeze out of the almanac a single drop! So also many good sayings are to be found in holy books, but merely reading them will not make one religious. One must practise the virtues taught in such books in order to acquire love of God.

144.* In the kingdom of God reason, intellect and learning are of no avail. There the dumb speak, the blind see, and the deaf hear.

145. To explain God after merely reading the scriptures is like explaining to a person the city of Benares after seeing it only in a map.

146. The intoxication of hemp is not to be had by repeating the word 'hemp' even a thousand times. Get some hemp, pound it with water into a solution and drink it; you will then really get intoxicated. What is the use of crying aloud, "O God, O God!" Regularly practise devotion, and you will see God.

147. This knowledge of God comes not to the person who is proud of his learning or wealth. You may say to such a person, "There is a holy man in a certain place. Do you like to see him?" He is however, sure to put forward excuses and say that he cannot go. He thinks he is too big a man to pay a visit to such a person. Such pride is born of ignorance.

148. Those who have read a little become puffed up with pride. I had a conversation with a certain person on God. He said, "Oh, I know all this." I said to him, "Does one who had been to Delhi go about boasting of it? Does a gentleman ever tell us that he is a gentleman?"

149. Grantha does not always mean a holy scripture, but often it comes to mean a 'Granthi' or a knot. If a man does not read it with an intense desire to know the Truth, and renouncing all vanity, the mere reading of books only gives rise to pedantry, presumption, egotism, etc., which will be an encumbrance on his mind like so many knots.

150. Water is dried up at once if poured on a heap of ashes. Vanity is like this heap of ashes. Prayer and

contemplation produce no effect upon the heart puffed up with vanity.

VANITY OF DISPUTATION

151. Water poured into an empty vessel makes a bubbling noise, but when the vessel is full, no sound is heard. Similarly, the man who has not found God is full of vain disputation about His existence and nature. But he who has seen Him, silently enjoys the bliss Divine.

152. Common men talk 'bagfuls' of religion but do not act even a 'grain' of it. The wise man speaks little, even though his whole life is religion expressed in action.

153. When a large number of guests are invited to a feast, you first hear a tremendous noise produced by them; but it continues only till they commence eating. When the dishes are served and the guests fall to, threefourths of the noise subside. Then comes the course of sweetmeats. The more they are served, the more does the noise subside; and finally, when the turn comes for curds (the last course), only one sound is heard *viz.*, 'soop-soop'. The feast over, the next thing for the guests to do is to go to sleep!

The nearer you come to God, the less you are disposed to questioning and reasoning. When you actually attain Him, when you behold Him as the reality,—then all noise, all disputations, come to an end. Then is the time for sleep, *i.e.*, for enjoyment which comes in Samadhi, the state of communion with the Divine.

154. So long as the bee is outside the petals of the flower and has not tasted the sweetness of the nectar within, it hovers round humming; but when it gets into the flower, it drinks it noiselessly. So long as a man disputes about doctrines and dogmas, he has not tasted the nectar of true faith. Once he tastes that, he becomes silent.

155. One who has just taken to the study of a foreign language, while talking, constantly resorts to words belonging to that language in order to make a show of his attainments; but he who knows the language well seldom uses it when speaking in his own mother tongue. Such indeed is the case with those who are well advanced in religion.

156. At a distance from the market, we hear only a loud buzzing noise; but entering the market, we hear it no longer, and perceive the bargains that are being carried on. Similarly, so long as a person is far away from God, he cannot but be in the midst of the confusion of sophistry, vain argument and discussion; but once he approaches God, all arguments and discussions cease, and he gains a clear and vivid perception of the mysteries of God.

157. Throw an unbaked cake of flour into hot ghee, and it will make a sort of noise. But the more it is fried, the less is the noise; and when it is fully fried, the bubbling ceases altogether. So long as a man has a little knowledge, he goes about talking and preaching; but when the perfection resulting from true Knowledge is gained, he no more makes vain display.

158*. When the grace of the Almighty descends on any one he immediately understands his mistakes; knowing this, you should not dispute.

THE TRUE END OF THE LEARNING

159. Sacred books only point out the way to God. Once you have known the way, what is the use of books? Then comes the time for the culture of the soul in solitary communion with God. A person received a letter from his village-home, asking him to send certain things to his kinsmen. When he was going to order for them, he wanted to ascertain from the letter the articles requisitioned. So he searched for the letter, which was then missing. At last, to his great delight, it was found out after a long search. He took it up eagerly, and went through the contents, which ran as follows: "Please send five Seers of sweetmeats, a hundred oranges and eight pieces of cloth." Knowing the contents, he threw the letter aside and set about procuring the articles.

How long then does one care for such a letter? So long as one does not know the contents. The contents being known once, the next step is to put forth the necessary effort to get the things desired. Similarly the sacred books tell us only the way to God, *i.e.*, of the means for the realisation of God. That being once known, the next step is to work one's way to the goal. Realisation is the goal.

160. Para-vidya, *i.e.*, higher knowledge, is that by which we know God. All else, mere scriptures, philosophy, logic, or grammar, as such, only burden and puzzle the mind. The Granthas (books) are sometimes Granthis (knots). They are good only when they lead to the higher knowledge.

161. Many think that knowledge of God cannot be attained except through the study of books. But higher

than reading is hearing, and even higher than hearing is seeing or realising. The hearing of the truth from the lips of the preceptor makes a greater impression on the mind than the mere reading of books; but seeing makes the greatest impression. Better than reading about Benares is hearing about the place from the lips of one who has actually visited it; but the best is to see Benares with one's own eyes.

162*. Only two kinds of people can attain to self-knowledge: those who are not encumbered at all with learning, that is to say, whose minds are not over-crowded with thoughts borrowed from others; and those who, after studying all the scriptures and sciences, have come to realise that they know nothing.

163. People talk of errors and superstitions, and feel proud of their book-learning; but the sincere devotee finds the loving Lord ever ready to lend him a helping hand. It matters not if he had been walking along a wrong path for a time. The Lord knows what he wants and in the end fulfils his heart's desires.

164. Two friends went into an orchard. One of them possessing much worldly wisdom, immediately began to count the mango trees there and the number of mangoes each tree bore, and to estimate what might be the approximate value of the whole orchard. His companion went to the owner, made friendship with him, and then, quietly going to a tree, began, at his host's desire, to pluck the fruits and eat them. Whom do you consider to be the wiser of the two? Eat mangoes! It will satisfy your hunger. What is the good of counting the trees and leaves

and making calculations? The vain man of intellect busies himself uselessly with finding out the 'why' and 'wherefore' of creation, while the humble man of wisdom makes friends with the Creator and enjoys His gift of supreme bliss.

165. One ray of light from my Divine Mother, Who is verily the Goddess of Wisdom, has power to cow down even the most learned of Pandits and make him appear like an insignificant worm crawling upon the earth.

166. Utter the word Gita, in quick succession, a number of times—Gi-ta-gi-ta-gi-tagi. It is then virtually pronounced as 'Tagi', 'Tagi', which means one who has renounced the world for the sake of God. Thus, in one word, the Gita teaches, "Renounce, ye world-bound men! Renounce everything, and fix the mind on the Lord."

167. In the course of his pilgrimage through the southern parts of India, Chaitanya Deva came across a certain devotee who was in tears all the while a Pandit was reading from the Gita. Now this devotee knew not even the alphabet. He could not follow a single text of the Gita. On being asked why he shed tears, he replied, "It is indeed true that I do not know a word of the Gita. But all the while it was being read, I could not help seeing with my inner eye the beautiful form of my Lord Sri Krishna seated before Arjuna in a chariot in the field of Kurukshetra, and giving out all those sublime thoughts embodied in the Gita. This it was that filled my eyes with tears of joy and love."

This man, who knew not letters, had the highest Knowledge, for he had pure love for God and could realise Him.

CHAPTER VI

RELIGIOUS TEACHERS—FALSE AND TRUE

[*Pitfalls of teachership—True teachers*]

PITFALLS OF TEACHERSHIP

168. Do you, O preacher, carry the badge of authority? The humblest servant of the king, authorised by him, is heard with awe and respect, and can quell a riot by showing his badge; so must you, O preacher, first, obtain your commission and inspiration from God Himself. So long as you do not have this badge of Divine inspiration, you may preach all your life, but it will be mere waste of breath.

169. None has patience or desire to dive deep into Divine love. None cares for discrimination and dispassion for worldly things (Viveka and Vairagya), or for devotional practices (Sadhana). On the other hand, all will rush to lecture and to teach with only a bit of book-learning. Strange indeed! To teach others is the most difficult of tasks. He alone can teach, who gets commission from God after having realised Him.

170. What do you think of the man who is a good orator and preacher, but whose spiritual powers are undeveloped? He is like the person who squanders another's property entrusted to him. He can easily advise others, for it costs him nothing since the ideas he expresses are not his own but borrowed.

171. A well-known speaker was lecturing once in a Harisabha (religious association). In the course of his speech he said, "The Lord is totally devoid of Rasa (sweetness); we must make Him sweet by lending to Him the sweetness of our own nature." By Rasa he meant love and other divine attributes. When I heard this, I was reminded of the boy who said that his mother's brother had many horses, and sought to convince his hearers by explaining that they occupied a whole cowshed. Of course, the intelligent could at once see that cowsheds are not meant for horses, that the youngster was telling a lie, and that he had no experience or knowledge of horses.

To say that God is devoid of Rasa was an absurdity, which proved that the speaker was totally ignorant of what he was saying. He had never realised the Supreme Being, Who is the very fountain of eternal love, wisdom and joy.

172. What is your opinion about the method employed by present-day religious preachers? It is like inviting a hundred persons to a dinner with food enough only for one. It is only pretending to be a great religious teacher with a small stock of spiritual experience.

173. First install God in the temple of your heart; first realise Him. Speeches, lectures and the rest may be taken up after you have seen God, not before. People

talk glibly of God and Brahman, while they are attached to the things of the world. What does all this amount to? Mere blowing of the conch (Sankha) for Divine Service without God to worship within the temple.

174. One day as I was going through Panchavati, I heard the frightful croaking of a frog. I guessed it must have been caught by a snake. When after a long time I was returning that way, I again heard the same noise. Peeping through the bushes, I saw a water snake with a frog in its mouth. It could neither swallow it, nor let it go, and there was no end to the agony of the frog. Then I thought, "Well, had it been the victim of a cobra, it would have been silenced for ever after three croaks at the most (and then there would have been no more suffering either for the frog or the snake). But here the snake's suffering is almost equal to the frog's." So if an unenlightened man takes upon himself in his foolhardiness the responsibility of saving another, there is no end to the misery of both. Neither does the ego of the disciple vanish, nor are his worldly ties cut asunder. If the disciple comes under the influence of an unworthy teacher, he never gets liberation. But under a competent teacher the egotism of the Jiva perishes with three croaks."

175. There was a professional preacher who could rouse strong devotional feelings in the hearts of his hearers whenever he delivered religious discourses; but personally he was not a man of character. Pained at the kind of life he led, I asked him one day how it was that he moved so many hearts to devotion, while he himself lived such an unworthy life. The man bowed and said, "Yes, Sir, the

broom though a contemptible thing, removes the dust and dirt on the floor and the street!" Of course I could not answer him.'[1]

WHO IS A TRUE TEACHER?

176. He alone is the true teacher who is illumined by the light of true Knowledge.

177. As many people have merely heard of snow but not seen it, so many religious preachers have only read in books about the attributes of God, but not realised them for themselves. And as many others have seen snow but not tasted it, so many religious teachers have obtained only a glimpse of Divine glory but have not understood its real essence. Only he who has tasted the snow can say what it is like. Similarly, he alone can describe the attributes of God, who has associated with Him in His different aspects in the relationship of a servant, a friend and a lover, and has realised his oneness with Him in complete absorption in Him.

178. If one has the idea that one is a leader and has formed a sect, one's ego is 'unripe'. But if one gets commission from God after realising Him, and preaches for the good of others, there is no harm. Sukadeva had such a commission to reveal the Bhagavata to Parikshit.

179. When the jar is full, it does not make noise any more. So the man of realisation too does not talk

[1] This need not be taken as a contradiction of the main theme of this chapter. For the effect which preaching of this type produces is temporary and is unlike the permanent change which the words of men of true spiritual realisation produce in their disciples.

much. But what then about Narada and others? Yes; Narada, Sukadeva and a few others like them came down several steps after the attainment of Samadhi, and out of mercy and love they taught mankind.

180. There are two classes of perfect men in the world—those who, on attaining Truth, become silent and enjoy it all by themselves without any thought of others; and those who attain Truth, but finding no pleasure in keeping it to themselves, cry out in a trumpet voice to all—"Come ye, and enjoy the Truth with us."

181. Bees come of themselves to the full-blown flower when the breeze wafts its fragrance all around. Ants come of themselves to the spot where sweets are placed. No one need invite the bee or the ant. So when a man becomes pure and perfect, the sweet influence of his character spreads everywhere, and all who seek the Truth are naturally drawn towards him. He need not go in search of an audience to listen to him.

182. Ants gather of themselves where the sweetmeats have fallen. Try to become sugar candy, *i.e.*, have within yourselves the sweetness of an enlightened spiritual consciousness, and the ants (devotees) will come to you of themselves. If you preach without commission from God, your preaching will be powerless, and none will listen to it. Onc must attain God by devotion or by any other means, and then, if one receives His word, one may teach and preach anywhere and everywhere. For only thus can one get power and strength from Him; and only then can one rightly discharge the responsible duties of a preacher.

183. When fire burns, the moths come, one knows not whence, and fall into it. The fire never goes about inviting the moth. Such is the preaching of the perfect. They do not go about inviting others, but hundreds and thousands, of their own accord, go to them—one knows not whence—seeking instruction from them.

184. What is true preaching like? Instead of preaching to others, if one worships God all the time, that is preaching enough. He who exerts himself to attain emancipation from birth and death is the real preacher. To him who is free hundreds of people come from all sides anxious to be taught. When a rose blossoms, bees come from all sides uninvited.

185. When corn is measured out to a purchaser from the granary of a big merchant, the man engaged in measuring out goes on unceasingly with his work, having a constant supply of grain. A petty dealer's store, on the other hand, is soon exhausted. Similarly, it is God Himself Who unfailingly inspires thoughts and sentiments in His devotees, and that is why they are never lacking in what is new and wise. But the book-learned, like petty grocers, soon find themselves short of thoughts and ideas.

186. Gas-light illumines different parts of the city in varying degrees. But the life of the light, namely, the gas, comes from one common source. So the true religious teachers of all climes and ages are like lamps through which is revealed the life of the Spirit flowing constantly from the one source, the Almighty Lord.

187. Rain-water falling upon the roof of a house flows down to the ground through spouts shaped grotesquely like

a tiger's head. One gets the impression that the water comes from the tiger's mouth, but in reality it descends from the sky. In the same way the holy teachings that come from the mouths of godly men seem to be uttered by those men themselves, while in reality they proceed from God.

CHAPTER VII

THE WORLDLY-MINDED AND THEIR WAYS

[*Characteristics of the worldly-minded—Fickle devotion of the worldly-minded—The worldly-minded and spiritual practices*]

CHARACTERISTICS OF THE WORLDLY-MINDED

188. Men are of two classes—men in name only (Manush) and the awakened men (Man-hush). Those who thirst after God alone belong to the latter class; those who are mad after 'woman and gold' are all ordinary men—men in name only.

189. As one mask may be worn by various persons, so also various kinds of creatures have donned the garb of humanity. Some are tearing wolves, others are ferocious bears, and some again are cunning foxes or venomous snakes, though they all look like men.

190. Just as it is the nature of the sieve to reject the fine grains and to keep the coarse ones, so it is the nature of evil souls to reject the good and retain the evil. Just the opposite is the nature of the winnowing basket and of good souls.

191. There are people who are so situated in life that naturally they have nothing in the world to attract them, but would yet create for themselves some attachment and get themselves bound by it. They neither want nor like to be free. A man who has no family to care for, nor relatives to look after, generally takes a cat or a monkey or a dog or a bird for a pet and fondles it, and thus 'slakes his thirst for milk with mere whey'. Such is the snare that Maya's charm has set for humanity.

192. The new-born calf looks very lively and gay. It runs and frisks about all day long, only stopping now and then to suck the sweet milk from its dam. But no sooner is the rope tied round its neck than it begins to pine away gradually, and, far from being merry, wears a dejected and sorrowful look, and gets emaciated. In the same way, so long as a boy has no concern with the affairs of the world, he is quite merry and gay. But when he once gets himself locked in the world, as it were, with the strong bar of wedlock, and is harnessed with the responsibilities of family life, all his joy vanishes. He wears a look of dejection, care and anxiety; no more is there the glow of health on his cheeks, and deep wrinkles gradually furrow his forehead. Blessed is he that remains a boy throughout his life, free as the morning air, fresh as a newly opened flower, and pure as a dew-drop.

193. As a little boy or girl can have no idea of conjugal pleasure, even so a worldly man cannot at all comprehend the ecstasy of Divine communion.

194. The worldly man cannot easily resist the lure of 'woman and gold', and turn his mind to God, although he

may be relentlessly buffeted by the miseries and sufferings of life.

195. A worldly man is best known by his antipathy to whatever savours of religion. Not only does he himself dislike to hear any hymn or sacred music or the chanting of the holy 'name' of God, but he dissuades others from listening to them. He who scoffs at prayers, religious societies and pious men, is indeed a true worldling.

196. Sometimes I see worldly-minded men coming to me with pious devotees. These worldly men have no liking for religious conversations. So they become very impatient and restless while the others are having long talks about God and spirituality. They find it very difficult even to sit still, and hence whisper in their friends' ears, "When are you going? How long will you stay?" Occasionally their friends would say, "Wait a little. We are coming presently." Disgusted with their words, these worldly men would reply, "Then you had better continue your talk. We shall go now and wait for you in the boat" (which was to take them back to Calcutta).

197. While talking with a worldly man, one can see clearly how his heart is stuffed with all kinds of worldly thoughts and desires, just as the crop of the pigeon is filled with grain.

198. The heart of a sinful man is like curly hair. You will never succeed in straightening it, howsoever you may try. So also the heart of the wicked cannot be easily made upright and pure.

199. The mendicant's calabash jug (Kamandaḷu) may have been to the four Dhamas (the four chief places of

pilgrimage which a Sadhu is expected to visit), yet it remains as bitter as ever. Such is the nature of worldly-minded men.

200. The potter shapes various forms with unburnt clay, but he cannot work the clay that has once been burnt. In the same way the heart that has been burnt in the fire of worldly desires cannot be acted upon by any higher sentiment, and is incapable of being moulded into any lovely form.

201. As water can never soak a piece of stone, so religious teachings can produce no impression on a soul in bondage (Baddha-jiva).

302. As a nail cannot be driven into a stone but enters easily into the earth, so the advice of the pious does not affect the soul of a worldly man while it goes deep into the heart of a believer.

203. As soft clay easily takes an impression, but not hard stone, so also Divine wisdom impresses itself on the heart of a devotee, but not on a bound soul.

204. As the water under a bridge enters from one side and passes out at the other, so religious advice given to the worldlings enters the mind through one ear and goes out by the other, without leaving any impression.

205. What is the characteristic of the worldly-minded man? He is like the mongoose in the tamer's pot. The mongoose-tamer fixes a pot high up in a wall to serve as a nest for the animal. He ties one end of a rope round the neck of the mongoose while the other end is fastened to a weight. Coming out of the pot, the mongoose goes down the wall and wanders about here and there, but when

frightened, runs back into the pot to hide itself there. Unfortunately it cannot stay there long, as the weight at the other end of the rope drags it down from its comfortable home. Similarly, the worldly man is often forced by the chastening influence of the sufferings and miseries of life to soar high above the world and take refuge in God, but the dead weight of the world with all its attraction soon pulls him down.

206. Seeing the gleaming water pass through the valve of the bamboo trap placed in rice fields, small fish enter the trap with great glee. But having once entered, they cannot come out. Similarly, foolish men enter the meshes of the world, lured by its false glitter; but it is much easier to enter than to escape; and they are caught like little fish and imprisoned for good.

207. The fettered ones—the worldlings—are never awakened. How sorrows assail them, how frauds deceive them, and how dangers threaten them! Yet they do not 'wake up', even as the camel, so fond of the prickly bush and the nettle, does not cease browsing on them though they make its mouth bleed. The man of the world suffers so much, yet in a few days he forgets everything. Perhaps his wife has died or proved faithless; and lo! he marries again. Or perhaps his child has died, and he weeps; but in a short while everything has slipped out of his memory. And the mother of the child, who has been so overwhelmed with grief, is again looking to her toilet, and wearing ornaments and jewels. Parents are impoverished by their daughter's marriage, and yet annually children are born to them. And these men, though ruined by

law-suits, will yet go for litigation. They have not the wherewithal to provide well for their children, yet they will beget more children every year!

The worldling is sometimes like a snake that has caught hold of a mole which it can neither swallow nor throw out. Possibly he has come to see that there is nothing substantial in the world, that it is all skin and stone like sour-sop (Amrah fruit), yet he cannot forget the world and set his heart on God. If you remove him from worldly environment and place him in holy surroundings, he will lose heart and pine away, even as a worm which lives and thrives on filth will die if kept in a pot of rice.

208. None would keep milk in an earthen pot which has once been used for preparing curd lest the milk should get curdled. Nor can it be safely used for cooking, because it may crack upon the fire. It is therefore almost useless. So also a good and experienced Guru does not entrust valuable and exalted precepts to a worldly man, for he is sure to misinterpret and misuse them for his own mean ends. Nor will he ask him to do any useful work which may cost a little labour lest he should think that the preceptor is taking undue advantage of him.

209. Man cannot renounce the world even if he wishes, because he is thwarted by the Karmas that are bearing fruit in the present birth and by the impressions of previous actions left on the mind (Prarabdha and Samskara). Once a Yogi asked a king to sit down near him and meditate upon God. To him the king replied, "No, Sir, that cannot be. I can remain near you, but still the thirst for worldly enjoyment will be with me. If I remain in

this forest, perhaps there will arise a kingdom within it, as I am still destined to enjoy."

FICKLE DEVOTION OF THE WORLDLY-MINDED

210. Worldly persons may perform many pious and charitable acts in the hope of earthly rewards, but at the approach of misfortune, sorrow and poverty, their piety and charity forsake them. They are like the parrot that repeats, 'Radha-Krishna, Radha-Krishna' the livelong day, but cries, 'Kang, Kang' when caught by a cat, forgetting the Divine name.

Therefore, I say unto you, preaching religion to such men will prove useless. In spite of all your sermons they are sure to remain as worldly as ever.

211. A spring cushion is pressed down when one sits upon it but soon resumes its shape when the pressure is removed. So it is with worldly men. They are full of religious sentiment as long as they hear religious talk; but as soon as they enter upon the routine of their daily life they forget all those high and noble thoughts, and become as impure as before.

212. Iron appears red-hot in the furnace, but becomes black soon after it is taken out. In the same way worldly men are full of religious emotion as long as they are in a temple or in the society of the pious; but no sooner do they leave these associations, than the flood of devotion in them subsides.

213. As the fly now sits on an unclean sore and next on offerings to God, so the mind of the worldly man is at

one time engaged in religious topics and at the next loses itself in the pleasures of wealth and lust.

214. The heart of the worldly man is like the worm in a dung-hill. The worm always lives in the dung and loves to live therein. If by chance someone takes it out of that filthy habitation and put it on a lotus-flower, it will soon die of the fragrance of the flower. So the worldly man cannot live even for a moment outside the dirty atmosphere of worldly thoughts and desires.

215. Do you know what worldly people's idea of God is like? It is like the children's prattle while they play among themselves. Sometimes they swear, saying, "By God, I say!" They learn this from their elders when they hear them taking an oath. Or, at best, it is like the utterance of the dandy who with all his foppish airs goes to a garden in one of his idle promenades, whistling and twirling his stick about, and picks up a flower and exclaims, "O what a beautiful flower God has made!" It is only a momentary mood like the sprinkling of a drop of water on a bar of redhot iron. So, I say, you must thirst for Him. You will have to take a deep plunge into the ocean.

THE WORLDLY-MINDED AND SPIRITUAL PRACTICES

216. A husbandman was watering a sugar-cane field throughout the day. After finishing his task he saw that not a drop of water had entered the field; all the water had run underground through several big rat-holes. Such is the state of the devotee who worships God, secretly cherishing ambitions and worldly desires in his heart.

Though he may be praying daily, he makes no progress, because his entire devotion runs to waste through the rat-holes of these desires, and at the end of his lifelong devotion, he remains the same as before.

217. Why does the mind become unsteady when engaged in contemplation? The fly sits at times on the sweetmeats kept exposed for sale in the shop of the confectioner; but when a scavenger passes by with a basketful of filth, the fly leaves the sweets and at once settles on the filth. On the other hand, the bee in search of honey sits only on flowers and never on filthy objects. Worldly men, like flies, get occasionally a momentary taste of the sweetness of Divine love, but their natural hankering after filth soon brings them back to the dung-hill of worldliness. The great Paramahamsas are, however, always absorbed in the contemplation and enjoyment of Divine love.

218. An evil spirit is exorcised by throwing charmed mustard seeds on the possessed; but if the evil spirit has possessed the mustard seeds themselves, how can they be of any use in exorcising it? If the mind with which you contemplate the Deity is tainted with the vicious thoughts of the world, how can you expect to do your religious devotions successfully with such a corrupt instrument?

219. A wet match does not ignite, however hard you may strike it; it only smokes. But a dry match lights at once, even with the slightest rubbing. The heart of the true devotee is like the dry match; the slightest mention of the name of the Lord kindles the fire of love in his heart, while the mind of the worldly man, soaked in lust and attachment for wealth, resists all warmth like the

moistened match. Though God may be preached to him several times, the fire of Divine love can never be kindled in him.

220. A worldly man may be endowed with as much intelligence and knowledge as a Jnani, may take as much pains and trouble as a Yogi, and may make as great sacrifices as an ascetic; but all his exertions are in vain since his energies are misdirected, and since he does all these for the sake of worldly honour and wealth, and not for the sake of the Lord.

221. The soiled mirror never reflects the rays of the sun; similarly those who are impure and unclean at heart and are deluded by Maya never perceive the glory of the Lord. But the pure in heart see the Lord as the clear mirror reflects the sun. Therefore be pure.

222. When a certain quantity of pure milk is mixed with double the quantity of water, it requires a good deal of time and labour to condense it into Kshira (condensed milk). The mind of a worldly man is largely diluted with the filthy water of evil and impure thoughts, and he has to work long and hard to purify it and give it the proper strength and consistency characteristic of a truly pious heart.

223.* Q. Why is it that worldly men do not give up everything to find God?

A. Can an actor coming on the stage throw off his mask at once? Let worldly men play out their part, and in time they will throw off their false appearance.

224. The soul that is wholly world-bound is like the worm that lives for ever in filth, and dies there and has no idea of anything better. The soul whose worldliness is

of lesser intensity is, however, like the fly that sits now on filth and now on sugar. The free soul alone is like the bee that always drinks honey and tastes nothing else.

225.* The worldly man is like the alligator. As the body of the alligator is not pervious to the strokes of any weapon, and as it cannot be put to death except by striking at the belly, so no matter how much good advice you give to the worldly man, and no matter how much self-disgust you arouse in him, he will never realise his situation fully unless you wean him from the objects of his attachment.

226. Worldly men will not act up to your advice if you ask them to renounce everything and devote themselves to the lotus-like feet of the Lord. Hence, after much deliberation as to how to attract such souls, Gour and Nitai [1] hit upon a plan of alluring them, and said, "Come, take the name of Hari, and you will have a nice soup of Magur fish and the caress of a young damsel." These two items tempted many to join them and take the name of the Lord. When by and by they came to have a little taste of the nectar of the holy name, they understood the hidden meaning of Nitai's teaching. The soup of the Magur fish is nothing but the streams of tears they shed in love of God. The earth is 'the young damsel', and to be caressed by her, means to roll on earth in the rapture of Divine love.

[1] Lord Chaitanya and his companion Nityananda.

BOOK II

THE ASCENT OF MAN

He who has not given up sinful ways, whose senses have not been restrained, who is unmeditative, and whose mind is devoid of peace, cannot attain Him even by a highly cultivated intelligence.

O good-looking youth, taking hold of that bow, the mighty weapon of scriptural wisdom (embodied in Om, the sound symbol of the Most High) and fixing the arrow (of the self) rendered sharp by devoted worship, draw it with the mind absorbed in His thought, and hit the mark—even that Imperishable Being.

He in whom are woven the heaven, the earth, the sky, and the mind together with the vital energies, know Him, that Atman alone, and give up all other vain talk. This is the path to Immortality.

The Upanishads

CHAPTER VIII

VARIETIES OF ASPIRANTS AND THEIR IDEALS

[Some types of aspirants—Characteristics of true aspirants—Kinship of the spiritually-inclined—Ideals of the aspirant entangled in the world—Ideals of the Sannyasin]

SOME TYPES OF ASPIRANTS

227. Out of the myriads of paper kites that are seen flying in the air, only one or two gets free by the snapping of the string. So out of hundreds of aspirants practising spiritual disciplines only one or two gets free from worldly bondage.

228. There is a fabled species of birds called 'Homa'. They live so high up in the heavens and love those high regions so dearly that they never come down to the earth. And it is said that they even lay their eggs in the sky, and that their young ones are hatched in mid-air as the eggs fall, pulled down by gravity. No sooner do these fledglings find out that they are falling downwards, than they immediately change their course and instinctively fly up towards their

home. Men like Sukadeva, Narada, Jesus and Sankaracharya are like these birds. Even in their boyhood they become free from all attachment to the things of the world and betake themselves to the highest regions of true Knowledge and Divine light.

229.* There are two classes of Yogis, hidden and open. The former go through religious practices in secret and keep themselves hidden from public gaze. The latter carry about them the external symbols of the Yogi, such as a staff, and converse freely on spiritual subjects.

230.* Though it is the general rule that flowers appear first and then fruits, there are some plants and creepers which bear fruits first and then flowers. Similarly, ordinary persons have to go through Sadhanas before they realise God but there is a class of aspirants who realise God first, and then perform the Sadhanas.

231. Of the grains of paddy fried in a frying pan, the few that leap out of the pan and burst outside are the best fried, for they are without any mark of charring. On the other hand, every one of the properly fried grains in the pan is sure to have some charred mark on it, however small. So of all good devotees, those few who give up the world altogether and go out of it are perfect without any spot, while even the best of those who are in the world must have at least some small spot of imperfection in their character.

232. Butter churned early in the morning is the best; that churned after sunrise is not so good. Addressing his young disciples who became Sannyasins later on, the Master used to say, "You are like butter charned early in

the morning while my householder disciples are like butter churned late in the day."

233. The young bamboo can be easily bent, but the full grown bamboo breaks when it is bent with force. It is easy to bend the young heart towards God, but the untrained heart of the old escapes the hold whenever it is so drawn.

234. The parrot cannot be taught to sing when the the vibrating membrane in its throat has hardened too much due to age. It must be taught to sing while young, before the collar line appears on its neck. So in old age it is difficult to learn how to fix the mind on God, but it can be easily learnt in youth.

235. A ripe mango may be offered to God, or used for some other purpose; but if it is pecked by a crow even once, it is unfit for any use. It can neither be offered to the Deity, nor presented to a Brahmin, nor may it be eaten by the pure. So boys and girls should be dedicated to the service of God before the impurities of worldly desires taint their hearts. Once worldly desires enter their minds, or the demon of sensual pleasures casts his baneful shadow over them, it is very difficult indeed to make them tread the path of virtue.

236. The love in the heart of a boy is whole and undivided. When he gets married in time, half of his heart, if not more, is given away to his wife, and when children are born to him, he loses another quarter thereof, while the remaining quarter is divided among father, mother, honour, fame, pride, dress, and the rest; therefore he has no love left to offer to God. Hence if the undivided

mind of a boy is directed early enough to God, he may gain His love, and realise Him easily. But it is not quite so easy for grown-up people to do so.

237. If you ask whether there is any difference between the Jnanis who live in the world and those who renounce it, I would say that the two are the same. Both of them have the same Jnana in common. But if the Jnani is in the world, he has cause to fear; for life in the midst of sensual attractions is attended with the fear of fall, slight as it is. If you live in a sooty room, you are sure to get a little tainted by the soot, however careful you may be.

238. To some one the Master said: "Well, you have now come to seek God when you have spent the best part of your life in the world. Had you entered the world after realising God, what peace and joy you would have found!"

239. *Q.* What is the difference between the Sattvic, the Rajasic and the Tamasic ways of worship?

A. The man who worships from the very depth of his heart without the least ostentation or vanity is a Sattvic worshipper. The man who gives much attention to decorating his house, makes much fuss about music and dancing, and makes all costly and elaborate arrangements for a rich feast when celebrating the worship of the Deity, is a Rajasic worshipper. The man who immolates hundreds of innocent goats and sheep on the altar, has dishes of meat and wine for offerings, and is absorbed only in dancing and singing while conducting worship, is a Tamasic worshipper.

CHARACTERISTICS OF TRUE ASPIRANTS

240. The flint may remain for myriads of years under water and still not lose its inner fire. Strike it with steel whenever you like, and out flashes the glowing spark. So is the true devotee firm in his faith. Though he may remain surrounded by all the impurities of the world, he never loses his faith in, and love of, God. He warms up with devout enthusiasm as soon as he hears the 'name' of the Lord.

241. Just as gold and brass are tested by a touchstone, so are the sincere and the hypocritical Sadhus distinguished by persecution and calumny.

242. The railway engine easily drags with it a train of heavily loaded carriages. So the loving children of God, firm in their faith and devotion, feel no trouble in passing through life in spite of all troubles and anxieties, and at the same time they lead many to God along with them.

243. When does the attraction of the pleasures of the sense die away? When one realises the consummation of all happiness and of all pleasures in God—the indivisible, eternal ocean of bliss. Those who enjoy Him can find no attraction in the cheap, worthless pleasures of the world.

244. He who has once tasted the refined crystal of sugar candy finds no pleasure in tasting the dirty treacle. He who has slept in a palace will not find pleasure in lying down in a dirty hovel. The soul that has tasted the sweetness of Divine bliss finds no happiness in the vulgar pleasures of the world.

245. The lady who has a king for her lover will not accept the addresses of a street beggar. The soul that has found favour in the eyes of the Lord does not fall in love with the paltry things of the world.

246. It is the nature of the winnowing basket to reject whatever is light and useless, and retain whatever is weighty and good. Such is the nature of all pious souls.

247. Sugar and sand may be mixed together, but the ant rejects the sand and carries away the grains of sugar. So the holy Paramahamsas and pious men successfully sift the good from the bad.

248. The water of a rapid stream moves round and round in eddies and whirlpools in some places; but passing these it resumes again a straight and swift course. So the heart of the devotee is caught every now and then in the whirlpool of despondency, grief and unbelief; but this is only a momentary aberration and does not last long.

249. Wherein is the strength of a devotee? He is a child of God, and his devotional tears are his mightiest weapon.

250. The more you scratch the part affected by ring-worm, the greater grows the itching, and the more the pleasure you derive from scratching. So the worshippers of God never get tired of singing His praise.

251. That man whose hair stands on end at the mere mention of the 'name' of God, and from whose eyes flow tears of love—he has indeed reached his last birth.

252. What happens when an impure woman tempts a pious man and tries to cast her evil influence upon him? Just as the skin of a ripe mango, when pressed hard, is left

in the hand, the stone and the kernel having slipped out of it, so does the mind of the pious man glide away to God, leaving behind its earthly tabernacle to be acted on by the woman.

253. The truly religious man is he who does not commit any sin even when he is alone, and when no man observes him, because he feels that God sees him even then. He who can resist the temptations of a young and seductive woman in a lonely forest, where he is unobserved by human eye, through the fear that God sees him and who, through such fear, will not even cast an immoral glance at her,—he is truly a religious man. He who finds a bag full of gold in a lonely and uninhabited house, and resists the temptation of appropriating it, he is a truly religious man. But he who practises religion for the sake of show, through fear of public opinion, cannot be called truly religious. The religion of silence and secrecy is the true religion, but it is all sham and mockery when attended with vaunting and vanity.

KINSHIP OF THE SPIRITUALLY-INCLINED

254. The spiritually-minded belong to a caste of their own, beyond all social conventions.

255. A woman naturally feels shy to relate to all the conversation she daily holds with her husband. She neither communicates it to anyone nor feels inclined to do so; and if it gets divulged in any way, she feels annoyed. But she would herself relate it to her intimate companion without reserve; nay, she would even be impatient to tell it to

her and would find pleasure in doing so. Similarly, a devotee of God does not like to relate to any one but a true Bhakta the ecstatic joy that he experiences in Divine communion; nay, sometimes he is impatient to relate his experiences to such a person and feels happy to do so.

256. If a strange animal were to approach a herd of cows, it would soon be driven off by the combined attack of the whole herd. But let a cow come, and all the cows would make friends with her, with much mutual licking of bodies. Thus, when one devotee meets another devotee, both experience much delight and are loth to part from each other. But when a scoffer enters their circle, they sedulously avoid him.

257. Why is it that one who loves the Lord does not like to live in solitude? The hemp-smoker finds no pleasure in smoking without company. The pious man, like the hemp-smoker, finds no pleasure in chanting the sacred 'name' of God away from the company of other devotees.

IDEALS OF THE ASPIRANT ENTANGLED IN THE WORLD

258. It is said that, when a Tantrika tries to invoke the Deity through the medium of the spirit of the dead, he sits on a fresh human corpse and keeps near him food and wine. In the course of the invocation, if at any time the corpse is, as they say, vivified temporarily and opens its mouth, the intrepid invoker must pour the wine and thrust the food into its gaping mouth to appease the elemental that has, for the time being, taken possession of it. If he does not do so, the invocation is interrupted by the elemental, and the higher spirit does not appear.

So, remaining on the carcass of the world, if you desire to attain beatitude, first provide yourself with all the things necessary to pacify the clamour of worldly demands on you; otherwise your devotions will be broken and interrupted by the cares and anxieties of life.

259. There is necessity of money, no doubt, in worldly life; but do not ponder much over it and other material gains. Contentment with what comes of its own accord is the best attitude. Do not be anxious to hoard. Those who dedicate their very life and soul to Him, those who are His devotees and have taken refuge in Him, can never think of such worldly matters. With them, expenditure is commensurate with income. As money comes into their hands in one way, it is spent in another.

260.* A householder disciple: Sir, may I try to earn a larger income?

The Master: Yes, if you mean to devote it to the life in the family based on discrimination. But take care that you earn money by honest means. For it is not earning money but the service of the Lord that is your aim; and wealth devoted to God is beyond cavil.

Disciple: How long, Sir, have I obligations to the family?

The Master; So long as the family is not provided with enough to maintain itself. But if your children can support themselves, you have no more duty to them.

261.* To some householder devotees the Master said: "You will look upon money only as a means of getting food, clothes and shelter, of worshipping the Deity and serving Sadhus and devotees. But it is wrong to hoard it. Bees labour hard to build their hives, but man comes and robs them. You need not renounce 'woman' completely. But after a few children are born, you and your wife should live like brother and sister."

262. *Q*. How can I go through my devotional practices when I have always to think of my daily bread?

A. He for whom you work will supply you with your necessaries. God made provisions for your support before He sent you into this world.

263.* We possess home, family and children for a short time, but these are all ephemeral. The palm tree itself is real, but when one or two of its fruits fall to the ground, why should we regret it?

264.* Renunciation of 'woman and gold' has been laid down only for those that lead a monastic life. Monks must not even look at the pictures of women. Even the thought of spiced pickles causes the mouth to water—not to speak of the sight or the touch of those dainties. But this hard rule is not meant for men of the world, like you (addressing the householder devotees present); it is intended purely for monks. As for you, you may go amongst women with a mind unattached and fixed upon God. That your mind may be thus unattached and fixed upon God, it is good that you should often retire into solitude—a place away from either men or women; a place where you may be left absolutely to yourself, praying to the Lord with a yearning heart for true knowledge; a place where you may stay at least for three days, if not more, or for at least one day, if not three.

Your path, again, as married men, is to live with your wife just as brother and sister, after one or two children are born to you, and to pray to the Lord constantly that both of you may have strength to live a perfect life of spirituality and self-control.

265. Live in the world, but be not worldly. As the saying goes, make the frog dance before the snake, but let not the snake swallow the frog.

266. A boat may stay in water, but water should not stay in the boat. An aspirant may live in the world, but the world should not live within him.

267. It matters not if you live the life of a house-holder, only you must fix your mind on God. Do your work with one hand, and hold the feet of the Lord with the other. When you have no work in the world to do, hold His feet fast to your heart with both your hands.

268. What is the state of a man who is in the world but is free from its attachments? He is like a lotus-leaf in water, or like a mud-fish in the marsh. Neither of these is polluted by the element in which it lives. The water wets not the leaf, nor does the mud stain the glossy coat of the fish.

269.* It does not matter much whether you are a family man or not. Always perform your duties unattached, with your mind fixed on God. As for instance, the man who has got a carbuncle on his back talks with his friends and others, and even carries out undertakings, but his mind is all the while on his pain.

270.* Living in the world one is safe, if one has Viveka (discrimination of the Real from the unreal), and

Vairagya (dispassion for worldly things), and along with these intense devotion to God.

271.* What are you to do when you are placed in this world? Give up everything to Him, resign yourself to Him, and there will be no more trouble for you. Then you will come to know that everything is done by His will.

272. It may be given even to the householder to see God. It was the case with Raja Janaka, the great royal sage. But one cannot rise to the height of Raja Janaka all of a sudden. Janaka spent many long years in solitude, away from the din and bustle of the world, practising devotional exercises. Thus it would do infinite good to men of the world, if they would retire now and then into solitude, even for three days at a time, so that God might be realised.

273. Some Brahmo boys once told me that they followed Janaka's example—they lived in the world but quite unattached to it. I said to them that it was easy to say one was Janaka but quite a different matter to be actually one. It is so hard to move among worldly objects without being contaminated. What terrible austerities did not Janaka practise at the outset! But I do not advise you to go through similar hardships. What I want you to do is to practice devotion, and to live alone for some time in some quiet place. Enter the world after gaining Jnana and Bhakti. The best curd is formed when the milk is left quite still; shaking, or even changing the pot, spoils it. Janaka was unattached; hence one of the epithets applied to him is Videha—literally 'bodiless'. He led the life of a Jivanmukta. The annihilation of the idea of the body

is exceedingly difficult to accomplish. Truly Janaka was a great hero. He handled with ease the two swords —one of Knowledge (Jnana) and the other of work (Karma).

274. Men always quote the example of king Janaka as a man who lived in the world and yet attained spiritual illumination. But throughout the whole history of mankind he is the solitary example of this type. He was not the rule but the exception. The general rule is that no one can attain spiritual perfection without renouncing 'woman and gold'. Do not think yourself to be a Janaka. Many centuries have rolled away, and the world has not yet produced a second Janaka.

275. If you desire to live in the world unattached, you should first practise devotion in solitude for some time —a year, six months, a month, or at least twelve days. During this period of retirement, you should constantly meditate upon God and pray to Him for Divine love. You should think that there is nothing in the world which you may call your own, that those whom you consider as your own are sure to pass away some day or other. God alone is really your own. He is your all-in-all. How to obtain Him?—this should be your only concern.

276. When you are engaged in devotional practices, keep aloof from those who scoff at them, and also from those who ridicule piety and the pious.

277. If you first smear your palms with oil and then cut open the jack, the milky exudation of the fruit will not stick to your hands and inconvenience you. If you first fortify yourself with the true knowledge of the

Universal Self, and then live in the midst of wealth and worldliness, surely they will in no way affect you.

278. The magnetic needle always points to the North, and hence it is that the sailing vessel does not lose her direction. So long as the heart of man is directed towards God, he cannot be lost in the ocean of worldliness.

279. In the game of hide-and-seek, if the player succeeds in touching the 'Grand-dame' (Boori), he is no longer liable to be made a 'thief' by the seeker. Similarly by once seeing God, we are no longer bound by the fetters of the world. Just as the person touching the Boori is free to go about wherever he chooses, without being pursued and made a 'thief', so also in the world's play-ground there is no fear for him who has once touched the feet of God. He attains freedom from all worldly cares and anxieties, and nothing can ever bind him again.

280. Alligators love to float on water, but as soon as one rises up, it is made a mark by the hunters. Necessarily it is obliged to remain under water and cannot rise to the surface. Yet, whenever it finds a safe opportunity, it rises up with a deep whizzing noise, and swims happily on the expanse of water. O man, entangled in the meshes of the world, you too are anxious to swim on the surface of the ocean of bliss, but are prevented by the importunate demands of your family. Yet be of good cheer. Whenever you find leisure, call upon God eagerly, pray to Him earnestly and tell Him all your sorrows. In due time, He will surely emancipate you and enable you to swim merrily on the ocean of bliss.

281. When you are forced by circumstances to go to a place of temptations, always remember the Divine Mother. She will protect you from the many evils that may be lurking even in your heart. The presence of the Mother will shame you away from evil deeds and evil thoughts.

282. The world and God—how is it possible to harmonise these two? Look at the carpenter's wife, how diversely busy she is! With one hand she stirs the flattened rice in the mortar of a Dhenki, with the other hand she is nursing her child, and at the very same time she bargains with a customer about the flattened rice. Thus, though her occupations are many, her mind is fixed on the one idea that the pestle of the Dhenki does not fall on her hand and bruise it. So be in the world, but always remember Him, and never go astray from His path.

283. As a boy holding to a post or pillar whirls about it with headlong speed without any fear of falling, so perform your worldly duties, fixing your hold firmly upon God, and you will be free from danger.

284. As the village maidens in India carry four or five pots of water placed one over the other upon their heads, talking all the way with one another about their joys and sorrows, and yet do not allow a single drop of water to spill, so must the traveller in the path of virtue walk along his route. In whatever circumstances he may be placed, let him always take heed that his heart does not swerve from the true path.

285. As an unchaste woman, busily engaged in household affairs, will all the while be thinking of her secret lover

so do you, O man of the world, perform your round of worldly duties, but let your heart be fixed always on God.

286. As a wet-nurse in a wealthy family brings up her master's child, loving it as if it were her own, yet knowing well that she has no claim upon it, so you also think that you are but trustees and guardians of your children whose real father is the Lord Himself.

287. As the street minstrel plays the guitar with one hand and with the other strikes a drum, while at the same time he sings a song, so do you, O man of the world, perform all your worldly duties with your hands, never forgetting to repeat and glorify the 'name' of the Lord with all your heart.

288. The maidservant says with reference to her master's house, "This is our house." All the while she knows that the house is not her own, and that her own house is far away in a distant village of Burdwan or Naddia. Her thoughts are all really directed to her village home. Again, referring to her master's child in her arms, she says, "My Hari has grown very naughty," or, "My Hari likes to eat this or that," and so on. But all the while she knows for certain that Hari is not her own. I tell those who come to me, to lead a life unattached like the maid-servant. I tell them to live unattached to this world—to be in the world, but not of the world—and at the same time to have their mind directed to God, the heavenly home whence all come. I tell them to pray for Bhakti, and base their lives on it.

289. Always consider that your family concerns are not yours; they are God's and you are His servant come

here to obey His commands. When this idea becomes firm, there remains nothing indeed that a man may call his own.

290.* He is a true hero who performs all the duties of the world with his mind fixed on God. None but a strong man can, while carrying a load of two maunds (more than a hundredweight) on his head, stop to admire a bridal procession passing his way.

291. Those who live in the world and still try to gain salvation are like the soldiers that fight from behind the ramparts of a fort, while the ascetics who renounce the world in search of God are like the soldiers fighting in the open field. To fight the enemy from within the fort is more convenient and far safer than to fight in the open field.

292. Before soldiers go out to meet the enemy, they learn the art of fighting in their barracks, where they do not have to put up with the hardships incidental to action in the open field. So avail yourselves of the conveniences of your home-life to raise your spiritual condition before you take to the austerities of an ascetic life.

293. He indeed is blessed, in whom all the qualities of head and heart are fully developed and evenly balanced. He acquits himself admirably well in whatever position he may be placed. He is full of guileless faith and love for God, and yet his dealings with others leave nothing to be desired. When he is engaged in worldly affairs, he is a thorough man of business. In the assembly of the learned he establishes his claims as a man of superior learning, and in debates he shows wonderful powers of reasoning. To

his parents he is obedient and affectionate; to his relations and friends he is loving and sweet; to his neighbours he is kind and sympathetic and always ready to do good; to his wife he is the god of love. Such a man is indeed perfect.

IDEALS OF THE SANNYASIN

294. The first birth of a man is from his father; Upanayana marks his second birth, and Sannyasa the third.

295. The mind is much wasted while one is engaged in worldly pursuits. And that loss can be made good, only if one takes to the life of renunciation (Sannyasa).

296. Who is a fit candidate for the holy order of Sannyasins? He who gives up the world altogether without having any thought of the morrow, as to how he will eat or how he will be clothed, is fit to be a true Sannyasin. His mentality must be like that of a man who can, if need be, let himself fall fearlessly from the top of a tall tree, without any thought of saving his own life or limbs.

297. Yogins and Sannyasins are like snakes. The snake does not dig out a hole for itself, but lives in the hole made by the mouse. When one hole becomes uninhabitable, it enters into another hole. Just so Yogins and Sannyasins make no house for themselves. They pass their days in other men's houses—today in one house, tomorrow in another.

298.* Sadhus never settle down in a place where there are 'no jungles' near by and where 'food and drink' is hard to get. 'Jungles' means solitary spots for answering the calls of nature; and 'food and drink' means alms. As

Sadhus live on alms, they select only those places for their temporary residence where alms can be easily procured. When they get tired in the course of their journey they may halt at a place for a day or two, in spite of the difficulty of procuring alms. But they never stay anywhere if there is scarcity of water and of solitary spots for answering the calls of nature. Good Sadhus never attend to these matters of physical cleanliness in places where they may be observed by others. They finish these things in solitude, far away from the haunts of men.

299. If a white cloth is stained even with a small spot, the stain appears very ugly indeed. So the smallest fault of a holy man becomes painfully prominent.

300.* A Sannyasin may himself be perfectly unattached and may have full control over his senses. Yet to set an example to mankind he must make a rigorous renunciation of 'woman and gold'. For only when they notice the thoroughness of the Sannyasin's renunciation, will men take courage; only then will they make efforts to renounce sex and riches. And who indeed will impart this lesson on renunciation, if not the Sannyasin?

301.* What is the sign of a genuine Sannyasin and a Tyagi? Both must be entirely unconnected with lust and gold. Should they feel an attachment for gold, or be troubled by pollution even in a dream, all their spiritual exercises would come to naught.

302. When one has taken up the garb of a Sannyasin, one has to conduct oneself precisely like a true Sadhu. Don't you see in the drama how the person playing the

part of a king always acts like a king and how he who is in the roll of the minister always plays the minister? Once a village clown put on the garb of a Sannyasin and appeared before the Zamindar of the place. The Zamindar wanted to present him with a purse, but he refused to accept it and went away. After a while he came back, having washed himself and changed his dress, and asked for the money that the Zamindar wanted to give. When he dressed like a Sadhu, he could not even touch the money, but now he was ready to feel gratified even with a four-anna bit.

303. A person went to a holy man to get some medicine for his sick child, carrying the little patient in his arms. The holy man asked him to come next day. Next day, when the man went, the Sadhu said, "Give no sweets to the child, and the child will soon be cured." The man replied, "Sir, you could have told me this yesterday itself." The Sadhu said, "Yes, I could have, but yesterday I had a quantity of sugar lying before me, and seeing that, your child would have thought that the Sadhu who advised others not to take sugar but ate it himself was a hypocrite."

304. The man who becomes an ascetic owing to some misunderstanding with his father, or mother, or wife may be called an 'ascetic-by-disgust'. His asceticism is momentary; he gives up the ascetic way of life as soon as he gets a good lucrative job in a wealthy family.

305. A disciple: How can we recognise a truly pious man (Sadhu)?

The Master: He is truly pious whose heart and soul are wholly dedicated to God. Truly pious is he who has renounced 'woman and gold'. The truly pious man never views women in the ordinary worldly light. He always remains at a distance from them, and if they happen to come near, he looks on them as his mother and shows respect to them. He thinks constantly of God, and serves all creatures, knowing that He resides in all. These are the general traits of the truly pious.

306.* Trust not a Sannyasin, who practises medicine, uses spells and incantations, receives money, and displays his piety with the sign-boards of elaborate external marks.

307. Forgiveness is the true nature of the ascetic.

CHAPTER IX

SOME AIDS TO SPIRITUAL LIFE

[*Caste and external observances—Worship of images—Value of pilgrimages—Pious company—Repetition of Divine 'names'*]

CASTE AND EXTERNAL OBSERVANCES

308. Honour both spirit and form, the sentiment within as well as the symbol without.

309. In a grain of paddy the germ is commonly considered to be the only thing necessary for germination and growth, while the husk is regarded as of no importance; but if the husked grain is sown, it will not sprout and grow up into a plant and yield rice. To get a crop one must needs sow the grain with its husk intact. If, however, one wants to get the pure grain itself for eating purposes, one must remove the husk from the seed. So rites and ceremonies are necessary for the growth and perpetuation of a religion. They are the receptacles that contain the germinating seeds of truth; and consequently every man must perform them till he reaches the central truth therein.

310. The oyster that contains the precious pearl is in itself of very little value, but it is essential for the growth

of the pearl. The shell itself may prove to be of no use to the man who has secured the pearl. So ceremonies and rites may not be necessary for him who has attained the highest truth, namely, God.

311.* Rituals are to be observed. But when one advances in spirituality, it is not necessary to observe them for long. Then the mind gets concentrated on God, resulting in communion with Him.

312. When a wound is perfectly healed, the scab falls off of itself; but if the scab be taken off earlier, it bleeds. In the same way, with the advent of Divine illumination all distinctions of caste vanish; but it is wrong for the ignorant to override such distinctions, lest they should lead to undesirable consequences.

313. A fruit that has ripened on the tree and fallen down of itself, tastes very sweet, but the one that has been picked and ripened artificially is not so sweet, and soon shrivels up. In like manner, the rules of caste fall away of themselves from him who has attained perfection and has realised the unity of all things; but those who have had no such exalted experience cannot escape the consciousness of superiority and inferiority in others, and have to observe caste distinctions. If in this state of ignorance a man feigns perfection by overriding all caste distinctions and by living a free life, he is surely like the green fruit artificially ripened.

314. Is it proper for one who has attained Divine wisdom to keep the Brahminical thread? When the knowledge of the Self is gained, all fetters drop off of themselves. Then there is no distinction between Brahmin and

Sudra, between high caste and low caste. Thus the sacred thread, a sign of caste, falls off of itself. But so long as a man is conscious of any distinction and difference, he should not forcibly throw it away.

315. While a storm is blowing, we cannot distinguish between an Asvattha (fig tree) and a Vata (banyan tree). So when the storm of supreme Knowledge blows, there can be no distinction of caste.

316. A true devotee who has drunk deep of Divine love is like a veritable drunkard, and as such cannot always observe the rules of propriety.

317. Once Krishna Kishore asked me, "Why have you cast off the sacred thread?" When this change came over me,[1] everything was blown away, as if by the great cyclone of Ashvin.[2] The old landmarks were swept away. There was no outward consciousness itself. What to speak, then, of taking care of either the holy thread or even of the piece of cloth I used to wear? Lost in intense God-consciousness, I could not even know that I was nude for the greater part of the day. Therefore when Krishna Kishore took me to task for having parted with the sacred thread, I only observed, "You will see it all clearly if you are once seized with madness for the Lord."

318. Those who utter the 'name' of God are holy. Krishna Kishore was a holy man of Ariadaha. Once he had been to Brindavan on a pilgrimage. There, one day, in the course of his walk he felt thirsty, and seeing a person standing near a well, he asked him to draw a little water

[1] Through God-vision and spiritual realisation.

[2] The great cyclone of 1864 in Bengal.

for him. The man said that he was of a very low caste and so was not fit to draw water for a Brahmin. Krishna Kishore said, "Will you pronounce the name of God and thus make yourself pure?" The man did so and fetched some water for him; and he, an orthodox Brahmin, drank the water! How great was the power of his faith!

319. As a drunkard sometimes puts his coat on his head and at other times uses it as breeches, so the God-intoxicated man behaves as if he is not conscious of the external world.

320. People of this age care for the essence of everything. They will accept the essentials of religion and not its non-essentials (that is, the rituals, ceremonials, dogmas and creeds).

321. Those who take fish do not want the useless head and tail of the fish, but only the soft middle portion of it; so the ancient rules and commandments of our scriptures must be pruned of all their accretions to make them suit modern times.

WORSHIP OF IMAGES

322. While raising a building, the scaffolding is indispensable; but when the work is completed, no one feels the necessity of it. So also image-worship is necessary in the beginning, but not afterwards.

323. As a man begins to learn writing by drawing big scrawls before he tries to write a smaller hand, so a person must acquire the power of concentrating his thoughts by fixing the mind first upon forms, and then, after succeeding therein, by fixing it upon the formless.

324. A marksman learns to shoot by first having big objects to shoot at; and as he acquires more and more facility in shooting, he aims more and more easily at the smaller marks on the target. So when the mind has been trained to focus on images having form, it is easy for it to do so on things having no form.

325. As a toy fruit or a toy elephant reminds one of the real fruit and the living animal, so do the images that are worshipped remind one of God Who is formless and eternal.

326. The Master once said to a disciple of his: "You were talking of images made of clay. There arises a necessity for them too. These various forms used for worship have been provided to suit the needs of different men at different stages of spiritual evolution."

327. The mother so arranges food for her children that each one gets what agrees with him. If she has five children and she gets a big fish to cook, she makes different dishes out of it, and gives each one what suits him exactly. One is given rich Polao with fish; another, of weak digestion, only a little soup; and so on, according to the digestive power of each. (The same in the case with the various symbols and disciplines prescribed for spiritual aspirants.)

328. A disciple: One may believe that God is 'with form'. But surely He is not the earthen image that is worshipped.'

The Master: Why call it an earthen image? The Divine image is made of the Spirit.

329. The Master once said to Keshab Chandra Sen, who was a great iconoclast in his days: "Why

do these images rouse the idea of mud and clay, stone and straw, in your mind? Why can you not realise the presence of the eternal, blissful, all-conscious Mother, even in these forms?"

330. If a worshipper is convinced that the images of the Deity in the shape of various Gods and Goddesses are verily divine, he reaches God by their worship. But if he holds them to be nothing better than mud and straw and clay, to him the worship of snch images does no good.

331. If there is anything wrong in image-worship, does He not know that all worship is meant for Him? He will surely be pleased to accept the worship, knowing that it is meant for Him alone. Love God; that is the duty nearest to you.

332. When one sees God, one realises that everything, images and all, is a manifestation of the Spirit. To him the image is not made of clay but of Spirit.

VALUE OF PILGRIMAGES

333. The Milk of the cow in reality pervades the whole body of the animal through its blood, but you cannot milk it by squeezing the ears or the horns; you can get the milk only from the teats. Similarly, God pervades the universe everywhere, but you cannot see Him everywhere. He manifests Himself more readily in sacred temples which are full of the spirit of devotion diffused by the life and spiritual practices of the devotees of former times.

334. Know that there must be manifestation of God in places where countless people have for long practised

austerity, Japa, meditation, prayer and worship with a view to realise Him. Through their devotion, spiritual ideas are present in these places in a solidified form, as it were. Hence there man easily feels the awakening of spirituality and realises Him. From time immemorial, numberless Sadhus, devotees and men of realisation have come to these holy places to have a vision of God, and have prayed to Him with an outpouring of their hearts, setting aside all worldly desires. Therefore, though equally present everywhere, God manifests Himself specially in these places. Water can be had anywhere by digging into the earth. When, however, there is a well or a tank or a lake, one has not to dig for water, but can get it whenever one likes.

335. As cows, after eating their fill, lie down quietly at a place and chew the cud, so after visiting a sacred spot or a place of pilgrimage, you must take hold of the holy thoughts that rose in the mind while there, sit down in a solitary corner and think of them till you are immersed in them. You must not devote yourself to the pursuit of the senses and drive away such higher ideas from your mind immediately after you leave those places.

336. Travel in all the four quarters of the earth, you will find nothing (no true religion) anywhere. Whatever there is, is only here (*i.e.* in one's own heart).

337.* When the Master was alive, many of his disciples used to express to him their desire to visit holy places, and to them he used to reply: "Well, he who has got it (spirituality) here (*i.e.* in the company of the Master or within himself) has got it there (i.e. in holy places) also. Whereas he who has not got it here, has not got it there either", or, "He who has got the spirit of devotion already within his heart, will find it more intensified in holy places. But of what profit will it be to him who has no devotion at all? We often hear that the son of so-and-so has run away from home and has gone to Benares or some such place. But later on we hear again that with great effort he has managed to secure a job there, and has sent money and news about himself to his family. People go to live in some sacred place, but many there are who open shops there and take to business. Going to the western provinces in the company of Mathuranath, I found the environment there just the same as here. The mango trees, the tamarind trees or the bamboo groves—they were exactly similar to those of these parts. Hence I told Hriday, 'Well what have we come to see here? Things are just the same here as well as there, with this one point of difference, that the inhabitants of these places seem to have better digestion.'"

BENEFITS OF PIOUS COMPANY

338.* Milk and water, when brought into contact, are sure to get mixed, and the milk can never be separated again. Similarly if the aspirant thirsting after self-improvement mixes indiscriminately with all sorts of worldly people, not only does he lose his ideal, but also his former faith, love and zeal; they die away imperceptibly.

339. The companionship of the holy and the wise is one of the main elements of spiritual progress.

340. Many warm themselves in the fire kindled by someone else who has taken the trouble of collecting the firewood and other necessary things; similarly, many fix their mind on the Lord by associating with, and following the instruction of, holy men who have come to know the Lord after a good deal of hard penance.

341. If a man sees a pleader, he naturally thinks of lawsuits and courts. Similarly, on seeing a pious devotee, one is reminded of God and of the life hereafter.

342. How should one pass one's life? As the fire in the hearth is stirred from time to time with a poker to make it burn brightly and prevent it from going out, so the mind should be occasionally invigorated by the society of the pious.

343. As the blacksmith keeps alive the fire of his furnace by blowing the bellows, so the mind should be kept clean and glowing with the help of pious company.

344. The society of pious men is like the water in which rice is washed. This rice-water has the potency of dissipating alcoholic intoxication. So does the society of the pious relieve worldly men, drunk with the wine of vain desires, from their intoxication.

345. The agent of a rich Zemindar, when he goes into rural localities away from the seat of his master, tyrannises over the tenants various ways. But when he comes back to the headquarters, and is under the eyes of his master, he changes his ways, becomes very pious, treats the tenants kindly, investigates into all their grievances fully, and tries to mete out justice impartially to all. The tyrannical agent becomes good through the fear of the master and also by

reason of his society. Similarly does the society of the pious make even the wicked righteous, awakening awe and reverence in them.

346. Even moist wood placed upon a fire soon becomes dry and finally begins to burn. Similarly, the Society of the pious drives away the moisture of greed and lust from the hearts of worldly persons, and then the fire of Viveka (discrimination) burns steadily in them.

347. In the Puranas, we are told that when Uma, the Mother of the universe, incarnated Herself as the daughter of the Himalayas, She blessed Her father with the vision of the various manifestations of the omnipotent Mother. But when, Giriraj (the king of mountains) asked Her to show him the Brahman of the Vedas, Uma said, "O father, if you wish to realise Brahman, you must live in the company of holy men—men who have entirely given up the world!"

348. If you wash an elephant well and leave it at large, it is sure to make itself dirty in no time; but if, after the wash, you tie it down in its stable, it will remain clean. So, if by the good influences of holy men you once become pure in spirit, and then allow yourself to mix freely with worldly men, you are sure to lose that purity soon; but if you keep your mind fixed on God, you will never more get soiled in spirit.

REPETITION OF DIVINE NAMES

349.* The best thing for people whose minds are attracted by sense-objects is to cultivate the dualistic attitude and chant loudly the 'name' of the Lord as mentioned in Narada-Pancharatra (a work on devotion).

350.* The Master said to a devotee: "Through the path of devotion the subtle senses come readily and naturally under control. Carnal pleasures become more and more insipid as Divine love grows in your heart. Can the pleasures of the body attract a husband and wife on the day their child has died?"

Devotee: But I have not learnt to love Him.

The Master: Take His 'name' constantly. This will cleanse all sin, lust, anger and all desire for the pleasures of the body will vanish.

Devotee: But I do not find delight in His 'name'.

The Master: Then pray with a yearning heart that He may teach you to relish His 'name'. Undoubtedly He will grant your prayer . . . "I find no delight in Thy 'name'!"—If a delirious patient loses all taste for food, despair of his life.. But if he relishes food even slightly, you may hope for his recovery. So I say, "Find joy in his 'name'." Durga, Krishna, Siva—any name will do. And if you daily feel a greater attraction for taking His 'name' and a greater joy in it, you need fear no more. The delirium must get cured, and His grace will surely descend on you.

351.* Why, is the 'name' insignficant? He and His "name' are not different. Satyabhama failed to balance the Lord with gold and jewels. But Rukmini succeeded when she placed a Tulsi leaf and the 'name' of Krishna in the other pan of the balance.

352. If you wish to see God, have firm faith in the efficacy of repeating the 'name' of Hari and try to discriminate the real from the unreal.

353.* Sri Chaitanya has said: "Very powerful indeed is the Lord's 'name'. It may not bring about immediate result, but it must one day bear fruit, just as we find that a seed left long ago on the cornice of a building at last reaches the ground, germinates, grows into a tree, and bears fruit, perhaps when the building cracks and is demolished."

354. Knowingly or unknowingly, consciously or unconsciously, in whatever state of mind a man utters God's 'name', he acquires the merit of such utterance. A man who voluntarily goes to a river and bathes therein gets the benefit of the bath; so does he also who has been pushed into the water by another, or who, when sleeping soundly, has water thrown upon him.

355. In whatever way one falls, whether consciously or unconsciously, into the lake of immortality, one becomes immortal by the mere immersion. Whoever utters the 'name' of God, howsoever pronounced, whether voluntarily or involuntarily, finds immortality in the end.

356.* To a religious teacher who said that His 'name' alone is sufficient for Divine realisation, the Master said: "Yes, no doubt the holy 'name' is very effective; but is it sufficient without Love? The soul must hunger for God. What will it avail if I repeat His 'name' while I allow my mind to be attached to 'woman and gold'? Mere muttering of magic incantations will not heal up a scorpion-sting. You must also apply the smoke of burning cow-dung.[1] No doubt, man is purged of his sins by once

[1] The reference is to a simple recipe of the village housewife for scorpion-sting.

uttering His 'name'. But the next moment he takes to various sinful ways of living. He has no strength of mind to take a vow that he will no more commit any sin. Ablutions in the Ganges take away all sins, but little do they avail. The story goes that the sins lie in ambush on the trees on the banks, and when the man returns after his bath, those old sins jump down on his shoulders. So, you see, before he has proceeded a few steps, they are on him again, they have possessed him once more. Therefore take the 'name' of the Lord always, but pray to him at the same time that you may gain love for Him, and that your attachment to money, fame and physical comforts—all transient things—may grow less and less.

357. Sing with Bhakti the hallowed 'name' of the Lord, and the mountain of your sins will vanish, just as a mountain of cotton will burn to ashes and disappear if but a spark of fire falls on it.

358. The devotional practices of the worldly-minded are only for the time being. They leave no lasting impression behind. But those who are solely devoted to God chant His 'name' with every breath. Some chant 'Om Ram Om' constantly within themselves. The votaries of the path of Knowledge chant 'Soham'. Of some, again, the tongue moves constantly (*i.e.*, utters prayers or some Mantra).

359. Japa means repeating the 'name' of the Lord silently, sitting in a quiet place. If one continues the repetition with concentration and devotion, one is sure to be blessed with Divine visions ultimately—one is sure to have God-realisation. Suppose a big log of

wood is immersed in the Ganges with one end attached to a chain, which is fixed on the bank. Following the chain, link by link, you can gradually dive into the water and trace your way to it. In the same manner, if you become absorbed in the repetition of His holy name, you will eventually realise Him.

360. The Master would often say: "Chant the 'name' of Hari (God) morning and evening, clapping your hands all the while; all your sins and afflictions will then leave you. If you clap your hands standing under a tree, the birds perching on it will fly away. So if you chant the 'name' of Hari clapping your hands at the same time, the birds of evil thoughts will fly away from the tree of your body."

CHAPTER X

WAYS OF SPIRITUAL LIFE

[Some obstacles to spiritual life—Influence of past impressions—Pitfalls of occult powers—Alms and charity—Dress and food—Attitude towards the body—Attitude towards sufferings—Forbearance—Reticence—Humility and self-respect—Simplicity—Conquest of desires—Attitude towards women—Devotee and his family—Prayer and devotion]

SOME OBSTACLES TO SPIRITUAL LIFE

361. God comes not where reign timidity, hatred and fear.

362.* The heavier scale of a balance goes down while the lighter rises up. Similarly, he who is weighed down by the many cares and anxieties of the world sinks down into it, while he who has fewer rises up towards the feet of the Lord.

363. One who spends his time in discussing the good and bad qualities of others simply wastes his own time. For it is time spent neither in thinking about one's own self nor about the Supreme Self, but in fruitless thinking of others' selves.

364. In what condition of mind is the vision of God obtained? When the mind is perfectly tranquil.

When the sea of one's mind is agitated by the wind of desires, it cannot reflect God, and then God-vision is impossible.

365. Though a person's stomach may be full and he is suffering from dyspepsia in addition, his tongue will water naturally at the sight of sweet delicacies and savoury sauces. Similarly a man may not have the slightest covetousness in him; yet the sight of wealth and other objects of temptation will unsettle his mind, howsoever holy he may be.

366.* Be not like the frog in the well. The frog in the well knows nothing bigger and grander than its well. So are all bigots. They do not see anything better than their own creed.

367. The great Sankaracharya had a foolish disciple who used to imitate his Master in all matters. Sankara uttered 'Sivoham' (I am Siva); the disciple also repeated 'Sivoham'. To correct his disciple's folly, Sankara one day, while passing by a smithy, took a potful of molten iron and swallowed it; and then he asked that disciple also to do the same. Of course, the disciple could not imitate this act of his Master, and thenceforward he left off saying 'Sivoham'. Base imitation is always bad, but an attempt to correct one's own self by the noble examples of the great ones is always good.

INFLUENCE OF PAST IMPRESSIONS

368. How strong is the influence of Samskaras (impressions of the past)? In a certain place there were seated some Sannyasins, when a young woman chanced to pass by. All continued as before to meditate upon God, except one

person, who stole a glance at her. This man who was attracted by her beauty had been a householder formerly, and was the father of three children when he became a Sannyasin.

369. Once I saw two castrated bulls at a certain place. just then a cow passed that way, and I noticed that at the sight of it one of the bullocks got excited with passion while the other remained quiet. Seeing the strange behaviour of this bullock, I made enquiries into its past history, and came to know that it was castrated after it had grown up and had mated with cows, while the other was castrated quite young. Such is the effect of the impressions of past habits on the mind. The Sadhus who renounce the world without enjoying sexual pleasures never get excited at the sight of women, but those who assume the yellow garb in their advanced age, after having tasted the pleasures of family life, are liable to have the impressions of their past revived, even after years of self-control.

370. When the mind dwells in the midst of evil propensities, it is like a high-caste Brahmin living in the quarters of the outcastes , or like a gentleman dwelling in the slums of a big town.

371. A person once said, "After my boy Harish has grown up, I shall get him married, and then leaving the family in his charge, I shall renounce the world and take to the practice of Yoga." At this, the Master remarked, "You will never find any opportunity to cultivate devotion to God. You will hereafter say, 'Harish and Girish are very much attached to me. Oh! they will miss my company if I retire from the

world. Let Harish have a son first, and let me see his son also married.' Thus there will be no end to your desires."

PITFALL OF OCCULT POWERS

372. Visit not miracle-mongers and those who exhibit occult powers. These men are stragglers from the path of Truth. Their minds have become entangled in psychic powers, which are like veritable meshes in the way of the pilgrim to Brahman. Beware of these powers, and desire them not.

373. Those that are of low tendencies seek for occult powers which help in healing diseases, winning lawsuits, walking on the surface of water and such other matters. True devotees seek nothing but the lotus-feet of the Lord.

374. Krishna once said to Arjuna, "If you desire to attain Me, know that it would never be possible so long as you possess even a single one of the eight psychic powers (Ashta Siddhis)." For occult powers increase man's egotism and thus make him forgetful of God.

375. A man, after fourteen years of hard penance in a solitary forest, obtained at last the power of walking on water. Overjoyed at this acquisition, he went to his Guru and said, "Master, I have acquired the power of walking on water." The Guru rebuked him, saying: "Fie upon you. Is this the result of your fourteen years' labour? What you have attained is only worth a pice. What you could accomplish only after fourteen years' labour ordinary men can do by paying a pice to the boatman."

9

376. Siddhis or psychic powers are to be avoided like filth. These come of themselves by virtue of Sadhanas or religious practices, and Samyama or control of the senses. But he who sets his mind on Siddhis remains stuck thereto, and he cannot rise higher.

377. There was a man named Chandra[1] who acquired the power called Gutika-siddhi. Keeping an amulet (Gutika) with him, he could roam anywhere at will or penetrate into any place without being seen by any person. The man was at first devoted to God and was austere in his spiritual disciplines. Later on, however, when he came to possess that power, he began to use it for satisfying the demands of his lower nature. I warned him against doing so, but he paid no heed. He used to frequent unseen a gentleman's house and had illicit amour with a young lady of the family. He lost all his power thereby, and became a fallen soul.

378. Sometimes it is very dangerous to have occult powers. Tota Puri told me that once a great Siddha (a spiritual man possessing psychic powers) was sitting on the sea-shore when there came a great storm. The Siddha, being greatly distressed by it, exclaimed, "Let the storm cease!" and his words were fulfilled. Just then a ship was going at a distance with all sails set, and as the wind suddenly died away, it capsized, drowning all who were on board the ship. Now the sin of causing the death of so many persons accrued to the Siddha, and for that reason he lost all his occult powers and had to suffer in purgatory.

[1] This Chandra also was a disciple of the Master's Guru, Bhairavi, the Brahmin woman, of whom we have made mention in the Introduction. Thus the Master had occasion to be acquainted with him.

379. At the time of my practising austere Sadhanas under the Panchavati, a man named Girija came there. He was a great Yogi. Once when I wanted to come to my room in the dark night, he raised his arm and a strong light emanated from his arm-pit and lighted the whole path. On my advice he gave up using that power and turned his mind to the realisation of the highest Reality. He lost that power subsequently, no doubt, but gained in true spirituality.

380.* A beggar would be acting very foolishly were he to go to the king's palace and beg for such insignificant things as a gourd or pumpkin. Similarly, a devotee would be acting foolishly were he to appear at the threshold of the King of kings and beg for psychic powers, neglecting the priceless gifts of true Knowledge and love of God.

381. A youthful disciple of the Master once acquired facility in thought-reading. Overjoyed at this he spoke to the Master about his attainment. The Master thereupon rebuked him, saying, "Shame on you, child; do not waste your energies on these petty things."

382. A disciple once told Sri Ramakrishna that in the course of his meditation he could see things as they actually happened at a distance and also what some people were doing at the time, and that on subsequent enquiry the visions proved to be true. The Master said to him, "My boy, for some days don't meditate. These powers are obstacles to the realisation of God."

ALMS AND CHARITY

383. Why is it that people are fed at a religious feast? Do you not think that it is the same as offering a sacrifice

to God, who is the Fire of Life in all creatures? But bad men, not God-fearing, guilty of adultery and so forth, should on no account be entertained at such feasts. Their sins are so great that even several cubits of earth under where they sit become polluted.

384. Once a butcher was taking a cow to a distant slaughter-house. Being ill-treated by the butcher, the cow got unruly on the way, and the man found it very difficult to drive her. After several hours, he reached a village at noon, and being thoroughly exhausted, he went to an alms-house near by and partook of the food freely distributed there. Feeling himself quite refreshed after a full meal, the butcher was able to lead the cow easily to the destination. Now, a part of the sin of killing that cow fell to the donor of the food distributed at the alms-house. So even in giving food and alms in charity, one should discriminate and see that the recipient is not a vicious and sinning person likely to use the gift for evil purposes.

385.* Thus goes the law: Those who made large charities in former life are born rich in this. But then this world is His Maya, and the process of Maya is beset with many irregularities—none can comprehend it.

DRESS AND FOOD

386. What is the good of wearing the orange coloured dress of an ascetic? What is there in the dress? The orange dress brings with it pure associations. The wearing of worn out shoes and torn clothes brings thoughts of one's low state into the mind; dressing smartly

in trousers and coats, with patent leather shoes on, makes one naturally feel rather elated with pride and vanity; by wearing the black-bordered Dhoti of fine muslin, one feels impelled to be lively and to sing love songs perhaps. The wearing of the orange garb of the Sannyasin causes sacred thoughts naturally to rise in the mind. Every kind of dress has its own associations, although dress in itself has no special significance.

387. A young plant should always be protected against goats and cows and the mischief of little urchins by a fence. But when it becomes a big tree, a flock of goats or a herd of cows can freely find shelter under its spreading boughs and fill their stomachs with its leaves. So when your faith is yet in its infancy, you should protect it from the evil influences of bad company and worldliness. But when you grow strong in faith, no worldliness or evil inclination will dare approach your holy presence; and many who are wicked will become godly through your holy contact.

388. Once a student questioned Sri Ramakrishna; " Sir, as the same God dwells in every being, what harm is there in accepting food from any and every man's hands? In reply the Master asked him whether he was a Brahmin. When the student said "Yes", the Master remarked, "That is why you put me the question. Suppose you light a match and heap over it a lot of dry wood. What would become of the fire?" The student replied, "The fire will get extinguished, being choked by the pile." Again the Master said, "Suppose a wild fire is blazing and you throw into it a lot of green banana trees. What would become of these trees?" The student replied,

"Surely they will be reduced to ashes in a moment." "Similarly," said the Master, "if the spirituality in you is very weak, there is every danger of its being smothered by eating indiscriminately from all hands. But if it is strong, no food will affect you."

389. Once I was initiated by a Mohammedan teacher and was given the 'name' of Allah to repeat. I repeated the 'name' for several days, strictly observing their ways and eating their food. During that period, I could not go to the temple of Mother Kali, or take the names of Hindu gods and goddesses.

390. Eat not in the feast given at a funeral ceremony; for such food destroys all devotion and Love. Also do not take food in the house of a priest who lives by conducting sacrificial rites for others.

391. *Q.* As regards eating, should not one eat what one gets?

A. That depends upon the spiritual state. In the path of Jnana it produces no harm. When a Jnani eats, he offers the food as an oblation in the fire of Kundalini. But for a Bhakta, it is different. A Bhakta should eat only pure food, such food as he can freely offer to his beloved Lord. Animal food is not for a Bhakta. At the same time I must say that if a man loves God, even while living upon pork, he is blessed; and wretched is he who lives on milk and rice or on Havishyanna (unspiced food) but whose mind is absorbed in 'woman and gold'.

392. He who eats simple non-stimulating vegetable food, but does not desire to attain God,—for him that simple food is as bad as beef. But he who eats beef and

desires to attain God,—for him beef is as good as the food of the gods.

393. Eat to your satisfaction in the day, but let your meal at night be light and small in quantity.

394. That food alone should be taken by the devotee which does not heat the system or unsettle the mind.

ATTITUDE TOWARDS THE BODY

395.* *Q.* How is one to conquer the love of the body?

A. The human frame is made up of decaying matter. It is a collection of flesh, bone, marrow, blood and other unclean substances subject to putrefaction. By such constant analysis of the body one's love of it vanishes.

396. One does not care for the cage when the bird has flown away from it. And when the bird of life flies away, no one cares for the body left behind.

397. If this body is worthless and transitory, why do pious and devout men take care of it? No one takes care of an empty box, but all protect with care a chest full of precious jewels, gold and costly articles. The pious soul cannot help taking care of the body because God dwells in it. All our bodies form the treasure-house of the Deity.

ATTITUDE TOWARDS SUFFERING

398. Disease is the tax which the soul pays for the use of the body, as the tenant pays house-rent for the use of the house.

399. Iron must be heated again and again and hammered a hundred times before it becomes good steel.

Then only it becomes fit to be made into a sharp sword, and can be bent in any way you like. So man must be heated several times in the furnace of tribulations and hammered with the persecutions of the world before he becomes pure and humble, and fit to enter the presence of God.

400. The Master once said to Keshab Chandra Sen while the latter was ill: "You are suffering; but your illness has a deep meaning. In this body you have gone through various stages of spiritual development; the body is now suffering from the reaction. When the spiritual waves arise, the consciousness of the body vanishes, but it tells upon the body in the end. When a big steamer plies on the Ganges, the waves dash against the shore for some-time after the steamer has passed. The larger the boat, the bigger the waves; and sometimes they even break down the banks. If an elephant enters a small hut, the hut shakes and falls down. So also the experience of spiritual ecstasy shakes and sometimes shatters the body of the devotee. Do you know the consequence of this? If a house catches fire, many things are burnt. Similarly, the fire of Divine wisdom burns all passions, anger and other evils, and in the end destroys the consciousness of 'I, me and mine'. The body suffers then a severe shock and is shattered. You may think that everything is finished, but as long as there is the least vestige of the ego, He will not make you free. If you are admitted as a patient in a hospital, you will not be discharged unless you are perfectly cured."

401. The Master said to Keshab while the latter was ill: "The gardener sometimes exposes the roots of rose

bushes, so that the dew may fall upon them. Sometimes he trims off some of the roots, so that the flowers may become larger. Perhaps the Lord is preparing you to do greater works."

402. Expressing his own attitude towards illness, the Master said: "Let the disease run its course and let the body suffer, but, O mind, be thou ever in bliss."

403. The power and glory of Knowledge and faith never fail a true devotee, whatever be the joy and suffering his body undergoes. His Knowledge and faith never get dim. See how severe were the tribulations that visited the Pandavas, yet not for a moment did the light of Knowledge desert them.

FORBEARANCE

404. In the Bengali alphabet no three letters are alike in sound except the three sibilants (Sa, Sha, and Sa); and they all mean for us, 'forbear', 'forbear', 'forbear'. (In Bengali Sa means forbear. It is derived from the Sanskrit root Sah.) This shows that even from our childhood we are made to learn forbearance through our very alphabet. The quality of forbearance is of the highest importance to every man.

405. Look at the anvil of a blacksmith—how it is hammered and beaten; yet it moves not from its place. Let men learn patience and endurance from it.

RETICENCE

406. Keep your own sentiments and faith to yourself. Do not talk about them abroad. Otherwise you will be a great loser.

407. The more a person conceals his devotional practices from others, the better for him.

HUMILITY AND SELF-RESPECT

408. It is a great degradation to be conceited. Look at the crow—how wise it thinks itself to be! It never falls into a snare. It flies off at the slightest approach of danger, and steals food with the greatest dexterity. But the poor creature cannot help eating filth. This is the result of being over-wise or having the wisdom of a pettifogger.

409.* To become great one must be humble. The nest of the sky-lark is on the earth below, but it soars high into the sky. High ground is not fit for cultivation; low ground is necessary, so that water may stand on it.

410. The tree laden with fruits always bends low. If you wish to be great, be lowly and meek.

411.* Our duty is to fall down and adore where others only bow.

412.* One should not entertain egotistical feeling, such as the conceit of the preacher, "I am lecturing, hear me, all of you!" Egotism exists in ignorance, not in Knowledge. He attains the Truth who is devoid of conceit. The rain water stands in low places, but runs off from high places.

413. In a balance, the scale that is heavy bends down, but the lighter one rises up. So the man of merit and ability is always humble and meek, while the fool is puffed up with vain conceit.

414. Be as devoid of vanity as the cast-away leaf carried by the high wind.

415. If you wish to thread a needle, make the thread pointed and remove all protruding fibres. Then it will easily pass through the eye of the needle. So, if thou wish to concentrate your heart and soul on God, be meek, humble and poor in spirit and remove all the spreading filaments of desire.

416. Many a man with a show of humility says, "I am like an earth-worm grovelling in the dust." In this way, thinking themselves always to be worms, in time they become weak in spirit like worms. Let not despondency ever enter into your heart. Despair is the greatest enemy in the path of progress. As a man thinks, so he becomes."

417. A true man (Manush) is only he who is a Man-hus—one endowed with a sense of self-respect. Others are men only in name.

418. No pride is pride that expresses the glory of the soul. No humility is humility that humiliates the self.

SIMPLICITY

419. Till one becomes simple like a child, one cannot get divine illumination. Forget all the worldly knowledge that you have acquired and become as ignorant of it as a child; then you will get the knowledge of the Truth.

420. Simple-mindednes takes one easily to God. If a person is simple, spiritual instructions easily fructify in him, as seeds germinate easily and grow to bear fruit soon when sown in tilled soil free from stones.

421*. The Master used to say: "People become generous and simple-minded only in consequence of much penance. God can never be attained except with a simple mind. It is to the simple-minded that He reveals His own nature." But to safeguard people from developing into simpletons in the name of simplicity and truthfulness, the Master would also sound a note of warning; "You are to be a devotee but not a simpleton on that account," or again, "Always you must discriminate in your mind between the true and the false, the eternal and the transient; and then leaving aside all that is transient, you should fix your mind upon that alone which is eternal."

CONQUEST OF DESIRES

422. He is a true man who is dead even in this life—that is, whose passions and propensities have been curbed to extinction as in a dead body.

423. So long as the heavenly expanse of the heart is troubled and disturbed by the gusts of desire, there is little chance of our beholding therein the brightness of God. The beatific vision dawns only in the heart that is calm and rapt in Divine communion.

424. God cannot be seen so long as there is the slightest taint of desire. Therefore have your minor desires satisfied, and renounce the major ones by right reasoning and discrimination.

425. As one who is standing by the brink of a deep well is always careful lest he should fall into it, even so should one living in the world be always on his guard against its temptations. He who has once fallen into the well of the world, so full of temptations, can hardly come out of it uninjured and stainless.

426. On being asked when the enemies of man, such as lust, anger, etc., will be vanquished, the Master replied: "So long as these passions are directed towards the world and its objects, they behave like enemies. But when they are directed towards God, they become the best friends of man, for then they lead him unto God. The lust for the things of the world must be changed into the hankering for God, the anger that man feels in relation to his fellow man should be turned towards God for not revealing Himself to him. One should deal with all the passions in the same manner. These passions cannot be eradicated but can be educated."

427. Mandodari told her royal husband Ravana, "If you are so intent upon having Sita as your queen, why don't you impose on her by assuming the form of her husband Rama with the help of your magical powers?" "Fie on you!" explained Ravana, "Can I stoop to the pleasures of the senses while I am in the holy form of Rama—a form the very thought of which fills my heart with such unspeakable joy and blessedness that even the highest heaven appears to me worthless?"

428. When an elephant is let loose, it goes about uprooting trees and shrubs; but as soon as the driver applies the hook on its head it becomes quiet. So the mind, when unrestrained, wantons in the luxuriance of idle thoughts, but becomes at once calm when pulled up with the goad of discrimination.

429.* The more a man's attachment to the world, the less he is likely to attain Knowledge. The less his attachment to the world, the more is the probability of his gaining Knowledge.

430. When butter is produced by churning curds, it should not be kept in the same vessel with the buttermilk, for then it will lose something of its sweetness and hardness. It should be kept in pure water and in a different vessel. Similarly after attaining partial perfection in the world, if one still continues to mix with the worldly and remains in the midst of the temptations of the world, one is likely to become tainted, but can remain pure by living out of it.

431. *Q.* How may we conquer the old Adam that is in us?

A. When the flower develops into fruit, the petals drop off of themselves. So, when the divinity in you increases, the weakness of human nature in you will vanish of its own accord.

432.* If once through intense Vairagya (dispassion) one attains God, then the inordinate temptations of lust fall off, and a man finds himself in no danger from his own wife. If there are two magnets at an equal distance from a piece of iron, which of them will draw it with a stronger force? Certainly the larger. Verily God is the larger magnet; what can the smaller magnet ('woman') do against it?

433.* *Q.* How does the attraction of sensual pleasures die away?

A. In God, who is at once the embodiment of all happiness and pleasures. They who realise Him can find no attraction in the mean and worthless pleasures of the world.

434. Taking Helancha (a medicinal herb) is not the same as taking a pot-herb, and taking a piece of sugar

candy is not the same as taking common sweets; for Helancha and sugar candy are not injurious to health and even a sick man may use them. The mystic Pranava, too, is no mere word but a phonetic symbol of the Divinity. In the same way the desire for holiness and devotion cannot be deemed to be equal to the common polluting desires of the world.

ATTITUDE TOWARDS WOMEN

435. All women are parts of the Divine Mother, and therefore they should be looked upon as mothers by all.

436. Women, whether naturally good or not, whether chaste or unchaste, should always be looked upon as images of the blissful Divine Mother.

437. *Q.* How should we look upon the fair sex?

A. He who has known the Real, who is blessed with the vision of God, does not regard them with any fear. He sees them as they really are—parts of the Divine Mother of the universe. So he not only pays all honour and respect to women, but actually worships them as a son does his mother.

438.* *Q.* How can we conquer lust?

A. Look upon all women as your own mother. Never look a woman in the face, but always look at her feet. All evil thoughts will then fly away.

439. The woman who observes continence even while living with her husband, is veritably the Divine Mother Herself.

440. *Q.* Sir, what do you think of the mode of devotional practices in the company of women, as enjoined by the Tantras?

A. Those are not safe 'paths'; they are very difficult, and are often attended with slips. There are three ways of practising devotion (according to the Tantras) —one may cultivate the attitude of the 'hero', or the 'hand-maid', or the 'son' towards the Divine Mother. Mine is the attitude of the 'son'. To think of oneself as the hand-maid of the Divine Mother is also good. But the path of the 'hero'[1] is frought with danger. Very pure is the path of 'sonship' (*i.e.* thinking of oneself as the son of the Divine Mother).

441.* Do you aspire after Divine grace? Then propitiate the Mother, the Primal Divine Energy (Sakti). Yes, She is Mahamaya Herself. She it is Who has deluded the whole world, and is conjuring up the triple device of creation, maintenance and dissolution. She has spread a veil of ignorance over all, and unless She unbars the gate, none can enter the 'Inner Court'. Left outside, we see only the external things, but the Eternal One, Sachchidananda, remains ever beyond our ken.

The Divine Sakti has two aspects—Vidya and Avidya. Avidya deludes and is the mother of Kamini-Kanchana, 'woman and gold'; and it binds. But Vidya is the source of devotion, kindness, knowledge and love, and it takes us towards God.

[1] It is called Virachara in the Tantras. In this path the devotee has to worship the Goddess as his Divine Consort, taking a woman as the *vice deus*.

This Avidya has to be propitiated, and hence the institution of Sakti worship. Various are the ways of worship for gratifying Her—as Her 'handmaid', or 'hero', or 'child'. Sakti-sadhana is no joke. There are very strenuous and dangerous practices in it. I passed two years as Mother's 'hand-maid' and 'friend'. Mine, however, is the mood of the 'child', and to me the breasts of any women are like unto my mother's.

Women are so many images of Sakti. In the western parts of this country the bridegroom holds a knife in his hand during marriage, and in Bengal, a nut-cracker. The idea is that he will cut the bonds of Maya with the help of the bride who is Sakti Herself. This is Virabhava, 'the way of the hero'. But I never practised it. Mine is the attitude of the 'child'.

DEVOTEE AND HIS FAMILY

442. *Q*. Suppose a wife tells her husband who is given to religious practices, 'If you do not look after me properly, I will commit suicide.' What should one do in that case?

A. One should give up such a wife—the wife that stands in the way to God-realisation. Let her commit suicide or let her not! The wife who thus puts obstacles in one's path to God is an embodiment of Avidya (nescience). But then all become amenable to one who has a sincere devotion to God—even the king, wicked persons and the wife. If one has true devotion, then one's wife also gradually turns Godward. If one is good-natured, it is quite possible that she too becomes good through the grace of God.

443. Father and mother are of prime importance to man. Unless they are pleased, no devotional practice will be of any avail. Look at Sri Chaitanya. Though mad with love of God, he took much pains to console his mother before he took Sannyasa. He told her, "Mother, do not be sorry. I will come now and then to see you." There are so many debts that one has to repay—the debt to the gods, the debt to the Rishis, and also the debt to the parents and the wife. No pious work can succeed unless the debt to the parents is paid off. There is a debt even to the wife. Harish is staying here, having renounced his wife. If his wife had not been provided for, I would have called him a wicked fellow. Ramaprasanna is always wandering about for milk and opium for the Hatha Yogi. He says that Manu has enjoined service to Sadhus. Meanwhile, his old mother is starving and has to do her own shopping. I feel so angry at this.

444.* But there is one consideration. If a man becomes mad with love of God, then who is father, who is mother and who is wife? He loves God so deeply that he becomes mad. He has no duty, he is absolved from all debts. When a man reaches that state, he forgets the whole world; he becomes unconscious of even the body which is so dear to everyone.

445.* The parents deserve the highest respect in this world. As long as they live, they should be served to the best of one's capacity, and after their death, their post-funeral rites ought to be performed according to one's means. Even if the son be the poorest of the poor, and has no means to perform the post-funeral rites of his parents, he should resort to the forest and shed tears there, remembering his inability. Only then can he free himself from his obligation to them. For the sake of God alone, one may disobey one's parents without incurring sin. As for instance, Prahlada did not refrain from taking the name of Lord Krishna, although prohibited by his father to do so. And Dhruva went to the forest in order to practise austerities, even though forbidden by his mother. They had not done any wrong in this.

PRAYER AND DEVOTION

446. Q. Should we pray aloud to God?

A. Pray to Him in any way you like. He is always sure to hear you. He can hear even the footfall of an ant.

447. Q. Is there really any efficacy in prayers?

A. Yes. When mind and speech unite in earnestly asking for a thing, that prayer is answered. Of no avail are the prayers of that man who says with his mouth, "These are all Thine, O Lord!" and at the same time thinks in his heart that all of them are his.

448. Be not a traitor to your thoughts. Be sincere; act according to your thoughts; and you shall surely succeed. Pray with a sincere and simple heart, and your prayers will be heard.

449. What you think, that you should speak. Let there be harmony between your thoughts and words. Otherwise, if you merely say that God is your all in all

while in your mind you have made the world your all in all, you cannot derive any benefit thereby.

450. To approach a mighty monarch a man must ingratiate himself with the officials who keep the gate and guard the throne. So, to reach the Almighty Lord and obtain His grace, one must practise much devotion, serve many devotees, and keep for long the company of the wise.

451. Do not let worldly thoughts and anxieties disturb your mind. Do everything that is necessary in the proper time, and let your mind be always fixed on God.

452. There is little fear that a ship will drift or run into danger as long as its compass points due North. So the ship of life steers clear of every danger, if the mind, its compass needle, is always turned towards God without oscillation.

453.* How to pray is the next question. Let us not pray for things of the world, but pray like saint Narada. Narada said to Ramachandra, "O Rama, grant that I may be favoured with Bhakti (love, devotion and self-surrender) for Thy lotus-feet." "Be it so, Narada," said Rama, "But will you not ask for anything else?" Narada replied, "Lord, may it please Thee to grant that I may not be attracted by Thy Maya, which fascinates the universe." Ramachandra said once more, "Be it so, Narada, but will you not ask for anything else?" Narada replied, "No, Lord, that is all I pray for."

454.* If you cannot settle whether God has form or not, then pray in this way: "O Lord, I cannot understand whether Thou art with form or without it. Whatever mayst Thou be, have mercy on me. Do reveal Thyself unto me."

455.* One may attribute the various forms and aspects of God that are current in society to imagination, and may have no faith in them. Yet God will shower His grace on a person if he believes in a Divine Power that creates and directs the world, and prays with a distressed heart, "O God, I do not know Thy real nature. Deign to reveal Thyself to me as Thou really art."

456.* God is extremely attentive, my boys. He has heard every time you have prayed to Him. He will surely reveal Himself to you some day or other, at least at the time of death.

CHAPTER XI

SPIRITUAL ASPIRANTS AND RELIGIOUS DIFFERENCES

[*God of all religions the same—Different religions as paths to God—Cause and cure of fanaticism—Right attitude towards religious differences—Attitude towards secret cults*]

GOD OF ALL RELIGIONS THE SAME

457. As one and the same water is called by different names by different peoples, some calling it 'water', some 'Vari', some 'Aqua' and some 'Pani', so the one Sachchidananda—Existence-Intelligence-Bliss Absolute—is invoked by some as God, by some as Allah, by some as Hari and by others as Brahman.

458. In a potter's shop there are vessels of different shapes and forms—pots, jars, dishes, plates, etc.—but all made of the same clay. So God is one, but He is worshipped in different ages and climes under different names and aspects.

459. As the same sugar is made into various figures of birds and beasts, so the one sweet Divine Mother is worshipped in various climes and ages under various names and forms.

460. Various ornaments are made of gold. Although the substance is the same, they are called variously and appear different in form. So one and the same God is worshipped in different countries and ages under different names and forms. He may be worshipped in various ways according to different conceptions—some loving to call Him as father and others as mother, some as friend and others as beloved, some again as the innermost treasure of their heart and others as their sweet little child—but it is always one and the same God that is worshipped in all these diverse relations.

461. Once a dispute arose among the learned men at the court of the Maharajah of Burdwan as to who was the greater of the two Deities, Siva and Vishnu. Some of the courtiers said that Siva was greater, while the others gave preference to Vishnu. When the dispute grew hot, a wise Pandit remarked, "Sir, I have seen neither Siva nor Vishnu. How can I say who is the greater of the two?" Similarly, do not try to compare one Deity with another. When you will see one of them, you will come to know that they are all the manifestations of the same Brahman.

DIFFERENT RELIGIONS AS PATHS TO GOD

462. There are several bathing ghats in a large tank. Whoever goes choosing whichever ghat he pleases to take a bath or to fill his vessel reaches the water, and it is useless to quarrel with one another by calling one's ghat better than another. Similarly, there are many ghats that lead to the water of the fountain of Eternal Bliss. Every

religion of the world is one such ghat. Go direct with a sincere and earnest heart through any one of these ghats, and you shall reach the water of Eternal Bliss. But say not that your religion is better than that of another.

463. Many are the names of God and infinite the forms through which He may be approached. In whatever name and form you worship Him, through that you will realise Him.

464. Different creeds are but different paths to reach the one God. Diverse are the ways that lead to the temple of Mother Kali at Kalighat in Calcutta. Similarly various are the paths that take men to the house of the Lord. Every religion is nothing but one of these paths.

465. Some years ago when the Hindus and the Brahmos were preaching their respective religions with true earnestness and great zeal, someone asked the Master what his opinion was regarding both the parties. To this the Master said, "I see that my Divine Mother is getting Her work done through both these parties."

466. Questioned by a pious Brahmo as to what constituted the difference between Hinduism and Brahmoism, the Master said that the difference is the same as that between a single note and the whole gamut. The Brahmo religion is content with the single note of the Brahman, while the Hindu religion is made up of several notes, which together produce a sweet harmony.

467. As one can ascend to the top of a house by means of a ladder, a bamboo, a staircase or a rope, so also diverse are the ways of approaching God, and every religion in the world shows one of the ways.

468. The light of the gas-lamp illuminates various localities with varying intensity, but the sustenance of light, namely, the gas, comes from one common store. So the religious teachers of all lands and of all ages are but so many lamps through which the light of the Spirit streams constantly from the one almighty source.

469. The cries of all jackals are the same. So are the teachings of all the wise ones are the same.

THE CAUSE AND CURE OF FANATICISM

470.* Through ignorance a common man considers his own religion to be the best and makes much useless clamour; but when his mind is illumined by true Knowledge, all sectarian quarrel disappears.

471. Two persons were hotly disputing as to the colour of a chameleon. One said, "The chameleon on that palm tree is of a beautiful red colour." The other contradicted him saying, "You are mistaken, the chameleon is not red, but blue." Being unable to settle the matter by argument, both went to a man who always lived under that tree and had watched the chameleon in all its phases. One of the disputants asked, "Sir, is not the chameleon on that tree of a red colour?" The man replied, "Yes, sir." The other disputant said, "What do you say? How is that possible? Surely it is not red, but blue!" The man again humbly replied, "Yes, sir." He knew that the chameleon constantly changed its colour. So he said 'Yes' to both the conflicting views. God who is Existence-Knowledge-Bliss Absolute, has likewise various forms. The devotee who has seen God only in one aspect knows that and that

aspect alone. None but he who has seen Him in manifold aspects, can say, "All these forms are of the one God, for God is multiform." He is formless and with form, and many are His forms which no one knows.

472. Dal (sedge) does not grow in large tanks with pure water. It grows only in small, stagnant and miasmatic pools. Similarly Dal (schism) does not occur in a party whose members are guided by pure, broad and unselfish motives. It appears only in the party whose members are selfish, insincere and bigoted.

473. Is it good to create sects (Dal)? (Here is a pun on the word 'dal' which means in Bengali both a 'sect' or 'party' and 'the rank growth on the surface of a stagnant pool'.) The 'dal' cannot grow in flowing water; it grows only in stagnant pools. He whose heart constantly flows towards the Lord has no time for anything else. He who seeks fame and honour forms sects.

474. Men may partition their lands by measuring rods and boundary lines, but no one can so partition the all-embracing sky overhead. The individual sky surrounds all and includes all. So the unenlightened man in his ignorance says that his religion is the only true one and that it is the best. But when his heart is illumined by the light of true Knowledge, he comes to know that above all these wars of sects and creeds is the one Existence-Knowledge-Bliss Absolute (Akhanda Sachchidananda).

RIGHT ATTITUDE TOWARDS RELIGIOUS DIFFERENCES

475.* Whoever performs devotional exercises, with the belief that there is but one God, is bound to attain

Him, no matter in what aspect, name or manner He is worshipped.

476.* You will advance, whatever way you meditate on Him or recite His holy names. The cake made of sugar candy will taste equally sweet, whether it is held straight or oblique when you eat it.

477. *Q.* If the God of every religion is the same, why is it then that God is painted differently by different religionists?

A. God is one, but His aspects are many. As the master of a house is father to one, brother to another and husband to a third, and is called by different names by different persons, so the one God is described in various ways according to the particular aspect in which He appears to His particular worshipper.

478. As a mother, in nursing her sick children, gives rice and curry to one, sago and arrowroot to another, and bread and butter to a third, so the Lord has laid out different paths for different men suitable to their natures.

479. Sankaracharya's exposition of the Vedanta is indeed true, and true also is what Ramanuja speaks of it—his Visishtadvaita philosophy.

480. Let a man be a Christian in the matter of mercy, a Moslem in the matter of strict observance of external forms, and a Hindu in the matter of universal charity towards all living creatures.

481. When you go out and mix with people, you should have love for them all; mix with them freely and become one with them. You should not shrug your shoulders and hate them, saying, "They believe in a Personal God, and not in the Impersonal," or "They believe in the Impersonal,

and not in the Personal," or "He is a Christian, a Hindu, or a Mussalman." Man understands about Him only so much as He makes him understand.

Moreover, knowing that men are of different tendencies, you should mix with them as much as you can. And you should love all. Then returning to your own 'home' (heart) you will enjoy bliss and peace. There you will meet your own real self.

482. Every man should follow his own religion. A Christian should follow Christianity, and a Mohammedan Mohammedanism. For the Hindu the ancient path, the path of the Aryan Rishis, is the best.

483. A truly religious man should think that other religions are also so many paths leading to the Truth. We should always maintain an attitude of respect towards other religions.

484. Dispute not. As you rest firmly on your own faith and opinion, allow others also equal liberty to stand by their own faith and opinion. By mere disputation you will never succeed in convincing another of his error. When the grace of God descends on him, every man will understand his own mistakes.

485.* One day the Master was heard talking to the Mother of the universe, in a God-intoxicated state: "Mother, every one says, 'My watch keeps correct time.' The Christians, the Hindus, the Mohammedans, all say, 'My religion is the true religion.' But Mother, nobody's watch is exact. Who can truly know Thee? But again, if one seeks Thee with a yearning heart, one can reach Thee by Thy grace through any path, through any religion."

ATTITUDE TOWARDS SECRET CULTS

486.* Some ardent moralists among the Master's disciples often found fault with certain people of great spiritual attainments, because some of the parctices they followed, being of the secret rites of the Saktas and Vaishnavas, seemed to violate the ordinary rules of morality. To them the Master used to reply always: "They are not to be blamed for that. For they had the thorough conviction that the paths they followed in themselves led to God-realisation. Whatever is ardently believed in and adopted as a means to God-realisation should not be found fault with. No aspirant's attitude should be condemned; since any attitude, if sincerely followed, is sure to lead to God, Who is the consummation of them all. Go on calling upon Him, each in his own way, and don't find fault with another's path or take to it as your own."

487.* With a view to remove the antagonism of his disciples towards these secret cults, the Master would sometimes speak to them about his views regarding them as follows: "Well, why should you cherish hatred towards them? Know them also to be paths, though they may be dirty. There may be diverse entrances to a house—the front gate, the back-door and the door for the scavenger who comes to clean the dirty places in the house. Know these cults to be akin to this last-mentioned door. No matter by which door one enters; when once within the house, all reach the same place. Are you therefore to imitate these people or mix with them? Certainly not. But do not hate them in any way."

CHAPTER XII

ESSENTIALS OF SPIRITUAL LIFE

[*Some conditions of spiritual enlightenment—Faith—Resignation to God—Necessity of Ishta or Chosen Deity—Truth—Brahmacharya or continence—Viveka or discrimination—Vairagya or aversion for worldly objects—Perseverance—Spiritual practice—Concentration and meditation*]

SOME CONDITIONS OF SPIRITUAL ENLIGHTENMENT

488. If a person possessed by an evil spirit becomes conscious that he is so possessed, the evil spirit at once leaves him. Similarly the Jiva which is possessed by the evil spirit of Maya, on realising that he is so possessed, becomes at once free from it.

489.* He alone enters the Kingdom of Heaven who is not a thief of his own thoughts. In other words, guilelessness and simple faith are the roads to that Kingdom.

490. A person once said: "The innate nature of a substance can never be changed." Another retorted, "When fire enters charcoal, it destroys its innate blackness." So when the mind is burnt by the fire of Knowledge, its innate nature too is destroyed, and it ceases to be a snare.

491. The mind is everything. If the mind loses its liberty, you lose yours. If the mind is free, you too are free. The mind may get dyed in any colour, like a white cloth fresh from the washing house. Study English, and you must mix English words in your talk in spite of yourself. The Pandit who studies Sanskrit must quote verses. If the mind is kept in bad company, the evil influence of it will colour one's thoughts and conversations. Placed in the midst of devotees, the mind is sure to meditate on God and God alone. It changes its nature according to the things amongst which it lives and acts.

492. The mind is everything. The attraction for the wife is of one kind, and the affection for the child is of quite a different nature. On one side is one's wife, on another side is the child; one caresses both, but is moved by quite different impulses.

493. Bondage is of the mind; freedom too is of the mind. If you say, "I am a free soul. I am a son of God! Who can bind me?" free you shall be. If one is bitten by a snake and can say with all the force of will and faith, "There is no venom, there is no venom", one will surely get rid of the venom.

494. *Q*. When shall I be free?

A. When 'I' shall cease to be. 'I and mine' is ignorance. 'Thou and Thine' is Knowledge.

FAITH

495.* To a disciple who criticised some people's faith as 'blind faith', the Master remarked: "Well, can you explain to me what you mean by 'blind faith'? Is not faith wholly 'blind'? What then are its eyes? Say either 'faith' or 'knowledge'. Or else, what is this queer notion that faith in some instances is 'blind' and in others is 'with eyes'?"

496. Man suffers through lack of faith in God.

497. There are physiological signs indicating who will be endowed with faith and who not. The bony sort of fellows, the hollow-eyed, the squint-eyed—all these types cannot have faith easily.

498. To kill another, sword and shield are needed, whilst to kill oneself even a pin will do. So to teach others one must study many scriptures and sciences, while to acquire spiritual illumination for oneself, firm faith in a single motto will suffice.

499. There are various sects and creeds among the Hindus. Which of them should we adopt? Parvati once asked Mahadeva, "O Lord, what is the root of the eternal, everlasting, all-embracing Bliss?" To her Mahadeva replied, "The root is faith." So the peculiarities of creeds and sects matter little or nothing. Let every one take to devotional practices and perform the duties of his own creed with faith.

500. Knowledge relating to God keeps pace with faith. Where there is little faith, it is idle to look for much Knowledge. The cow which is over-nice in matters of eating is not liberal in its supply of milk. But the cow which welcomes all kinds of food—herbs, leaves, grass, husks, straw and the rest—and eats them up with great appetite, gives an abundant supply. Her milk comes down from the udder into the pail in torrents.

501. He who has faith has all, and he who lacks it lacks all.

502. If you are keen on realising God, repeat His 'name' with firm faith, and try to discriminate the Real from the unreal.

503. Unless one becomes childlike in faith, it is difficult to realise God. If the mother says to the child, "He is your brother," the child fully believes that the person referred to is really its brother. If the mother says, "Don't go there, there is a bogy," the child is indeed convinced that there is a bogy. God is moved to pity when He sees in a man that kind of childlike faith. None can attain God with the calculating nature of the worldly-minded.

504.* One day, Sri Krishna, while going in a chariot along with Arjuna, looked up to the sky and said, "Behold! What a nice flight of pigeons there!" Arjuna at once turned his eyes in that direction and exclaimed, "Really, friend, very beautiful pigeons indeed!" But the very next moment Sri Krishna looked again and said, "No, friend, they are not pigeons, it seems." Arjuna, too, saw again and said, "True, they are not pigeons." Now try to understand the meaning of this. A great adherent of truth that Arjuna was, he did not possibly assent to whatever Sri Krishna said, simply for flattering him. But he had such an unflinching faith in Sri Krishna that he perceived at once actually whatever Sri Krishna said.

505. Boil your sugar well over a burning fire. As long as there is dirt or impurity in it, the sweet infusion will smoke and simmer. But when all the impurity and scum

are cast out, there is neither smoke nor sound; only the delicious crystalline syrup heaves in its unmixed worth. Then whether liquid or solid, it becomes the delight of men and gods. Such is the character of the man of faith.

506. A man wanted to cross a river. A sage gave him an amulet and said, "This will carry you across." The man, taking it in his hand, began to walk over the water. Before he had gone half the way, he was seized with curiosity, and opened the amulet to see what was in it. Therein he found, written on a piece of paper, the sacred name of Rama, the Lord. At this the man said depreciatingly, "Is this the whole secret?" No sooner did this scepticism enter his mind than he sank down. It is faith in the 'name' of the Lord that works wonders; for faith is life and want of faith is death.

507. A disciple who had firm faith in the infinite power of his Guru walked over a river by simply uttering his name. Seeing this, the Guru thought, "Well, is there such a power in my mere name? Then how much great and powerful must I be!" The next day, the Guru also tried to walk over the river uttering 'I', 'I', 'I', but no sooner did he step into the water than he sank down and was soon drowned; for the poor man did not know how to swim even. Faith can achieve miracles while vanity or egotism brings about the destruction of man.

508. Sri Ramachandra, who was God incarnate, had to bridge the ocean before he could cross over to Lanka (Ceylon). But Hanuman, his faithful monkey devotee and servant, crossed the ocean at one leap, because of his

firm faith in Rama. Here the servant achieved more than the master, simply through faith.

509. A king guilty of the heinous sin of killing a Brahmin went to the hermitage of a Rishi to learn what penance he must perform in order to be purified. The Rishi was absent, but his son was in the hermitage. Hearing the case of the king, he said, "Repeat the 'name' of God (Rama) three times, and your sin will be expiated." When the Rishi came back and heard of the penance prescribed by his son, he remarked indignantly, "Sins committed in myriads of births are purged immediately by uttering the 'name' of the Almighty but once. How weak must be your faith, O fool, since you have ordered the holy 'name' to be repeated thrice? For this weakness of your faith, you shall become an outcaste." And the son became Guhaka of the Ramayana.

510. The stone may remain in water for numberless years; yet the water will never penetrate into it. But clay is soon soaked into mud by the contact of water. So the strong heart of the faithful does not despair in the midst of trials and persecutions, but the man of weak faith is shaken even by the most trifling cause.

511.* One becomes as one thinks. They say that by constantly thinking of a particular kind of insect (Bhramarakita), a cockroach is transformed into that insect. Similarly he who constantly thinks of the Bliss Absolute himself becomes full of bliss.

512. Why talk of sin and hell-fire all the days of your life? Chant the 'name' of God. Do say but once, "I have, O Lord, done things that I ought not to have done,

and I have left undone things that I ought to have done. O Lord, forgive me!" Saying this, have faith in Him, and you will be purged of all sins.

513. The faith-healers of India order their patients to repeat with full conviction the words, "There is no illness at all." The patients repeat them, and this mental suggestion helps to drive off the disease. So if you think yourself to be morally weak, you will actually become so in a short time. Know and believe that you are of immense power, and then power will come to you at last.

514. He who thinks that he is a Jiva, verily remains as a Jiva; but he who considers himself to be God, verily becomes a God. As one thinks, so does one become.

RESIGNATION TO GOD

515. He who can resign himself to the will of the Almighty with simple faith and guileless love realises the Lord very quickly.

516. To live in the world or to leave it depends upon the will of God. Therefore work, leaving everything to Him. What else can you do?

517. A shallow pool of water in an open field will soon be dried up, though no one may lessen the quantity of its water by using it. So a sinful man is sometimes purified by simply resigning himself totally and absolutely to the mercy and grace of God.

518. Q. What are we to do when we are placed in this world?

A. Give up everything to Him, resign yourself to Him, and there will be no more trouble for you.

Then you will come to know that everything is done by His will.

519. There is no path safer and smoother than that of Ba-kalama (power of attorney). Ba-kalama means here resigning oneself to the will of the Almighty and having no feeling that anything is one's own.

520. The young of a monkey clasps and clings to its mother tightly when she moves about. The kitten on the other hand does not do so but mews piteously, and the mother grasps it by the neck. If the young of the monkey lets go its hold of its mother, it falls down and gets hurt. This is because it relies upon its own strength. But the kitten runs no such risk, as the mother herself carries it about from place to place. Such is the difference between self-reliance and entire resignation to the will of God.

521. A father was once passing through a field with his two little sons. He was carrying one of them in his arms while the other was walking along with him holding his hand. They saw a kite flying, and the latter boy, giving up his hold on his father's hand, began to clasp with joy, crying, "Behold, papa, there is a kite!" But immediately he stumbled down and got hurt. The boy who was carried by the father also clapped his hands with joy, but did not fall, as his father was holding him. The first boy represents self-help in spiritual matters, and the second self-surrender.

522. Blessed Radha was once called to prove her chastity. She was subjected to the ordeal of fetching water in a jar with a thousand holes. She succeeded in doing so without even a drop of water leaking out, and everyone

applauded her, declaring that such a chaste woman never was and never will be. At this Radha exclaimed, "Why do you heap praise on me? Say rather, 'Glory to Krishna! Glory to Him alone!' I am only a handmaid of His."

523. What is the nature of absolute reliance on God? It is like that happy state of relaxation felt by a fatigued worker when, reclining on a pillow, he smokes at leisure after a day's hard work. It is the cessation of all anxieties and worries.

524. Live here like a leaf cast off after being used for taking food. It is at the mercy of the winds; it is blown here and there; sometimes indoors and sometimes abroad in dirty places. Well, now you are placed here; all right, remain here. And when He will take you away and put you in a better place, then, too, you should say 'Amen' and resign to His will with perfect unattachment. Let things take care of themselves.

NECESSITY OF ISHTA OR CHOSEN DEITY

525. The young wife in a family respects her father-in-law and mother-in-law, ministers to their wants, and does not despise or disobey them; but at the same time she loves her husband more than any of them. In the same way be firm in your devotion to your own Chosen Deity (Ishta), but do not despise other Deities. Honour them too; for they all represent one Authority and one Love.

526. In the play of dice called Ashta-kashta, the pieces must pass through all the squares of the chequer before they reach the central square of rest and non-return. But so long as a pawn does not reach that central square, it is

liable to return again and again to its starting point and commence its weary journey over and over again. If, however, two pawns happen to start their journey in unison and move jointly from square to square, they cannot be forced back by any winner. Similarly, those who start on their career of devotional practices, first uniting themselves with a Guru and an Ishta, have no fear of reverses and difficulties on the way. Their progress will be smooth, unimpeded and without any retrogression.

527. Many roads lead to Calcutta. Dr. Doubtful started from his home in a distant village to go to the metropolis. He asked a man on the road, "Which is the shortest route to Calcutta?" The man said, "Follow this road." Proceeding some distance, he met another man and asked him, "Is this the shortest road to Calcutta?" The man replied, "Oh no! You must retrace your steps and take the road to your left." The man did so. Going along that new road for some distance, he met a third man who pointed out another road to Calcutta. Thus Dr. Doubtful made no progress, but spent the whole day in changing roads. One who really wishes to reach Calcutta must stick to a single road pointed out by an honest man; so also those who want to reach God must follow steadily one particular guide.

528. A man began to sink a well, but having dug down to a depth of twenty cubits, he could not find any trace of water there. So he gave up that site and selected another spot for the purpose. There he dug still deeper, but even then could not find any water. So he selected yet another site and dug deeper than before, but it was also of no avail.

At last in utter disgust he gave up the task altogether. The total depth of all these three wells was only a little short of one hundred cubits. Had he the patience to devote even half of the whole of this labour to his first well, instead of changing the site again and again, he would surely have succeeded in getting water. The same is the case with men who continually change their faith. In order to succeed we have to devote ourselves wholeheartedly to one object of faith without being in the least doubtful as to its worth.

529. As a chaste woman wholly devoted to her husband is united with him for ever even after death, so the man who is solely devoted to his own Chosen Deity certainly obtains union with God.

TRUTH

530.* Have Bhakti within, and give up all cunning and deceit. Those who are engaged in business, such as work in office or trade, should also stick to truth. Truthfulness is the Tapasya (austerity) of this age of Kali.

531. Unless one always speaks the truth, one cannot find God Who is the soul of truth.

532.* One must be very particular about telling the truth. Through truth one can realise God.

533. Everything false is bad. Even false garb is bad. If your mind is not quite in accord with the garb, then terrible ruin shall visit you. In this way, one grows hypocritical, and all fear of doing wrong or uttering falsehood disappears.

534. A certain person, deeply involved in debt, feigned madness to escape the consequences of his liabilities.

Physicians failed to cure his disease; and the more medicines were administered to him the greater became his madness. At last a wise physician found out the truth, and taking the man feigning madness aside, rebuked him saying, "Sir, what are you doing? Beware that by feigning madness you do not become actually mad. Already I see some genuine signs of insanity in you." This warning roused the man from his folly and he left off feigning madness. You will actually become what you constantly pose yourself to be.

BRAHMACHARYA OR CONTINENCE

535. As one's face may be seen reflected in a sheet of glass coated with quick silver, so the glorious image of the Almighty God can be seen reflected in the heart of a person who has preserved his power and purity through perfect continence.

536. Unless one practises absolute continence, one cannot comprehend the subtle truths of spirituality.

537.* Sukadeva was an Urdhvaretas (a man of complete and unbroken continence); he had never any emission of semen. There was another class called Dhairyaretas, who had discharge of semen at one time but subsequently practised absolute continence. If a man remains a Dhairyaretas continually for twelve years, he acquires a superhuman power. A new nerve is developed in him. It is called the 'nerve of intelligence' (Medhanadi), and he can remember everything and know everything.

538.* If a man practises absolute continence for twelve years, the Medhanadi will open (*i.e.*, his powers and understanding will blossm). His understanding will become capable of penetrating and comprehending the subtlest of ideas. With such an understanding man can realise God. God can be attained only through a purified understanding of this type.

539. Waste of the vital fluid entails loss of energy. Involuntary emission, however, is not of much consequence. That is due to food. But still one (a truely spiritual man) should not know any woman carnally.

540. He who has relinquished sexual enjoyment has indeed renounced the world! God is indeed very near him!

VIVEKA OR DISCRIMINATION

541.* Practise discrimination. 'Woman' and 'gold' are both unreal; the one reality is God. Of what use is money? Why, it gives us food and clothing and a place to live in. Thus far it is useful, and no further. Surely you cannot see God with the help of money. Money is certainly not the end of life. This is the process of discrimination. What is there in money or in the beauty of women? Using your discrimination you shall find that the body of the most beautiful woman is made up only of flesh and blood, skin and bones, fat and marrow, nay, as in the case of all animals, of entrails, urine, excreta, and the rest. The wonder is that man can lose sight of God, and give his mind entirely to things of such kind!

542.* Viveka and Vairagya—Viveka means the sifting of the real from the unreal; and Vairagya, indifference to the objects of the world. They do not come all on a sudden; they have to be practised daily. 'Woman and gold' have to be renounced, first mentally, and God willing, they should be renounced afterwards both internally and externally. It is said in the Gita that by Abhyasa Yoga (continuous practice of meditation) dislike for 'woman and gold' is engendered. Continuous practice brings to the mind extraordinary power; then nobody feels difficulty in subjugating the senses, passions and lust. It is like a tortoise that never stretches out its limbs, once it has drawn them in. Even if you cut it to pieces, it would never stretch them out.

543. *Q.* Is this world unreal?

A. It is unreal so long as you do not know God. For you do not see Him in everything, and so fasten yourself to the world with the tie of 'I and mine'. Being thus deluded by ignorance, you become attached to sense-objects and sink deeper and deeper into the abyss of Maya. Maya makes men so utterly blind that they cannot get out of its meshes even when the way lies open. You yourself know how unreal this worldly life is. Think a little of the very house that you are in. How many men were born and how many died in it! Things of the world appear before us for a moment and vanish in the next. Those whom you know to be your 'own' will cease to exist for you, the moment you close your eyes in death. How strong is the hold of attachment upon a worldly man! There is nobody in the family who requires his attention, yet for the sake of a grandson he cannot go to Benares to practise devotion. "What will become of my Hari," is the one thought that keeps him bound to the world. In a Ghuni (a trap for catching fish) the way out is always open, yet the fish do not get out of it. The caterpillar shuts itself up in its own cocoon and perishes. Being of such a nature, is not this mundane life (Samsara) unreal and evanescent?

544. Do you know how egotism is to be destroyed? When they husk corn, they stop from time to time to examine the grain, and see if the husking is complete. When they weigh some fine things in a delicate balance, they often stop and adjust the needle to test if the point is accurate. So now and then I used to abuse myself with strong denunciations to see whether my ego still rose within me are not. At times I used to ponder thus over the nature of the body: "Look at this body. What is it but a cage of flesh and bones! It contains nothing but blood, pus and such other impure matter. It is strange that so much pride is felt with regard to this!

545.* Suppose rice is boiling in the pot. To test whether it is properly boiled, you take one grain from it and press the same between your fingers. At once you come to know whether the whole pot of rice is boiled or not. Surely you would not press each and every grain of rice? Just as you know the condition of the rice by testing only a few grains, so also you can know whether the world is real or unreal, eternal or ephemeral, existent or non-existent, by examining two or three objects in it. Man is born, lives for some days, and then dies. So too are animals and trees. Discriminating like this, you come to know that the same is the fate of all things endowed with name and form, even of the earth, the sun and moon. Do you not thus come to understand the nature of all things in the universe? When you thus recognise the world to be unreal and ephemeral, you will no longer have any love of it. You will renounce it from the mind, and become free from all desires. When you succeed in this act of renunciation, you come to know God who is the cause of the universe. One who gains the realisation of God in this way—if he is not all-knowing, what else is he?

VAIRAGYA

546.* Even when we are blinded to reality by the fulfilment of every worldly desire, there may arise in us the question, "Who am I who enjoy all this?" This may be the moment in which a revelation of the secret begins.

547. In a forest full of thorns and briars it is impossible to walk bare-footed. One can do so if the whole forest is covered with leather, or if one's own feet are protected with leather shoes. It is impossible to cover the whole forest with leather, so it is wiser to protect one's feet with shoes. Similarly, in this world man is troubled with innumerable wants and desires, and there are only two possible ways of escape from them, *viz.*, either to have all those wants satisfied, or to give up all of them. But it is impossible to satisfy all human wants; for with every attempt to satisfy them, new wants arise. So it is wiser to decrease one's wants by contentment and the knowledge of Truth.

548. It is very pleasant to scratch an itching ringworm, but the sensation one gets afterwards is very

painful and intolerable. So the pleasures of this world are very attractive in the beginning, but their consequences are terrible to endure and contemplate.

549. A kite with a fish in its beak was chased by a large number of crows and screaming kites, pecking at it and trying to snatch away the fish. In whichever direction it went the flock of kites and crows also followed it. Tired of this annoyance, the kite threw away the fish which was instantly caught by another kite. At once the flock of kites and crows turned to the new possessor of the fish. The first kite was left unmolested; it calmly perched upon the branch of a tree. Seeing it in this quiet and tranquil state, the Avadhuta saluted it and said, "You are my Guru, O kite; you have taught me that so long as man does not throw off the burden of worldly desires, he cannot escape from worldly distractions and be at peace with himself."

550. A shy horse does not move straight when its eyes are not protected by eyeflaps. Similarly, the mind of a worldly man, restrained from looking around by the eyeflaps of discrimination and aversion for worldly objects, will not stumble, or stray into evil paths.

551. When paper is wetted with oil, it cannot be written upon. So the soul stained by the oil of vice and luxury is unfit for spiritual devotion. But when the paper wetted with oil is overlaid with chalk, it may be written upon; so when such a soul is 'chalked' over with renunciation, it becomes fit again for spiritual progress.

552. There is a venomous spider whose poison no medicine can counteract till the wound is magnetised by

passes with turmeric roots held in the hand. After the wound is thus treated, other remedies are seen to produce their effect. So when the spider of lust and wealth has infected a man, he must first get thoroughly saturated with the magnetic remedy of renunciation before he can have any spiritual progress.

553.* If you put a purifying agent, say, a piece of alum, into a vessel of muddy water, the impurities settle down at the bottom and the water is made clear. Discrimination and dispassion for worldly objects are the two purifying agents. It is through these that the worldly man ceases to be worldly and becomes pure.

554. The caterpillar gets itself imprisoned in its own cocoon. So the worldly soul is caught in the meshes of its own desires. But when the caterpillar develops into a bright and beautiful butterfly, it bursts the cocoon and flies out enjoying freely light and air. So the worldly soul can fly out of the meshes of Maya with the wings of discrimination and dispassion for worldly things.

555. Reverse turns the key of the room wherein God lives. To reach Him you have to renounce the world and all.

556. It is useless to pore over the holy scriptures if one's mind is not endowed with Viveka and Vairagya. No spiritual progress can be made without these.

557. How may one attain God? One has to sacrifice body, mind and riches to find Him.

558.* What must be the condition of the mind of a bound soul before he can hope to be liberated? If by the grace of God he can acquire intense dispassion for worldly things, then only can he be released from the attachment to 'woman and gold'. And what is this intense dispassion, this vehement desirelessness? "By and by I shall realise God"—this is the attitude of feeble Vairagya. But he whose Vairagya is acute and strong—his heart longs and pants for God, even as the mother's heart pants for her child. He never seeks anything but God, and to him the world appears as a veritable well wherein he fears he may be drowned any moment. To him his relations then seem so many venomous serpents from whom he is inclined to fly away. And such is the strength of his impulse and determination that he never thinks of settling his domestic affairs first before he would seek the Lord.

559. Why does a God-lover renounce everything for the sake of Him Whom he loves? The moth after seeing a light has no mind to return to darkness; the ant dies in the heap of sugar but does not turn back. So the God-lover gladly sacrifices his life for the attainment of Divine bliss, and cares for nothing else.

560.* One becomes a real Jnani, a true Paramahamsa, only when one has tested all possible conditions of life, from the humblest position of a scavenger to the highest role of a king, through observation, report of others and actual experience, and has become convinced thereby of the trivial nature of all worldly enjoyments.

561.* Jnana never comes without renunciation of lust and possessions. With the dawn of renunciation is destroyed all ignorance, all Avidya. Many things can be burnt by means of a lens held in such a manner that the rays of the sun falls on it directly, but you cannot use it so in the shade of a room. Even so with the mind. You must take it out of the dark cell of this world and expose it to the full blaze of self-effulgent Divinity. Then alone true renunciation will come, and with it all ignorance will be destroyed.

562. Knowledge (Jnana) cannot be communicated all at once. Its attainment is a question of time. Suppose a fever is of a severe type, the doctor cannot give quinine in that circumstance. He knows that it will do no good. The fever must first leave the patient, which depends upon time, and then quinine or any other medicine should be administered. Analogous is the case with a man who seeks Knowledge. Religious precepts often prove useless as long as one is immersed in worldliness. Allow a man a certain time for the enjoyment of the things of the world. When his attachment to the world has somewhat lessened, then comes the time for fruitful religious instructions. Till then all such instructions will only be lost upon him.

563. In a room away from their mother, little children play with dolls just as they like; but as soon as the mother comes in, they throw aside the dolls and run to her, crying "Mamma, Mamma". You also are now playing in this world, deeply absorbed in the dolls of wealth, honour and fame, without caring for anything else. But if once you see the Divine Mother in you, you will no more find pleasure in any of these, be it wealth, honour or fame. Leaving them all away, you will run to Her.

564.* Vairagya is of many kinds. One kind of it springs from acute pain due to worldly misery. But the better kind arises from the consciousness that all worldly blessings, though within one's reach, are transitory and are not worth enjoying. Thus, having all, he has not anything.

565. How many kinds of Vairagya are there? Generally two: the intense and the moderate. Intense Vairagya is like digging a large tank in one night until it gets filled with water then and there. Moderate Vairagya is slow in its growth and procrastinating. There is no knowing when it will become complete.

566. A person was going to a river to bathe when he heard that a certain gentleman had been preparing for some days past to renounce the world and become a sannyasin. This somehow produced a conviction in the man's mind that the Sannyasin's is the highest mode of life. He immediately determined to be a Sannyasin and without returning home went away in his half-naked condition. This illustrates intense Vairagya.

567.* Dive deep into the ocean of the Absolute Existence-Knowledge-Bliss. Fear not those deep sea-monsters—avarice and anger. Paint yourself thickly with the turmeric of Viveka and Vairagya and these alligators will not approach you; for the scent of this turmeric is too much for them.

PERSEVERANCE

568. Do you know how peasants buy their teams? Oh, they are expert in these matters, and know very well how to distinguish the good ones from the bad. They know how to find out the mettle of an animal. They simply touch the

tail, and the effect is miraculous. Those that have no mettle in them will offer no resistance, but lie down on the ground as if they are going to sleep. But those that have mettle will jump about, as if in protest against the liberty taken with them. The peasants will choose the latter.

One must have the true mettle of a man within, if one wishes to be successful in life. But there are many who have no grit in them—who are like popped rice soaked in milk, soft and cringing! No strength within! No capacity for sustained effort! No power of will! They are failures in life.

569. The angler, anxious to hook a big fish, waits calmly for hours together, having thrown the bait and the hook into water. Similarly the devotee who patiently goes on with his devotions is sure at last to find his God.

570. The hereditary peasant does not give up tilling the soil though it may not rain for twelve years; but a merchant who has recently taken to agriculture is discouraged by one season of drought. The true believer is never discouraged even if he fails to see God in spite of lifelong devotion.

571. He who will learn to swim must attempt swimming for some days. None can venture to swim in the sea after a single day's practice. So if you want to swim in the sea of Brahman, you must make many ineffectual attempts at first before you can successfully swim therein at last.

572. The new-born calf feels unsteady and tumbles down scores of times before it learns to stand steady. So in the path of devotion slips are many and frequent until success is finally achieved.

573. Two persons, it is said, together began invoking the Goddess Kali by the terrible rite called Savasadhana.[1] One invoker was frightened to insanity by the terrible visions appearing in the earlier portion of the night, while the other was favoured with the vision of the Divine Mother at the end of the night. The latter said to the Goddess, "Mother, why did the other man become mad?" The Deity answered, "You, too, O child, did become mad many times in your previous births, and now at last you have seen Me."

574. *Q.* Peace comes to our heart but rarely, and then it does not last long. Why is it so?

A. The fire made by burning bamboo is soon extinguished unless kept alive by constant blowing. Uninterrupted devotion is necessary to keep alive the fire of spirituality.

575. If you fill an earthen vessel with water and set it apart on a shelf, all the water in it evaporates in a few days; but if you keep it immersed in water, it will remain full as long as it is there. Such is the case with your love of God. If you cultivate love of God for a time, and afterwards employ yourself in other affairs forgetting Him, then you would soon find that your heart has become empty of that precious love. But if you keep your blissful heart immersed always in holy love and faith, it is sure to remain ever full to overflowing with the divine fervour of that sacred love.

576. So long as there is fire beneath the vessel, the milk in it boils and bubbles, but remove the fire and the

[1] This Tantric rite is performed in a cremation ground in the darkness of night, the Sadhaka seating himself on a corpse.

milk stands still again. So the heart of the neophyte boils with enthusiasm only so long as he goes on with his spiritual exercises.

577. How long does godliness remain in man? Iron is red so long as it is in the fire, but it becomes black the moment it is removed from fire. So man is imbued with God so long as he is in communion with Him.

578. The mind is like the curly hair of a Negro; you may draw it straight as long as you please, but the moment you let it go it again becomes curled. As long as the mind is forcibly kept straight and steady, it works well and to advantage; but when you slacken your vigilance, it turns away from the right path.

579. Tota Puri[1] used to say, "If a brass vessel is not scoured daily, it gets dim in colour. So if a man does not meditate daily on the Deity, his heart will get impure." To him the Master once replied that a gold vessel does not require daily cleaning. The man who has reached God no more needs the help of prayers and penances.

SPIRITUAL PRACTICE

580. To drink pure water from a shallow pond one should gently take the water from the surface without disturbing it in the least. If it is disturbed, the sediments rise up and make the whole water muddy. If you desire to be pure, have firm faith, and slowly go on with your devotional practices, without wasting your energy in useless

[1] The itinerant monk who initiated the Master into the practice of Advaita Vedanta.

scriptural discussions and arguments. Your little brain will otherise be muddled.

581. There are many who inquire about the houses and riches of a wealthy citizen of Calcutta like Jadunath Mullick, but only a few go to see him personally and cultivate his acquaintance. Similarly, many are the men who study scriptures and talk of religion, but very few are those who wish to see God or take pains to approach Him.

582. Adopt adequate means for the end you seek to attain. You cannot get butter by crying yourself hoarse, saying, "There is butter in the milk." If you wish to get butter, turn the milk into curd and churn it well, and then you will have butter. So if you long to see God, take to spiritual practices (Sadhanas). What is the good of merely crying, "O God! O God!"

583. If a man desires to see the king in his palace, he will have to go to the palace and pass through all the gates; but, if, after entering the outermost gate only, he exclaims, "Where is the king?" he will not find him. He must go through the seven gates, and then he will see the king.

584. Effort is necessary for realisation. One day in Bhava Samadhi (spiritual absorption), I saw the Haldar-pukur[1] and found there a rustic taking water. He removed the sedges from the surface and examined it now and again, taking it up in his hand. It was shown to me, as if to signify that just as water can never be seen unless one removes the sedge, love of God and realisation of Him cannot be had if one does not work for it. Meditation,

[1] A big tank situated just in front of the ancestral house of Sri Ramakrishna in his native village Kamarpukur.

repeating the 'name' of the Lord, singing His glories, praying to Him, charity, performance of sacrifices—these are the holy works that lead to God.

585. Even Sri Krishna went through tremendous spiritual practises relating to the worship of the Radha-yantra. The Yantra is the Brahmayoni (Creative Power of Brahman), and the Sadhana consisted of its worship and meditation. From this Brahmayoni there spring myriads of worlds!

586. The course of Sadhana is of three kinds, *viz.*, (1) of the nature of birds, (2) of the nature of monkeys and (3) of the nature of ants.

(1). The bird comes and pecks at a fruit which perhaps falls down at the jerk, and the bird cannot get it for eating. So there are devotees who try to rush on with devotional practices with such violence that it often frustrates their attempts.

(2) It is the nature of the monkey to jump from branch to branch, holding a fruit in its mouth, and while jumping, the fruit often falls down from its mouth. Thus at times, distracted by the changing events of life the aspirants lose sight of the devotional path, if the grasp is not firm.

(3) The ant creeps gently and steadily towards a grain of food, and carries it back to its hole where it enjoys it comfortably. The course of Sadhana like that of the ant is considered the best—there is sureness of attaining and enjoying the fruit.

587. He who is fond of fishing, and wishes to be informed if good fish abound in a certain pond, goes to

those persons who have already fished in it, and eagerly asks them: "Is it true that there are big fish in this pond? And what is the most suitable bait to catch them?" Having gathered the necessary information from them, he resorts to the pond with his fishing rod, waits there patiently after throwing his line, and allures the fish with dexterity. At last he succeeds in hooking a large and beautiful dweller of the deep. Similarly, with implicit trust in the sayings of holy saints and sages, one must try to secure God in one's own heart with the bait of devotion, and the rod and hook of one's mind. With unceasing patience one must wait for the fullness of time. Then only can one catch the Divine fish.

588. The Master used to say: "Will you be able to obey to the fullest extent the commands that I give you? Verily, I tell you, your salvation is assured if you put into practice even one-sixteenth of what I say to you."

589.* Spiritual practices (Sadhanas) are absolutely necessary for Self-knowledge, but if there is perfect faith, then a little practice is enough.

590.* Once a person comes to believe in the power of His holy 'name' and feels inclined to repeat it constantly, neither discrimination nor devotional exercises of any sort are necessary for him. All doubts are set at rest, the mind becomes pure, and the Lord Himself is realised through the force of His holy name.

591. The Vedas and the Puranas must be read and heard, but one must act according to the precepts of the Tantras. The 'name' of Lord Hari must be uttered by the mouth and heard with the ear as well. Indeed in some

diseases it is necessary not only to apply medicine externally but also to take it internally.

592. There are two kinds of Siddhas (perfect men) —Sadhana-siddhas and Kripâ-siddhas (those who have gained perfection through religious discipline and those who have gained perfection through grace). To get a good crop, some have to irrigate their fields with great labour by cutting canals, or by drawing water. But some others are lucky enough to be saved all this trouble for getting water; for there comes the rain and floods the whole field. Almost all have to perform devotional practices assiduously in order to get freedom from the shackles of Maya. But Kripâ-siddhas are saved from all this trouble; they attain perfection through the grace of God. Their number, however, is extremely small.

CONCENTRATION AND MEDITATION

593. Meditation and contemplation should be kept up always.

594. Throwing away all work, you must meditate upon God in the evening. The thought of God naturally comes to the mind at dusk. Everything was visible a while ago, but ah! now it is all shrouded in darkness. Who has done this? Such thoughts come to the mind. Haven't you marked how the Mohammedans give up all work and sit down to pray in the evening?

595. As it is very difficult to gather the mustard seeds that escape out of a torn package and are scattered in all directions, so it is not a very easy affair to ingather and

concentrate the mind which runs after worldly things in diverse directions.

596. Meditate on God either in an obscure corner, or in the solitude of forests, or within the silent sanctuary of your own heart.

597. In the beginning a man should try to concentrate his mind always in a lonely place; otherwise many things may distract him. If we put milk and water together, they are sure to get mixed; but if the milk is changed into butter by churning, the transformed milk (*i.e.* butter), instead of mixing with water, will float upon it. So when a man has gained the power of mental concentration by constant practice, his mind will always rise above his environment and rest in God, wherever he might stay.

598.* The Master sometimes used to instruct his disciples: "Before beginning your meditation, think of this (me) for some time. Do you know why I say so? Because, on account of your faith in this (me), your thoughts, if directed towards this (me), will at once turn Godward. It is just as a herd of cows reminds one of a cowboy; or the son, of the father; or the lawyer, of the law-court. The mind that remains scattered over a thousand and one objects will be collected together when you will think of this (me); and if the mind, thus concentrated, is then directed towards God, meditation in its true sense will be possible."

599. The easiest way of concentrating the mind is to fix it on the flame of a candle. Its inmost blue portion corresponds to the causal body or the Kâranasarira. By fixing the mind on it, the power of concentration is soon obtained. The luminous portion that envelops the blue

flame represents the Sûkshmasarira or the subtle body; and outside of that there is what represents the gross body or the Sthûlasarira.

600.* Referring to the days of his Sadhana, the Master used to tell his disciples: "Well, my boys, in those days before meditating upon God I would imagine as if I was thoroughly washing the mind of all the various impurities (evil thoughts, desires, etc.) that were there, and then installing the Deity therein. Do like this."

601.* During meditation you should imagine as if you are tying your mind to the lotus feet of the Deity with a silk thread, so that it may not wander away from there. But why must the thread be silken? Since His lotus feet are too delicate, any other band will give Him pain.

602. In the course of his meditation, a beginner sometimes falls into a kind of sleep that goes by the name of Yoganidra. At that time he invariably sees some kind of Divine visions.

603. Do you know how a man of Sâttvika (pure) nature meditates? He meditates in the dead of night, upon his bed within the mosquito-curtain, so that he may not be seen by others.

604. Be diluted in the Lord even as the crude medicine is diluted by spirit.

605. When all the clamourings of the mind are hushed, there comes the suspension of breath or the state of Kumbhaka. The Kumbhaka comes even through Bhakti Yoga; through intense love of God also the breath is suspended.

606. Deep meditation brings out the real nature of the object of meditation, and infuses it into the soul of the meditator.

607. An Avadhuta (a great Yogi) once saw a bridal procession passing along a meadow with much pomp, to the accompaniment of drums and trumpets. Hard by the way through which the procession was passing, he saw a hunter so deeply absorbed in aiming at a bird that he was perfectly inattentive to the procession and did not cast even a side glance at it. The Avadhuta, saluting the hunter, said: "Sir, you are my Guru. When I sit in meditation, let my mind be concentrated on the object of meditation as yours has been on the bird."

608. An angler was fishing in a pond. The Avadhuta, approaching him, asked, "Brother, which road leads to Benares?" The man was at that time all attention to his fishing-rod, as the float was indicating that a fish was nibbling at the bait. So he did not give any reply to the question. When the fish was caught, he turned round and said, "What was it you were saying, sir?" The Avadhuta saluted him and said, "Sir, you are my Guru. When I sit in contemplation of the Supreme Being, let me follow your example and not attend to anything else before finishing my meditation."

609. Once a heron was slowly moving towards the edge of a pond to catch a fish. Behind, there was a hunter aiming an arrow at it; but the bird was totally unmindful of this fact. The Avadhuta, saluting the heron, said, "When I sit in meditation, let me follow your example and never turn back to see who or what is behind me."

610. "To him, who is perfect in meditation, salvation is very near," is an old saying. Do you know when a man becomes perfect in meditation? When, on sitting down to meditate, he becomes immediately surrounded with divine atmosphere and his soul communes with God.

611. There comes deep concentration in meditation when nothing else can be seen or heard. Even perceptions and feelings disappear. A snake may crawl over the body, but one does not feel it. Neither the person meditating nor the snake feels it.

612. He who at the time of contemplation becomes so unconscious of everything outside that he would not know if birds were to nest in his hair—such a man has really acquired the perfection of meditative power.

613. In deep meditation all the functions of the senses are inhibited. The outward flow of the mind comes to a dead stop as if the door of the outer apartment is closed. All the five objects of the senses—light, sound, taste, touch and smell—lie outside unperceived. At first, visions of sense objects appear before the mind during meditation, but when it becomes deep, they ever rise at all—they lie outside, debarred.

614. The secret is that the union with God (Yoga) can never happen unless the mind is rendered absolutely calm, whatever be the 'path' you follow for God-realisation. The mind is always under the control of the Yogi, and not the Yogi under the control of his mind.

CHAPTER XIII

YEARNING FOR GOD

[*Be mad for God—Nature of true yearning—Sole condition of God-realisation*]

BE MAD FOR GOD

615.* If you must be mad, be it not for the things of the world. Be mad with the love of God.

616. Some men shed streams of tears because sons are not born to them, others eat away their hearts in sorrow because they cannot get riches. But alas! how many are there who sorrow and weep for not having seen the Lord! Very few indeed! Verily, he who seeks the Lord, who weeps for Him, attains Him.

617. He who yearns after God cannot bestow any thought on such trifles as food and drink.

618. He who feels thirsty does not discard the water of the river merely because it is muddy, nor does he begin to dig a well to find clear water. So he who feels real spiritual thirst does not discard the religion near at hand, be it Hinduism or any other, nor does he create a new

religion for himself. A really thirsty man has no time for such deliberations.

NATURE OF TRUE YEARNING

619. Let your heart pant for Him as a miser longs for gold.

620. As the drowning man pants hard for breath, so must one's heart yearn for the Lord before one can find Him.

621.* Do you know what kind of Love is required for gaining the Lord? just as a dog with a bruised head runs restlesssly, so must one become distressed for His sake.

622. O heart, call on to your almighty Mother sincerely and you will see how She quickly comes running to you. When one calls on God with heart and soul, He cannot remain unmoved.

623. Do you know how intense our love of God should be? The love that a devoted wife possesses for her beloved husband, the attachment that a miser feels for his hoarded wealth, and the clinging desire that the worldly-minded foster for the things of the world—when the intensity of your heart's longing for the Lord is equal to the sum of these three, then you will attain Him.

624. Jesus Christ was one day walking along the sea-shore when a devotee approached him and asked him, "Lord, how can one attain God?" Jesus directly walked into the sea with the enquirer and immersed him in the water. After a short time he released him, and raising him by the arm, asked him, "How did you feel?" The devotee replied, "I felt as though my last moment had

come—the condition was desperate." Upon this Jesus said, "You shall see the Father when your heart pants for Him as it has panted for a breath of air just now.[1] "

625. 'I must attain God in this very life; yea, in three days I must find Him; nay, with a single utterance of His name I will draw Him to me'—with such violent Love the devotee can attract the Lord and realise Him quickly. But devotees who are lukewarm in their Love take ages to find Him, indeed, if they find Him at all.

626.* Why this attitude of an idler, that if realisation is not possible in this birth, it will come in the next? There should not be such sluggishness in devotion. The goal can never be reached unless a man makes his mind strong, and firmly resolves that he must realise God in this very birth, nay, this very moment. In the countryside, when cultivators go to purchase bullocks, they first touch the tails of the animals. Some of the bullocks do not make any response to this. Rather, they relax all their limbs and lie down on the ground. At once the cultivators understand them to be worthless. There are some others that jump about and behave violently the moment their tails are touched; and the peasants can immediately know that they will be very useful. Their choice is then made from among this active type. Slothfulness is not at all desirable. Gather strength, firm faith, and say that you must realise God this very moment. Then only can you succeed.

[1] This story is not in the Bible and there is nothing in the Bible coming near it. It might be in an 'apocrypha', and Sri Ramakrishna might have heard it from somebody acquainted with it.

SOLE CONDITION OF GOD-REALISATION

627. What means should we adopt in order to get free from the clutches of Maya? He who yearns to be free from its clutches is shown the way by God Himself. Only ceaseless yearning is needed.

628.* A devotee asked the Master, "By what means can He be seen?" and the Master replied: "Can you weep for Him with intense longing? Men weep jugful of tears for children, wife, money, etc.; but who weeps for God? So long as a child is engrossed in play with its toys, the mother engages herself in cooking and other household works. But when the little one finds no more satisfaction in toys, throws them aside and loudly cries for its mother, she can no longer remain in the kitchen. She drops down the rice pot, perhaps, from the hearth, and runs in hot haste to the child and takes it up in arms."

629. He finds God quickest, whose concentration and yearning are strongest.

630. In this age of Kali three days' ardent yearning to see God is enough for a man to obtain Divine grace.

631.* Uncle moon is the uncle of all children. So also God is everyone's. All have got the right to call on the Lord. Whoever calls on Him becomes blessed by realising Him. If you call on Him, you too can realise Him.

632. Verily, I tell you, he who wants Him finds Him. Go and verify it in your own life. Try for three days, try with genuine zeal, and you are sure to succeed.

633. Pray to the Divine Mother, begging Her to give you unswerving Love and adamantine faith.

634. Where does the strength of an aspirant lie? He is a child of God, and tears are his greatest strength. As a mother fulfils the desires of a child who weeps and importunes her, so does the Lord grant to His weeping child whatever he is crying for.

635. A certain man once said to the Master: "I am now fifty-five years old. I have been engaged in the search for the Lord for fourteen years, have followed the advice of my teachers, had been to all the sacred places of pilgrimage, and have seen many a holy man; but I have gained nothing." Hearing this the Master replied: "I assure you, he who yearns for Him shall find Him. Look at me and take heart."

636. The child said, "Mother dear, wake me up when I shall be hungry." The mother replied, "Darling hunger itself will awaken you."

637. As a child beseeches its mother for toys and pice, weeping and teasing her, so he who weeps inwardly, intensely longing to see Him, like an innocent child, and knowing Him to be his nearest and dearest, is rewarded at last with the vision Divine. God can no longer remain hidden from such an earnest and importunate seeker.

638. In Yatras depicting the life of Krishna, the play commences with the beating of drums and the loud singing of 'O Krishna, come! Come, O dear!' But the person who plays the part of Krishna pays no heed to the noise and goes on complacently chatting and smoking in the green-room behind the stage. But as soon as the noise ceases, and the pious sage Narada, overflowing with love, enters the stage with sweet and soft music and summons

Krishna to appear, Krishna finds that he can no longer remain indifferent. Hurriedly he then enters stage. As long as the spiritual aspirant calls on the Lord with mere lip-prayers—'Come, O Lord'—the Lord will not appear. When the Lord comes, the heart of the devotee melts into divine emotion, and all loud utterances cease for ever. The Lord cannot tarry when His devotee calls on Him from the depth of his heart overflowing with profound Love.

BOOK III

MAN AND THE DIVINE

Knowing Him Who is the origin and dissolution of the universe—the source of all virtue, the destroyer of all sins, the master of all good qualities, the immortal, and the abode of the universe—as seated in one's own self, He is perceived as different from, and transcending, the tree of Samsara as well as time and form.

May we realise Him—the transcendent and adorable master of the universe—Who is the supreme Lord over all the lords, the supreme God above all the gods, and the supreme Ruler over all the rulers.

He has nothing to achieve for Himself, nor has He any organ of action. No one is seen equal or superior to Him. His great power alone is described in the Vedas to be of various kinds, and His knowledge and strength and action are described as inherent in Him.

No one in the world is His master, nor has anybody any control over Him. There is no sign by which He can be inferred. He is the cause of all, and the ruler of individual souls. He has no parent, nor is there any one who is His lord.

The Upanishads

CHAPTER XIV

THE LORD AND HIS DEVOTEES

[*Why the Lord is not seen—The Lord and His devotees—Worldly position of devotees—How the Divine reveals Himself—The Lord cares not for wealth —Divine grace and self-effort*]

WHY THE LORD IS NOT SEEN

639. The sun is many times larger than the earth, but distance makes it appear like a small disc. So the Lord is infinitely great, but being too far away from Him, we are incapable of comprehending His real greatness.

640. Because of the reeds and scum that cover the surface of a pond, one cannot see the fishes playing in it; similarly, because of the screen of Maya that shuts off God from human view, one cannot see Him playing in one's heart.

641. Why do we not see the Divine Mother? She is like a high-born lady transacting all her business from behind the latticed screen, seeing all but seen by none. Only Her devout sons see Her, going near Her behind the screen of Maya.

642. The policeman with his lantern (bull's eye) can see every one on whom he casts light, but no one can see him so long as he does not turn the light on himself. So does God see every one; but no one can see Him until He reveals Himself to him in His mercy.

THE LORD AND HIS DEVOTEES

643. A landlord may be very rich, but when a poor tenant brings a humble present to him with a loving heart, he accepts it with the greatest pleasure. So the Almighty Lord, though so great and powerful, accepts the humble offerings of a sincere heart with the greatest pleasure and satisfaction.

644.* I am content if I have realised Him. What if I do not know Sanskrit. He bestows His mercy equally on all His children who yearn to know Him, be they learned or ignorant. Suppose a father has five chidren. Some of them can call him 'Papa'; others can perhaps say only 'Ba' or 'Pa' and cannot pronounce the whole word. But will the father love the latter less than the former? He knows that they are mere infants and cannot correctly call him father. The father indeed loves them all in an equal measure.

645. It is the nature of a child to soil itself with dirt and mud, but the mother does not allow it to remain dirty always. She washes it from time to time. Similarly it is in the nature of man to commit sin; but if man is sure to commit sin, doubly sure is that the Lord devises methods for his redemption.

646. As the same fish is dressed into soup, curry, or cutlet, and each man has his own choice dish of it, so the Lord of the universe, though one, manifests Himself differently according to the different likings of His worshippers, and each one of them has his own view of God which he values most. To some He is a kind master or loving father, a sweet smiling mother or a devoted friend, and to others a faithful husband or a dutiful and obliging son.

647. The fish may be far away, yet when a sweet, savoury and attractive bait is thrown into the water, they hastily rise to it from all quarters. Similarly the Lord approaches quickly the holy devotee whose heart is full of devotion and faith.

648. The divine sages form, as it were, the inner circle of God's nearest relatives. They are like friends, companions and kinsmen of God. All ordinary persons form the outer circle, they are merely the creatures of God.

649. Sunlight is one and the same wherever it falls; but only a bright surface like that of water, or of a mirror or of polished metals, reflects it fully. So is the light Divine. It falls equally and impartially on all hearts but the pure and pious hearts of the good and holy Sadhus alone receive and reflect that light well.

650. It is the nature of a lamp to give light. With its help some may cook their food, some may forge deeds, and some others may read the sacred scriptures. So some with the help of the Lord's 'name' try to attain salvation, while others use it for accomplishing their evil purposes. His holy 'name', however, remains untainted in its purity.

651. Bhagavan (the Lord), Bhagavata (His word or scripture) and Bhakta (devotee) are all one and the same.

652. How does a true devotee look upon God? He looks upon Him as the nearest and dearest relative, just as the shepherd women of Brindavan (Gopis) saw in Sri Krishna not Jagannatha (the Lord of the universe), but their own beloved Gopinatha (the Lord of the Gopis).

653. Why does the God-lover find such ecstatic delight in addressing the Deity as Mother? Because the child is more free with the mother than with anybody else, and consequently she is dearer to it than anybody else.

654. A patient in high fever and excessively thirsty imagines that he can drink a sea of water; but when the fever subsides and he regains his normal temperature, he can barely take a single cupful of water and his thirst is easily quenched with even a very small quantity of it. So a man, being under the feverish excitement of Maya and forgetful of his own littleness, imagines that he can receive the whole of the Infinite God within his heart, but when the illusion passes away, a single ray of Divine light becomes sufficient to flood him with the eternal bliss of God.

655. Some get tipsy with even a small peg of wine, while others require two or three bottles to make them intoxicated. But both feel equally the pleasure of intoxication. Similarly, some devotees become full of ecstasy even by a ray of Divine glory while some others get intoxicated with the Divine bliss only on coming into the direct presence of the Lord. But both are equally fortunate, since both are deluged with the bliss of God.

656. God is like a hill of sugar. A small ant fetches from it a tiny grain of sugar, and a bigger one takes from it another grain considerably larger in size. But in spite of this the hill practically remains as large as ever. So are the devotees of God. They become ecstatic even with a little of a single Divine attribute. No one can contain within him the realisation of all His glories and excellences.

657. The breeze that comes from the ocean of Brahman affects every heart on which it blows. The ancient sages Sanaka, Sanatana and others were softened by this breeze. The God-intoxicated Narada obviously got a glimpse of that Divine ocean from a distance; and so forgetting his own self, he had been wandering over the world like a mad man, always singing the praise of Lord Hari. Sukadeva, a born ascetic, only touched the water of that ocean thrice with his hand, and ever since he had been rolling about like a child through the fullness of his ecstasy. And the great teacher of the universe, Mahadeva, drank three handfuls of the water thereof, and has since been lying motionless like a corpse, intoxicated with Divine bliss. Who can fathom the depth, or measure the mysterious power, of this ocean?

658. The Master said to Keshab Chandra Sen: "Why do they, the members of the Brahmo Samaj, dwell so much upon the glories of God's works and say, 'O Lord, Thou hast made the sun, the moon and the stars?' Many are they that are charmed with the beauty of the garden, its glorious flowers and sweet odours. But few seek the Lord of the garden! Which is the greater of the two—the garden or its Lord? Verily the garden is unreal as long

as death stalks in our midst; but the Lord of the garden is the one reality.

"After having taken a few glasses at the bar of a tavern, who cares to inquire how many tons the liquor in the barrels there weigh? A single bottle suffices for one.

"At the sight of Narendra I get inebriated with joy. Never have I asked him, 'Who is your father?' or 'How many houses have you got as your own?'

"Men value their own possessions; they value money, houses, furniture; hence they think that the Lord will view His own works—the sun, the moon, and the stars—just in the same light! Men think He would be glad if they speak highly of His works."

659. How sweet is the simplicity of the child! He prefers a doll to all the wealth and riches of the world. So is the faithful devotee. No one else can reject all wealth and honour, and be taken up with God alone.

660. The truly pious man gives three-fourths of his mind to God; only the remaining one-fourth he gives to the world. He is more alert in matters godly, like the snake which grows furious when its tail is trampled upon, as if its feelings are more located in its tail than anywhere else.

661. Referring to the Master, a well-known Brahmo missionary once said that the Paramahamsa was a mad man, and that too much cogitation over one and the same subject had unsettled his mind, as it had happened with many European thinkers. The Master afterwards said, addressing this missionary, "You say that even in Europe learned men become mad by continuously thinking of one subject. But is the subject of their thought matter or spirit? If it is matter, what

wonder if a man should become mad by constantly thinking of it. But how can a man lose his intelligence by thinking on that Intelligence whose light enlightens the whole universe? Is this what your scriptures teach you?"

662. Dive deep into the sea of Divine love. Fear not. It is the sea of Immortality. I once said to Narendra, "God is like a sea of sweetness. Would you not dive deep into the sea? Suppose, my boy, there is a vessel with a wide mouth containing syrup of sugar, and you are a fly anxious to drink of it. Where would you sit and drink?" Narendra replied that he would like to drink from the edge, for if he happened to fall into it, he was sure to be drowned. Thereupon I said to him, "You forget, my boy, that if you dive deep into the sea Divine, you need not fear danger or death. Remember that the sea of Sachchidananda is the sea of Immortality, having everlasting life for its waters. Be not afraid, like some foolish people, that you may 'run to excess' in your love of God."

WORLDLY POSITION OF DEVOTEES

663. Though Devaki was blessed in the prison with the sight of the Divine form of Krishna, yet that could not free her from imprisonment.

664. Once a blind man bathed in the holy waters of the Ganges and had all his sins expiated by the bath, yet his physical blindness was not removed.

665. Once a devout wood-cutter was blessed with the vision of the Divine Mother and became a recipient

of Her grace, yet his profession of a wood-cutter never ceased. The poor man had still to earn his scanty livelihood by the same hard profession of wood-cutting.

666.* As Bhishma lay dying on his bed of arrows, he was found shedding tears. Sri Krishna and the Pandavas were standing by. Arjuna exclaimed, "How strange, brother! Our grandfather Bhishma himself—so truthful and wise, the master of his self, and one amongst the eight Vasus (a class of deities)—even he is overcome by Maya in his dying hour and is shedding tears!" When this was communicated to Bhishma he replied: "O Krishna, you know full well that I am not crying for that. But when I think that even the Pandavas, whom the Lord Himself is serving as charioteer, have to pass through endless troubles and tribulations, I am overpowered with the thought that the ways of God cannot in the least be comprehended, and I cannot restrain my tears."

HOW THE DIVINE REVEALS HIMSELF

667. There is a dark room, and rays of light are coming into it from outside through a small chink. Now, the idea of light that a man inside will have, will be just commensurate to the rays of light. If there are a greater number of chinks in the doors and windows, the man within will see more of light; and if he flings open the doors and windows, he will get light still more. But then it is he who stands in the open field that receives the maximum degree of light. Just so the Lord reveals Himself to the devotees according to the varying capacity and nature of their mind.

668. The more one approaches the Universal Being, the newer and greater become the revelations of His infinite nature, and in the end he merges in Him through the consummation of Knowledge.

THE LORD CARES NOT FOR WEALTH

669. Does the Lord care for all the wealth that one may offer him? Oh, no! His grace lights on him alone who offers Him love and devotion. What He values are only love and devotion, discrimination and renunciation for His sake.

670. Sambhu Mallick once said to me, "Sir, bless me that I may die leaving all my wealth at the hallowed feet of the Divine Mother." I replied, "What do you say? It is all wealth to you, but to the Divine Mother, it is no better than the dust you trample under your feet!"

671. There was once a theft committed in Rani Rasmani's temple at Dakshineswar. The jewels with which the images in the shrine of Vishnu were adorned were stolen. Mathur (the manager of the temple and son-in-law of the Rani) and the Master went there to see what the matter was. Mathur cried out, saying, "Thou God art worthless! They took away all Thy jewels, and Thou couldst not prevent it!" Upon this, the Master retorted sharply, "How foolish it is of you to talk thus! The jewels of which you speak are as good as lump of clay to the Lord of the universe whom you worship in the image! Remember, it is from Him that the Goddess of fortune, Lakshmi, derives all Her splendour.

DIVINE GRACE AND SELF-EFFORT

672. We cannot say that God is gracious because He feeds us, for every father is bound to provide his children with food; but when He keeps us from going astray and holds us back from temptations, He is truly gracious.

673. Q. By what kind of work can God be attained?

A. There is no difference in work. Do not think that this work will lead to God and that will not.

Everything depends upon His grace. To have His grace, whatever work you perform, do it with sincerity and earnest longing for Him. Through His grace the environment will become favourable and the conditions of realisation will become perfect. If you want to renounce the world, and if your family depends upon you, perhaps your brother will assume its responsibility for you. Perhaps your wife will not hinder you in your spiritual life, but will rather help you; or perhaps you will not marry at all and be attached to the world in any way.

674. The darkness of centuries is dispersed as soon as a light is brought into a room. The accumulated sins of countless lives vanish hy a single glance of God.

675. There are some fish which have many sets of bones, but others have only one set. Fish-eaters, however, remove all of them, whether many or few. In the same way some men have many sins and others have few, but the saving grace of God purifies them all alike in time.

676. When the Malaya breeze blows, all trees having stamina in them are said to be converted into sandal trees, while the papaw, the bamboo, the plantain and other trees devoid of stamina remain unchanged. So when Divine

grace descends on men, those that have germs of piety and goodness in them are made holy and are filled with Divinity, while those that are worthless and worldly are unaltered.

677. A certain pious man used to tell the beads constantly, uttering the 'name' of the Deity silently. To him the Master said, "Why do you stick to one place? Go forward." The pious man replied, "It cannot be done without His grace." The Master said, "The breeze of His grace is blowing day and night over your head. Unfurl the sails of your boat (mind), if you want to make rapid progress through the ocean of life."

678. The wind of God's grace is incessantly blowing. Lazy sailors on the sea of life do not take advantage of it. But the active and the strong always keep the sails of their minds unfurled to catch the favourable wind and thus reach their destination very soon.

679. *Q.* Does nothing take place all of a sudden?

A. As a general rule, one must go through a long preparation before one can attain perfection. Babu Dwarka Nath Mitter was not made a Judge of the High Court in one day. He had to work hard and spend years of arduous toil and study before he was raised to the Bench of the High Court. Those who are not willing to undergo the trouble and labour must be prepared to remain mere briefless pleaders. However, through the grace of God, sudden exaltation does take place now and then, as was the case with Kalidasa, who, from the state of an ignorant rustic, became at once, through the grace of Mother Saraswati, the greatest poet of India.

680. A householder devotee: Sir, we have heard that you have seen God. So please make us also see Him. How can one get intimate knowledge of the Lord?

The Master: Everything depends upon the will of the Lord. Perseverance is necessary for God-vision. If you merely sit on the shore of a lake and say, "There are fishes in this lake," will you get any fish? Go and get the things necessary for fishing; get a rod and line and bait, and throw some food into the water to entice them. Then from the deep water the fish will rise and come near when you can see and hook them. You wish me to show you God while you sit quietly by, without making the least effort! You want me to set the curd, to churn the butter and hold it to your mouth. You ask me to catch the fish and put it in your hands. How unreasonable is your demand!

681. A bird perching upon the masthead of a ship in mid ocean, gets tired of its position and flies away to discover a new place of rest; but failing to find any other place, it returns at last to the old roost, weary and exhausted. In the same manner, an ordinary aspirant is disgusted with the monotony of the task and the discipline imposed upon him by his well-wishing and thoroughly experienced Guru. He loses all his hopes as well as confidence in the Guru and so goes out into the world with the belief that he can attain God with his self-effort alone; but after much fruitless exertion he is sure to return to his old master for his blessing and grace at last.

682. So long as no breeze is blowing, we fan ourselves to alleviate heat; but when the breeze begins to blow,

giving relief to all men, rich and poor alike, we give up fanning. We should ourselves persevere to reach our final goal so long as there is no help from above; but when fortunately that help comes to one, one might stop toiling, otherwise not.

683. Fans are of no use when the wind blows. Prayers and penances may be given up when the grace of God descends.

684. "Though a soul has received the grace of God, of a Guru and of a good devotee, yet it meets with destruction through the lack of the grace of (a fourth) one." One might have been fortunate enough to receive all the first three forms of grace, yet if one's own heart shows no grace to itself, *i.e.*, if it has no yearning to save itself, they are of no avail.

685. However much you may try, without God's grace nothing can be attained; He cannot be realised without Divine grace. But Divine grace descends not so easily. You shall have to banish your ego completely from the heart. If you have the egoistic feeling "I am the doer", you can never see God. If there is somebody in the store-room, and if the owner of the house is asked to fetch a certain thing from the store, he at once says, "Well, there is someone already in the store; please ask him to get it. There is no need of my going there." God never appears in the heart of him who thinks himself to be the doer.

686. Through His grace He reveals Himself. He is the sun of Knowledge. One ray of His has brought the power of understanding in this world. On account of it

we have the power to know each other and to acquire various forms of knowledge. We can see Him only if He turns His light on his own face.

CHAPTER XV

HELPERS IN THE SPIRITUAL PATH

[I. **Guru** : *Conception of the Guru—Necessity of having a Guru—Relation between Guru and disciple—* II. **Divine Incarnation** : *What is a Divine Incarnation? —Difficulty of recognising Divine Incarnations—Incarnations as revelations of God—Difference between Incarnations and ordinary perfect men*]

I

Guru

CONCEPTION OF THE GURU

687. Who is whose Guru (spiritual guide and teacher) ? God alone is the guide and Guru of the universe.

688. He who considers his Guru to be merely human, what good can he derive from his prayers and devotions? We should not consider our Guru to be a mere man. Before the disciple sees the Deity, he sees the Guru in the first vision of Divine illumination. And it is the Guru who afterwards shows the Deity, being himself mysteriously transformed into the form of the Deity. Then the disciple

sees the Guru and the Deity as one and the some. Whatever boon the disciple asks, the deified Guru gives him all, yea, the Guru even takes him to the highest bliss of Nirvana (the state of extinction of individuality in God). Or, the man may choose to remain in a dualistic state of consciousness, maintaining the relation of the worshipper and the worshipped. Whatever he asks, his Guru vouchsafes him.

689. The human Guru whispers the sacred formula (Mantra) in the ear; the Divine Guru breathes the spirit into the soul.

690. The Guru is a mediator. He brings man and God together, even as a match-maker brings together the lover and the beloved.

691. A Guru is like the mighty Ganges. Men throw all filth and refuse into the Ganges, but the holiness of that river is not diminished thereby. So is the Guru above all petty insult and censure.

692. There are three classes of religious teachers as there are three classes of doctors. There is one class of doctors who, when they are called in, look at the patient, feel his pulse, prescribe the necessary medicines, and ask him to take them. If the patient declines to do so, they go away without troubling themselves further about the matter. This is the lowest class of doctors. In the same way, there are some religious teachers who do not care much whether the disciples attach any value to their teachings and act up to them or not. Doctors of the second type not only ask the patient to take their medicine but go further. They expostulate with him in case he shows any reluctance

to take it. In the same way, those religious teachers who leave no stone unturned to make other people walk in the ways of righteousness, devotion and truth by means of gentle persuasion, can be said to belong to the next higher class. The third and the highest kind of doctors would proceed to use force with the patient in case their expostulation failed. They would go to the length of putting their knee on the chest of the patient and forcing the medicine down his throat. Similarly, there are some religious teachers who would use force, if necessary, with their disciples with a view to make them walk in the path of the Lord. These belong to the highest class.

NECESSITY OF HAVING A GURU

693. What is the necessity of calling a particular man our Guru instead of calling everyone who teaches us something, by that designation ? When going to a strange countrry, one must abide by the directions of the guide who knows the way. Taking the advice of many would lead to utter confusion. So in trying to reach God one must implicitly follow the advice of one single Guru who knows the way to God.

694. At a game of chess the on-lookers can tell what the correct move is, better than the players themselves. Men of the world think that they are very clever, but they are attached to the things of the world—money, honours, sense-pleasures, etc. Being actually engaged in the play, it is hard for them to hit upon the right move. Holy men who have given up the world are not attached to

worldly objects. They are like the on-lookers at a game of chess. They see things in their true light and can judge better than the men of the world. Hence, in living the holy life, one must put faith only in the words of those who meditate upon God and who have realised Him. If you seek legal advice, will you not consult lawyers who are in the profession? Surely you will not take the advice of the man in the street.

695. If you are in right earnest to learn the mysteries of God, He will send you the Sadguru, the right teacher. You need not trouble yourself about finding out a Guru.

696. He who can himself approach God with sincerity, earnest prayer and deep longing, needs no Guru. But such deep yearning of the soul is very rare; hence the necessity of a Guru. The Guru is only one but Upagurus (subsidiary teachers) may be many. He is an Upaguru from whom anything whatsoever is learned. The Great Avadhuta (an ascetic of high order mentioned in the Bhagavata) had twenty-four such Upagurus.

RELATION BETWEEN GURU AND DISCIPLE

697. The fabled pearl-oyster leaves its bed at the bottom of the sea and comes up to the surface to catch rain water when the star Svati is in the ascendant. It floats about on the surface of the sea with its shell wide open until it succeeds in catching a drop of the marvellous Svati rain. Then it dives down to the sea-bed and there rests until it has succeeded in fashioning a beautiful pearl out of that raindrop. Similarly, there are some true and eager aspirants who travel from place to

place in search of the Mantra, the saving word, from a godly and perfect preceptor (Sadguru), which can open for them the gate of eternal bliss; and if in his diligent search a man is fortunate enough to meet such a Guru and get from him the much-longed-for Mantra that has the power to break all fetters, he leaves society at once and retires into the deep recess of his own heart and rests there till he has succeeded in gaining eternal peace.

698. Do not fear if such a teacher (*i.e.*, spiritually enlightened Guru) does not seem to be learned and well up in scriptures and other books. Do not fear because he is not book-learned. No, he will never be found wanting in the wisdom of life. He has a never-failing supply of Divine wisdom—of truths directly revealed and superior to all knowledge contained in books.

699. A man was disputing about the character of his Guru when the Master said, "Why are you wasting your time in this futile discussion? Take the pearl and throw away the oyster-shell. Meditate on the Mantra given to you by the Guru and leave out of consideration the human frailties of the teacher."

700. Listen not to any one censuring your Guru. He is greater than your father and mother. Would you keep quiet when your father and mother are insulted in your very presence? Fight, if necessary, and maintain the honour of your Guru.

701. The disciple should never criticise his Guru. He must implicitly obey whatever the Guru says. A certain couplet in Bengali says: "Though my Guru may visit the tavern, still my Guru is holy Rai Nityananda; and though

my Guru may visit the unholy haunts of drunkards and sinners, still to me he is my own pure and faultless Guru."

702.* When the devotion is genuine, even the most ordinary things make the devotee remember God and lose himself in Him. Have you not heard how Lord Chaitanya was merged in Samadhi at the thought, "This is the earth of which drums are made?" Once, while passing through a village, Sri Chaitanya came to know that the inhabitants of that village earned their living by making drums. At once he exclaimed, "This is the earth of which drums are made," and immediately lost all external consciousness. For he thought that out of that earth drums were made which were used in congregational music; and that the music, again, was in praise of God who is the Soul of our souls and the Beauty of beauties. In this way a train of ideas was flashed upon him, and he was at once engrossed in God. Likewise, when a man has true devotion to his Guru, he will certainly be reminded of him at the sight of his relatives. Not only that. Even if he meets people from the Guru's village his thoughts are at once directed to the Guru himself. He prostrates before them constantly, sprinkles the dust of their feet over his body, feeds them sumptuously and renders all other kinds of service to them. At this stage the disciple fails to see any defect in his Guru. Now only can he say, "Even if my Guru frequents taverns, he is the Lord, the Eternal Bliss all the same." As a human being a Guru cannot be a repository of virtues alone and free from all defects whatsoever. The disciple, on account of his devotion, no longer sees him as man but as God Himself, just as one sees everything as yellow, due to one's jaundiced eye. His devotion then reveals to him that God alone is everything; it is He that has become the master, the father and the mother, man and beast, the animate and the inanimate.

II

Divine Incarnation

WHAT IS A DIVINE INCARNATION?

703. An Avatara (Incarnation) is a human messenger of God, He is like a viceroy of a mighty monarch. As the king sends the viceroy when there is any disturbance in some far-off province, to quell it, so whenever there is waning of religion in any part of the world, God sends there His Avatara to guard virtue and to foster its growth.

704. Think not that Rama and Sita, Krishna and Radha, are mere allegories and not historical personages, or that the scriptures are true only in their inner or esoteric meaning. Nay, they were human beings of flesh and blood just as you are; but because they were divinities, their lives can be interpreted both historically and allegorically. The Avataras are to Brahman as waves are to the ocean.

705. The Avatara is always one and the same. Having plunged into the ocean of life, the one God rises up at one point and is known as Krishna, and when after another plunge, He rises up at another point, He is known as Christ.

706. On the tree of Sachchidananda (Absolute Existence-Knowledge-Bliss) there hang innumerable bunches of Ramas, Krishnas, Buddhas, Christs, etc. Out of these, one or two now and then come down into this world and produce mighty changes and revolutions.

707.* The Avataras are born with Divine powers and Divine qualities. They can go into, and stay in, any state of realisation from the highest to the lowest. In a king's palace a stranger can go only to the outer quarters, but the king's own child, the prince of the house, is free to go to every corner.

708.* It is a thin ego that personages like the Incarnations possess. Through this ego God is always visible. For example, a man is standing on one side of a wall, on either side of which are boundless stretches of land. If there is an aperture in the wall, the whole of the other side is visible, and if this be big enough, one can pass through it as well. The ego of the Incarnations resembles that wall with the aperture. Even though they be on this side of the wall, they can see the boundless extent of land on the other. The meaning of this is that though they have taken up bodies, they are always in a state of Yoga, and can, if they like, enter into Samadhi on the other side of the big aperture. Again, if this be big enough, they can come and go through it; that is to say, can come down to a lower plane of consciousness even after Samadhi.

DIFFICULTY OF RECOGNISING DIVINE INCARNATIONS

709.* A Divine Incarnation is hard to comprehend. It is the play of the Infinite on the finite.

710. When Bhagavan Ramachandra came into this world, only twelve sages recognised that He was an Incarnation of God. So when God incarnates in this world, only a few recognise His divine nature.

711. What is the reason that a prophet is not honoured by his own kinsmen? The kinsmen of a juggler do not crowd round him to see his performances, while strangers stand agape, looking at his surprising tricks.

712. The seeds of the Vajrabantula plant (euphorbia) do not fall at the root of the tree. They are carried by the wind far off, and take root at distant places. So the spirit of a prophet manifests itself at a distance from his native home, and he is appreciated there.

713. There is always a shadow under the lamp, while its light illumines the surrounding objects. So men in the immediate proximity of a prophet do not understand him. Those who live far off are charmed by his spiritual glow and his extraordinary power.

714. The elephant has two sets of teeth, the tusks visible externally, and the grinders inside the mouth. Similarly God-men like Sri Krishna have an external manifestation and behave like common men in the view of all, while internally they rest in transcendental peace far beyond the pale of Karma.

INCARNATION AS A REVELATION OF GOD

715. God is indeed infinite. But He is omnipotent. He may so ordain that His divinity as love may be manifest in flesh, and be among us as God incarnate.

Love streams to us from God Incarnate. Divine Incarnation is a fact. Of course, one cannot make this perfectly clear by means of words. It is a fact to be seen and realised by spiritual eyes. One must see God to be convinced of this. By analogy we can at best faintly apprehend the matter. Suppose one touches the horn of a cow, or her feet, or the tail, or the udder. Would not this be the same as touching the cow herself? For us, human beings, the chief thing about the cow is its milk, which comes from the udder. Well, the milk of Divine love streams for us from the Incarnations of God.

716. Who can know God fully? It is not given to us, nor is it required of us, to know Him fully. It is enough if we can see Him—feel that He is the only reality. Suppose a person comes to the holy river Ganges and touches the water. He would say, "I have been blessed with the vision and touch of the holy river from Gomukhi to Gangasagar—from its source to the estuary!"

717. Do you seek God? Then seek Him in man. His divinity is manifest more in man than in any other object. Look around for a man whose heart overflows with the love of God, a man who lives, moves and has his being in God—a man intoxicated with His love. In such a man God manifests Himself.

718. He is the absolute, and again His is the Lila (relative existence conceived as a sport of the Divine). This Lila is of four kinds—Isvara Lila, Deva Lila, Jagat Lila and Nara Lila.[1] In Nara Lila His incarnation

[1] God has four distinct aspects of manifestation. One aspect of His is Isvara, the supreme Lord of the Universe; the Devas, another aspect of His,

becomes possible. Do you comprehend the nature of the Nara Lila? One may well say that it is like the gushing out of the water of a vast terrace in a big torrent through a wide channel. It is the power of that Absolute, the Sachchidananda, which flows out—becomes manifest—through a channel, as it were. All cannot truly recognise the Avataras. Only seven Rishis—Bharadwaja and the rest—could recognise Sri Rama as an Avatara. God incarnates in the human form to teach man true Jnana and Bhakti.

719. A Siddha (an ordinary perfect man) is like an archæologist who, by removing the superincumbent earth and dust, lays open an old well that has been covered up by disuse. The Avatara is like a great engineer who sinks a new well even in a place where there was no water before. Whereas the former can give salvation only to those men who have the waters of salvation near at hand, an Avatara saves him too whose heart is devoid of all love and is dry as a desert.

720. When the tidal wave comes, it inundates alike rivers, streams and land, and all the adjacent area presents one watery surface; but rain water merely flows away through the usual channel. When a Saviour appears, all are saved through His grace. But Siddhas can only save themselves with much pain and penance.

721. When a mighty log of wood floats down a stream, it carries on it hundreds of birds and does not sink. A reed floating down may sink with the weight of even a single

form the superhuman agencies who maintain the world-functions under the control of the Lord; the third aspect of His manifestation is the universe; and the fourth is man.

crow. So when a Saviour appears, innumerable men find salvation by taking refuge in Him. The Siddha can only save himself with much toil and trouble.

722. As a large and powerful steamer moves swiftly over the water, towing rafts and barges in its wake, so when a Saviour comes, he easily carries thousands to the haven of safety across the ocean of Maya.

723. The locomotive engine not only moves on and reaches its destination but also takes with it a long train of waggons behind. So are our Saviours. They carry multitudes of men burdened with sin, to the presence of the Almighty.

724. In ordinary seasons water from wells can be drawn from great depths and with much difficulty; but when the country is flooded with water in the rainy season, water is obtained with ease everywhere. So, ordinarily God is attained with great difficulty through prayers and penances; but when the flood of Incarnation descends on earth, God is seen everywhere.

725. There was a place enclosed by a high wall, and men outside did not know what sort of a place it was. Once four persons determined to scale the wall with the ladder, and find out what was inside. As soon as the first man ascended the top of the wall, he laughed out, "Ha ha! ha!", and jumped into the enclosure. The second person also, as soon as he ascended the wall, laughed aloud and jumped in like the first; and so did the third. When the fourth and last man got upon the wall, he found stretched before him a large and beautiful garden with pleasant groves full of delicious fruits. Though strongly tempted to

jump in and enjoy the scene, he resisted the temptation, and coming down the ladder, spoke of the glory of the garden to those outside of it. Brahman is like that walled garden. Whoever sees Him forgets his own existence and rushes headlong to Him to be absorbed in His essence. Such are the holy men and liberated saints. But the Saviours of humanity are those who see God, and being at the same time anxious to share their happiness of Divine vision with others, refuse the opportunity of passing into Nirvana (state of extinction of individuality), and willingly undergo the troubles of rebirth in the world in order to teach and lead struggling humanity to its goal.

726. In fireworks there is a type of flower-pot which sends off one kind of flower for a while, then another kind, and again still another, thus seeming to possess an infinite variety of flowers, as it were. So are the Avataras. Then there is another kind of flower-pot which, when lighted, burns a little and then goes off all at once. Similarly, ordinary Jivas, after long practice and devotional exercises, go into Samadhi and do not return.

727.* *Q.* Why should God incarnate Himself in the human form?

A. To make manifest to man the perfection of Divinity. Through these manifestations man can talk with God and see His play. In the Incarnation, God fully enjoys, as it were, His own transcendent sweetness. In the saints, God manifests Himself only in part, like the honey in a flower. You suck the flower, and get a little honey. In the Incarnations, it is all 'honey',—all sweetness and all blessedness.

728. Nothing is problematical to the Incarnation. He solves the most difficult and intricate problems of life as the simplest of things in the world, and his expositions are such as even a child can follow. He is the sun of Divine knowledge, whose light dispels the accumulated ignorance of ages.

729. Sometimes there appears that unique composite light which may be called the lunar-solar light, and to this may be compared unique Incarnations like Chaitanya Deva, who are marked alike by Bhakti (Love) and Jnana (Knowledge). It is like the sun and the moon appearing in the firmament at one and the same time. The manifestation of Jnana and Bhakti in one and the same person is as unique an occurrence as the phenomenon referred to above.

730.* The Lord takes the human body for the sake of those pure souls who love the Lord.

731. Those who come with the Avataras are either souls who are eternally free, or who are born for the last time.

CHAPTER XVI

JNANA, BHAKTI AND KARMA[1]

[I. **Path of Knowledge** : *What is Jnana Yoga?—Method of Jnana Yoga—Difficulties of Jnana Yoga—* II. **Path of Love :** *Bhakti and the conditions of its growth—Bhakti and worldly love—Effects of Bhakti—Stages and aspects of Bhakti—Prema or Parabhakti (ecstatic Love)—Love of the Gopis—Viraha and Mahabhava*—III. **Bhakti and Jnana :** *Bhakti and Jnana the same in the end—How Bhakti leads to Jnana—Difference in the temperaments of the Jnani and the Bhakta*—VI. **Path of Work :** *What is Karma Yoga?—Bhakti as a safeguard in Karma Yoga—Work as service equal to worship—Work a means and not an end—Work and worklessness.*]

I

Path of Knowledge

WHAT IS JNANA YOGA?

732. Jnana Yoga is communion with God by means of Knowledge. The Jnani's object is to realise Brahman,

[1] These Sanskrit words may roughly be translated into English as Knowledge, Love and Work; and Yogas or spiritual disciplines connected with them, as the path of Knowledge, the path of Love and the path of Work.

the Absolute. He says "Not this," "Not this" and thus leaves out of account one unreal thing after another until he gets to a point where all Vichara (discrimination) between the real and the unreal ceases, and Brahman is realised in Samadhi.

733. A thief enters a dark room and feels the various articles therein. He lays his hand upon a table perhaps, and saying "Not this" passes on. Next he comes upon some other article—a chair, perhaps—and again saying "Not this" continues his search, till, leaving article after article, he finally lays his hand on the box containing the treasure. Then he exclaims, "It is here!" and there his search ends. Such, indeed, is the search for Brahman.

734. I have seen that the knowledge derived by reasoning is of quite a different kind from the knowledge derived through meditation; and quite different from this again is the Knowledge that dawns by His revelation.

735. Knowledge (Jnana) varies in degree and kind. There is first the Jnana or insight of men of the world—ordinary mortals. This knowledge is not sufficiently powerful. It may be compared to the flame of a lamp which illumines only the interior of a room. The Jnana of a Bhakta (devotee) is a stronger light. It may be compared to the light of the moon which reveals things both inside and outside a room. But the Jnana of the Avatara is

respectively. But these terms mean more than their English equivalents. Thus Knowledge is not a mere intellectual affair, but spiritual insight affecting the whole man; Love is not worldly love, but a kindred feeling in relation to God; and Work is not mere action, but spiritualised pursuit of duties and altruistic undertakings. To indicate this technical sense we have used capitals for them in this chapter and elsewhere, wherever they stand by themselves without qualifying words pointing to their special significance.

still more powerful, and may be likened to the sun. He is the sun of Divine knowledge whose light dispels the accumulated ignorance of ages.

METHOD OF JNANA YOGA

736. If a man knows his own self, he knows other beings and God. What is my ego? Is it my hand or foot, flesh or blood, muscles or tendons? Ponder deeply, and you will know that there is no such thing as 'I'. As you peel off the skin of an onion, you find it consists only of skin; you cannot find any kernel in it. So on analysing the ego, it will be found that there is no real entity that you can call 'I'. Such an analysis of the ego convinces one that the ultimate substance is God alone. When egotism drops away, Divinity manifests Itself.

737. So long as God seems to be outside and far away, there is ignorance. But when God is realised within, there is true Knowledge.

738. Pointing to the heart, the Master used to say: "He who has God here, has Him also there (pointing to the external world). He who does not find God within himself, well never find Him outside of himself. But he who sees Him in the temple of his own soul, sees Him also in the temple of the universe."

739. A man woke up at midnight and desired to smoke. Therefore he wanted some fire, for which he went to a neighbour's house and knocked at the door. Someone opened the door and asked him what he wanted. The man said: "I wish to smoke. Can you give me a little

fire?" The neighbour replied: "Bah! What is the matter with you? You have taken so much trouble to come and awaken us at this hour, while in your own hand you have a lighted lantern!" What man wants is already within him; but he still wanders here and there searching for it.

740. Reasoning is of two kinds—Anuloma and Viloma. By the Anuloma process man rises from the contemplation of the creation to the Creator, in other words, from the effect to the First Cause. Then the Viloma process of reasoning commences. Having attained God, man learns to see His manifestation in every part or act of creation. The one process is analytical and the other is synthetical. The former is like the peeling off of the successive layers of the plantain trunk till one reaches the pith within. The latter is like lying these layers one over another.

741. Knowledge leads to unity: ignorance to diversity.

742.* To a young disciple who was much pre-occupied with the study of books on Vedanta, the Master said one day: "Well, my boy, are you not nowadays deeply engaged in inquiring into the mysteries of Vedanta? Very good. Brahman is real and the world is unreal—is this not the one teaching that forms the purport of all Vedantic studies? Is it anything more than this?" The young man admitted that that was the whole. The Master's words shed for him quite a new light on the truths of Vedanta. The words filled him with wonder. He thought that in fact if one could have a firm conviction of these truths, one would understand everything of Vedanta. The Master went on with his exposition: "Hearing, inquiry and meditation. That Brahman is real and the world is unreal is first to be heard. Then comes inquiry; for the truth of what is heard is firmly established by reasoning. The next step is meditation; that is, withdrawing the mind from the unreal world and concentrating it on Brahman, the Real. This is the order of Vedantic discipline. If, on the other hand, the Truth is heard and understood intellectually but no attempt is made to renounce the unreal, of what use is that knowledge? Such knowledge is like that of the men of the world, and does not help one to attain the Truth. Firm conviction and renunciation—these are the necessary things. With these alone can one realise the Truth. Or else a person may profess in mere words that the world is unreal and non-existent, and that Brahman alone is existent; but the moment sense-objects—colour, taste and the rest—appear before him, he takes them to be real and gets entangled just like a man who verbally asserts that there are no thorns, but bursts out screaming as soon as his hand comes in contact with a thorn and gets pricked. Once a Sadhu came to Panchavati. He used to talk much Vedanta before others. One day I heard that he had illicit connection with a woman. After a while, when I went that side, I found him sitting there, and said, 'You talk so glibly about Vedanta; but what is all this they talk about you?' 'What of that?' he replied, 'I shall show you that there is no harm in it. If the whole world is unreal at all times, how can my fall alone be real? That also is equally unreal.' I said in utter disgust, 'I spit on such knowledge of Vedanta! It is not real Knowledge but a mere sham, falsely professed by the worldly-minded, by wiseacres with gross worldly attachment.' "

DIFFICULTIES OF JNANA YOGA

743. Jnana Yoga is exceedingly difficult in this age of Kali. In the first place, our life in this age depends entirely upon food (Annagataprana). Secondly, the term of human life now is much too short for this purpose. Thirdly, it is almost impossible in this age to get rid of the illusion that the Self is one with the body (Dehatmabuddhi), which clings to us. Now the conclusion which the Jnani must come to is: "I am not the body, I am one with the Universal Soul, the Absolute and Unconditioned Being." "As I am not the body, I am not subject to the conditions of the body, such as hunger, thirst, birth, death, disease and the rest. One subject to these physical conditions and yet calling oneself a Jnani, is like a person who is suffering from intense pain caused by a thorn that has run into his hand and who nevertheless says, "Why, my hand is not at all scratched or torn. It is all right." This kind of talk will not do. First of all the 'thorn' of body-consciousness has to be burnt into ashes by the fire of Jnana.

744. Very few persons are fit for the attainment of Jnana. The Gita declares: "One among thousands desires to know Him, and even among thousands of those who are desirous to know, one perhaps can actually know Him." The less one's attachment to the world, *i.e.*, for 'woman and gold', the more will be one's Jnana (knowledge of God).

745.* The Jnana Yogi says, "I am He." But as long as one has the idea of the Self as body, this egotism is injurious. It does not help one's progress, and it brings about one's ruin. Such a person deceives himself and others.

746.* A certain Brahmachari (religious aspirant) named Ramachandra one day visited Sri Ramakrishna at the temple of Dakshineswar. The aspirant had allowed his hair to grow into long matted tresses after the way of ascetics. Having taken his seat, he began to exclaim from time to time, "Sivoham! Sivoham!" (I am the Lord Siva!), but was dumb otherwise. Sri Ramakrishna observed him silently for some time and then remarked: "What is the good of merely repeating the word 'Sivoham'? It is only when one, by perfect meditation on the Lord in the temple of one's heart, has lost all idea of self and realised the Lord Siva within, that one is entitled to utter this sacred word. What good can the mere repetition of the formula do without the realisation? So long as the stage of realisation is not reached, it is better to regard the Lord as the Master and oneself as His humble servant." The aspirant came to see his mistake, and became wiser by this advice and other similar teachings. Before he left the place, he wrote down on the wall of Sri Ramakrishna's room: "Taught by the Swami, from this day forward Ramachandra Brahmachari regards the Lord as his Master and himself as His humble servant."

II

Path of Love

BHAKTI AND THE CONDITIONS OF ITS GROWTH

747. Nothing can be impressed on smooth glass, but when the surface is coated with proper chemicals, pictures

can be impressed upon it, as in photography. In the same way, on the human heart coated with the chemicals of Bhakti, the image of Divinity can be impressed.

748. It is a rare thing—this love of God. Bhakti can arise only when there is whole-hearted devotion to God such as that of a chaste wife to her husband. Pure Bhakti is very difficult to obtain. Through Bhakti the mind and soul must be absorbed in God. Then comes Bhava (the higher form of Bhakti). In Bhava a man becomes speechless, his breath is stilled and the Kumbhaka (suspension of breath in Yoga practice) sets in of itself, just as, when one shoots at an aim, one becomes speechless and the breath is stopped.

749. Devotion to God increases in the same proportion as attachment to the objects of the senses decreases.

750. Verily these customers (worldly men) seek for Kalai pulse, (worthless commodity, *i.e.*, sensuous enjoyments). It is given to pure souls alone, uncontaminated by the world, to love God and to have a single aim, namely, to have the mind fixed wholly upon the Lord.

751. Unless one screens the eyes of unbroken horses, they will not move a single step. Is it possible to realise God unless one's passions have already been controlled? In a sense not. But that is true only of Jnana Yoga, the path of Knowledge. The knowing one says, "One must first be pure if one desires to see God. One must first control one's passions. First self-discipline, then knowledge of God." There is, however, another path leading to God—the path of devotion (Bhakti Yoga). If once man gains love of God, if once the chanting of His holy

'name' begins to thrill the devotee with joy, what effort is needed for the control of passions afterwards? The control comes of itself. Can a man suffering from intense grief be in a mood to enter into a quarrel, or to enjoy a feast, or to give his mind up to the pleasures of the senses? So one absorbed in the love of God cannot think of sense-pleasures.

752. As Srimati (Radha) was nearing Sri Krishna, she was getting more and more the fragrance of his hallowed person. The more one approaches God, the more becomes one's love of Him; the nearer the river approaches the sea, the more is it subject to ebb and flow.

753.* On one occasion the Master said to Keshab and his followers with regard to worship: "Why do you dwell upon the glory and powers of the Lord so much? Does the son, seated in front of the father, think, 'My father has so many houses, so many horses and cows, so many gardens and orchards'? Or, does he think fondly how very, very dear his father has been to him, and how much he has been loving him? Is it strange if a father feeds and clothes his children and makes their life happy? We are all the children of God, and his protecting care has ensured our safety. What is there in it to wonder at? Therefore a real devotee of the Lord, instead of indulging in such thoughts, enters into the most intimate relation with the Lord, makes Him his own, teases Him with importunities, takes pride in Him, and presses Him with the entreaties: 'You must fulfil my prayer and reveal Yourself to me.' If you reflect upon His glorious majesty so much, it won't be possible to think of Him as your own or as one close to you; nor is it possible for you then to press and compel Him. How great He is! how far removed from us!—such thoughts will come to you. Consider Him your own as much as you can, and then you will get Him."

754.* You must make Him your own by firmly adhering to one particular attitude. Then only will He be compelled to yield to your prayers. As for example, when two persons are only superficially acquainted with each other, they observe all rules of formality in their conversation. But with the growth of intimacy all such formal terms of respect completely disappear, and they speak to each other in the most familiar language. Similarly we must have the closest relation with God. An unchaste woman in the beginning of her liaison feels extremely shy, proceeds with great apprehension and keeps her love affair a strict secret. But when her love matures, all such feelings disappear. She then boldly leaves her hearth and home, and appears in public with her lover. If afterwards the lover does not take interest in her and wants to avoid her, she holds him by the neck and asks in a peremptory tone, "I have left my roof for your sake; now let me know whether you will provide for my maintenance or not."

BHAKTI AND WORLDLY LOVE

755.* J—'s mother grew old. She thought it was high time that she should retire from the world and spend the evening of her life peacefully in Brindavan. She expressed her intention to Sri Ramakrishna. But the Master knew her circumstances too well to endorse her proposal, and answered as follows: "You are very fond of your son's daughter. The thought of the child will force itself upon you and make you restless, wherever you go. You may live in Brindavan if you like, but your mind will always hover about your home. On the other hand, all the good of living in Brindavan will come of its own accord to you, if you cultivate the feeling of sweet affection for your grand-daughter, in the thought that she is Sri Radhika herself. Fondle her just as much as you are wont; feed and dress her to your heart's content; but always think within yourself that in those acts you are offering your worship to the goddess of Brindavan."

756.*. Finding a certain devotee inordinately attached to one of his relatives and unable to steady his mind on this acccount, the Master instructed him to look upon the object of his love as an image of God, and serve him in this attitude. In the course of explaining this point, sometimes the Master would thus refer to the similar views of Vaishnavacharan: "Vaishnavacharan would hold, 'If one looks upon the beloved as the Chosen Deity, the mind easily turns Godward.'"

EFFECTS OF BHAKTI

757. A devotee: Is it necessary, Sir, that one should first get one's senses controlled by right discrimination (Vichara)?

The Master: Well, that is one path—the path of right discrimination. In the path of Bhakti, self-control comes of itself—and it comes very easily. The more one's love of God increases, the more insipid will become the pleasures of the senses, just as parents cannot think of physical enjoyment on the day they have lost a child.

758. Devotional practices are necessary only so long as tears of ecstasy do not flow at once on hearing the 'name' of Hari. He needs no devotional practices whose heart is moved to tears at the mere mention of the 'name' of God.

759. A poet has compared devotion (to God) to a tiger. As the tiger devours animals, devotion also swallows up all the 'arch-enemies' of man, such as lust, passion and the rest. Once the devotion to God is fully awakened, all evil passions like lust and anger are completely destroyed. The Gopis of Brindavan attained that state through their strong devotion to Krishna.

760. Devotion is compared again to collyrium. Srimati (Radha) once declared, "Lo, friends, I see my Krishna everywhere!" To that the other Gopis replied, "You have applied the collyrium of Love to your eyes; hence you are seeing like that!"

761. Q. Why does a Bhakta forsake everything for the sake of God?

A. The insect flies from darkness as soon as it sees a light; the ant loses its life in the syrup without leaving it. So the Bhakta clings to God for ever and leaves all else.

762. The Master: Does the moth seek darkness once it has seen a light?

The doctor (smiling): Oh! it does not—it will rather rush into the flame and perish.

The Master: But that is not so with the true worshipper of God. The Divine Light to which he is drawn does not burn and cause death. It is like the lustre of a gem, shining yet soft, cool and soothing. It burns not but illumines the heart with peace and joy.

763. It may be that one does not know the right path and yet has Bhakti for God, the intense desire to know Him. Such a devotee gains Him through the sheer force of that Bhakti. There was a great devotee who started to see Jagannath, but not knowing the way to Puri (where the temple of Jagannath is situated), he went away from the city instead of going towards it. With an anxious heart he asked everybody he met on the way about the road. They all told him, "This is not the way; take that path." And the devotee reached Puri at last, and had his wish fulfilled. Thus even if one is ignorant of the path, one is sure to get somebody to direct one to it, provided one has the will. One may err at first, but in the end one is set on the right road.

764. Devotion effloresces into right discrimination, renunciation, love of all creatures, service of pious men, keeping company with the devoted, singing the praises of the Lord, truthfulness and other virtues.

765. There are signs of God-realisation. Know that there is no more delay for him to realise God, in whom you mark the efflorescence of devotion.

766. The magnetic rock under the sea attracts the ship sailing over it, draws out all its iron nails, separates plank from plank and sinks the vessel in the deep. In the same way when the human soul is attracted by the magnet that

is God, it destroys in a moment man's selfishness and sense of individuality, and plunges the soul into the ocean of God's Infinite love.

STAGES AND ASPECTS OF BHAKTI

767. Love is of three varieties: unselfish (Samartha), mutual (Samanjasa) and ordinary or selfish (Sadharana). Unselfish love is of the highest kind. The lover here seeks only the welfare of the beloved, and does not care whether he suffers pains and hardships thereby. The second kind of love is mutual love in which the lover desires not only the happiness of his beloved, but has an eye to his own happiness also. Selfish love is the lowest. It makes a man only care for his own happiness without having any regard for the weal or woe of the beloved.

768. As there are shades of Sattva, Rajas and Tamas in worldliness, so Bhakti has its corresponding aspects. There is one type of Bhakti that partakes of the humility of Sattva, another that is characterised by the ostentation of Rajas, and a third by the brute force of Tamas.

The Sattvic devotee performs his devotions in secret. He meditates in the night in his bed inside the mosquito-curtain, and therefore rises late in the morning—a fact explained by his friends as due to want of good sleep. The care he bestows on the body ends by providing it with plain food—perhaps a little rice and vegetables. Of luxury he has none, either in food or in dress. There is no show of fittings and furniture in his house, and he never seeks to rise in the world by flattery.

The Rajasic devotee has perhaps distinctive sectarian marks on his body and beads round his neck, with perhaps a few golden ones interspersed. He is particular about outward observances such as wearing silk at the time of worship and celebrating the worship of the Deity with pomp and splendour.

The Tamasic devotee has a fiery faith. He applies force to God like a robber seizing things by force. "What!" he says, "I have uttered His 'name' and yet I am to remain sinful! I am His son! I am duly entitled to the inheritance of His wealth!" Such is his vehement ardour.

769. *Q.* What is the violent form of devotion?

A. It is becoming mad with the constant and terrific uttering of 'Jai Kali' (Glory to the Divine Mother), or dancing like a maniac with arms upraised and shouting praise of Hari (Hari-bol). In this iron age (Kali Yuga) the violent form of devotion is more suitable than other forms; it brings speedier fruition than do milder forms of contemplation. The citadel of God must be taken by storm.

770. These are the stages of Sadhana (devotional practice) for the purification of the soul:

(1) Sadhu-sanga or the company of holy men; (2) Sraddha or faith in, and devotion to things relating to the Spirit; (3) Nishtha or single-minded devotion to one's ideal; (4) Bhakti or intense love of God; (5) Bhava or the state of speechless absorption in the thought of God; and (6) Mahabhava—When Bhava is intensified, it is called Mahabhava. The devotee sometimes laughs

and sometimes weeps like a mad man. He has completely conquered the flesh and has no consciousness of his body. This stage is not generally attained by ordinary souls but by Mahapurushas or Incarnations of God only. (7) Prema or the most intense love of God. It goes hand in hand with Mahabhava. The two marks of this stage are: first, forgetfulness of the world; second, forgetfulness of self, which includes one's own body. This brings the devotee face to face with God, and he thus attains the goal of life.

771. "This much of pious duties has been enjoined by the scriptures, so I am doing it"—this sort of attitude is called Vaidhi-bhakti. There is another kind of devotion known as Raga-bhakti, which comes through extreme love of God—as was the case with Prahlada. When that Raga-bhakti appears, there remains no necessity to do the "enjoined works" (Vaidhi-karma).

772. There is the kind of Bhakti which is called Vaidhi-bhakti (devotion as enjoined by the scriptures). Repeating the 'name' of God a certain number of times, fasting on certain occasions, making pilgrimages to certain shrines, worshipping with certain articles—these and other observances constitute Vaidhi-bhakti. Practice of this for a long time leads one to the higher aspect of devotion known as Raga-bhakti. Love is the one thing needful. Worldly ideas must go away completely; the mind should be set on Him "in all its sixteen annas" (*i.e.*, wholly) and only then you can reach Him. Without Raga-bhakti one cannot attain Him.

773. Love of God is of two kinds: First, the Bhakti which is enjoined by the scriptures. We are to worship in a certain way or repeat the 'name' of the Lord so many times, and so on. All this belongs to what is known as Vaidhi-bhakti, *i.e.*, devotion according to the Law. It may lead to pure devotion and Knowledge of the Absolute in Samadhi. The self is thus merged in the Universal Soul never to come back. This is the case with ordinary devotees. But quite different is the case with Divine Incarnations and those that are the Lord's own. Their love of God is not made up of mere scriptural formulas. It springs from within. It wells up from the soul. Divine Incarnations (like Sri Chaitanya) and those that are nearest to Him, have within their reach the Knowledge of the Absolute attainable in Samadhi, and at the same time may come down from that height, retaining their self and loving the Lord as Father, Mother, and so on. Saying, 'Not this,' 'Not this,' they leave behind them the stairs one after another until they get to the roof. Reaching there, they say, 'It is this.' But soon they find out that the staircase is made up of the same materials as the roof itself—brick lime and brick-dust. So they walk up and down, sometimes resting on the roof and sometimes on the steps of the staircase.

The roof symbolises the Absolute realised in Samadhi, in which the self responding to the sense-world is blotted out. The staircase is the phenomenal world, the world of name and form. When one has attained that roof of Samadhi, one realises the world as a manifestation of the Absolute to the human senses.

PREMA OR PARA-BHAKTI (ECSTATIC LOVE)

774. Prema or ecstatic Love comes not before the realisation of God.

775. In Persian books it is written that within the flesh are the bones, within the bones is the marrow, and so on, and within them all is Prema.

776. Prema is like a string in the hands of the devotee, binding him to that Sachchidananda, *viz.*, God. The devotee holds the Lord, so to speak, under his control. God comes to him whenever he calls.

777. The stage of devotion called Bhava (speechless absorption in God) is like an unripe mango; Prema or ecstatic Love is like the ripe fruit.

778. The worship from fear of hell fire and the like is intended for the beginner. Some people look upon the sense of sin as the whole of religion. They forget that it marks only the earliest and the lowest stage of spirituality. There is yet a higher ideal, a higher stage of spirituality, *viz.*, the love of God as our own Father or Mother.

779. What is Para-bhakti or the supreme ecstatic love of God? In the stage of ecstatic Love the worshipper contemplates God as his dearest and nearest relative. It is like the love of the Gopis to Lord Krishna. They always knew Him and addressed Him as the Lord of the Gopis and not as the Lord of the universe.

780. There is such a thing as loving God without knowing why. If this comes, there is nothing more to desire. One endowed with such Bhakti says, "O Lord, I do not want riches, fame, health, happiness or anything

else. Grant that I may have pure devotion to Thy lotus feet!"

781. The two characteristics of Prema are; (1) forgetfulness of the external world; (2) forgetfulness of one's own body.

782. There are two elements in this Prema-bhakti, *viz.*, 'I-ness' and 'my-ness' (*i.e.*, 'I am the devotee and my God is wholly mine'). Yasoda used to think that except herself none else could look after her Gopala; but for her care, her Gopala would fall ill. Yasoda never liked to perceive her Krishna as the Lord of the universe. And the 'my-ness' of the devotee makes him feel, "He is mine, my own; he is my Gopala!" Uddhava said to Yasoda, "Mother, your Krishna is the Lord Himself. He is the Chintamani (the wish-yielding gem) of the whole universe. He is not an ordinary person." To that Yasoda replied, "No, no, I am not asking about your Chintamani, I am asking how my Gopala is. Not Chintamani, but my Gopala!"

783. Prema or ecstatic Love is attainable only by a few. They are men of extraordinary powers, entrusted with Divine commission. Being heirs of Divine powers and glory, they form a class of their own. To this class belong Incarnations of God like Chaitanya Deva and their devotees of the highest order who are parts of the Lord.

784. There are a few who have this ecstatic Love naturally in them, perhaps even from their boyhood. Yes, like Prahlada they weep and long for God even in their childhood. They belong to the class of Nityasiddhas or men perfect from their very birth.

LOVE OF THE GOPIS

785. It is immaterial whether one believes or not that Radha and Krishna were Incarnations of God. One may believe (like the Hindu or the Christian) in God's Incarnations. Or one may not believe (like the modern Brahmos) in His assuming form, human or otherwise. But let all have a yearning for this Anuraga or intense love for the Lord. This intense Love is the one needful thing.

786. Speaking about the Gopis' love of God, the Master said to M., one of his disciples: "How wonderful was the intensity of their Love! At the very sight of the Tamala tree, they were seized with the madness of Love (Premonmada). (For the dark colour of the Tamala tree reminded them of Sri Krishna). This was also the case with Gauranga. Looking at a forest before him, he thought it was Brindavan. Oh! If one is favoured with but a particle of this ecstatic love! What a devotion! This devotion they had not only brim-full but in overflowing superabundance.

787. The unflinching devotion (Nishtha) of the Gopis is wonderful. When the Gopis went to see Krishna in Mathura, they got admission into the audience chamber after begging the sentinel at the gate several times. But when they saw Krishna there, with a turban on, they bent their heads and began to whisper among themselves, "Who is this turbaned man? We won't talk with him lest we should be culpable of infidelity to our Krishna. Oh, where is our Lord, that supremely Beloved, who wears yellow cloth and a crest of peacock tail!" Ah! mark the single-hearted devotion of the Gopis.

788. The devotion of the Gopis is Prema-bhakti (devotion of ecstatic Love). It is also called absolutely constant devotion (Avyabhicharini-bhakti), or passionate devotion (Nishtha-bhakti). And what is inconstant devotion (Vyabhicharini-bhakti)? It is devotion blended with knowledge; for instance, the knowledge, that Krishna has become all, that He is the supreme Brahman, that He is Rama, Siva and Sakti, that He is the Divine Energy, etc. But you will not find this element of knowledge mixed up with ecstatic Love. When Hanuman went to Dvaraka, he said that he would only see Sita and Rama. So Lord Krishna asked Rukmini to assume the form of Sita; otherwise Hanuman would not be reconciled. When the Pandavas celebrated the great Rajasuya sacrifice, Yudhishthira was seated on the throne and all the kings prostrated before him, but Vibhishana among them said that he would not prostrate to anybody save Narayana. So the Lord Himself began to prostrate before Yudhishthira, whereupon Vibhishana, too, did obeisance to Yudhishthira falling flat and touching his crowned head on the ground.

VIRAHA AND MAHABHAVA

789. Oh! immense is the suffering that arises from Viraha or the feeling of separation from God. It is said that when Rupa and Sanatana[1] sat under a tree in that state, the very leaves of it used to get scorched! I was almost unconscious for three days while in that state!

[1] These were two of the foremost disciples of Lord Chaitanya. They built the famous shrine of Govindaji in Brindavan.

I could not move, and I lay in one spot. When I became a little conscious, Brahmani[1] would take me to bathe; but she could not touch my skin. The whole body was covered with a thick cloth, and she held me by placing her hands over the cloth. The earth with which the body was smeared got burnt! When that state came, I used to feel as if a big spear had been passed through my spine. I would cry out at times that I was dying. But it was always followed by intense beatific feeling.

790. Mahabhava is the supreme God-consciousness; it brings about a terrible commotion both in the body and the mind, as if a mighty elephant enters into a small hut and shakes it furiously, sometimes even breaking it to pieces. There is as much bliss after that state, as there is suffering before it.

III

Bhakti and Jnana

BHAKTI AND JNANA THE SAME IN THE END

791. Pure Knowledge and pure Love are both one and the same.

792. The same Being whom the Vadantins call Brahman, is called Atman by the Yogis and Bhagavan by the Bhaktas. The same Brahmin is called priest when he conducts worship, and cook when he is employed in the kitchen.

[1] The Brahmin lady who initiated Sri Ramakrishna into the Tantrik Sadhanas.

793. What is Jnana (Knowledge) in the highest sense? Says the Jnani, "O Lord, Thou alone dost act in all this universe. I am but the smallest of tools in Thy hands. Nothing is mine. Everything is Thine. Myself, my family, my riches, my virtues—all are Thine."

794. A devotee: How can one know that one has attained Jnana, even while leading a family life?

The Master: By tears and thrill of the hair at the name of Hari. When, at the very mention of the sweet 'name' of the Lord, tears trickle down from a person's eyes and his hairs stand on end, truely he has attained Jnana.

795.* Here is a Puranic story which reconciles Jnana and Bhakti. Once Ramachandra, God incarnate, said to his great devotec Hanuman, "My son, tell Me in what relation you regard Me, and how you meditate upon Me." Hanuman replied: "O Rama, at times I worship Thee as Purna, the undivided one. Then I look upon myself as an Amsa, a part, a fragment as it were, of that Divinity. At other times I meditate upon Thee, O Rama, as my Divine Master and think of myself only as Thy servant. When, however, I am blessed, O Rama, with Tattva Jnana, or true Knowledge, I see, I realise that I am Thou and Thou art I."

796. If the scum on the surface of a tank is pushed aside a little, it spreads out again covering the water; but if it is well kept away with bamboo frames, it cannot come back any more. So if Maya is forced back merely once in a way, it comes again to trouble us; but when the heart is hedged in with Bhakti and Jnana, it is permanently

kept away. Indeed, it is only thus that God becomes manifest to human vision.

HOW BHAKTI LEADS TO JNANA

797. Knowledge of Non-duality is the highest; but God should be worshipped first as a master is worshipped by his servant, as the adored by the adorer. This is the easiest path; it soon leads to the highest knowledge of unity.

798. Though the non-dualistic Knowledge is the highest, you should proceed in your devotion first with the idea of the worshipper and the worshipped (*i.e.*, with the feeling, "God is the object of worship and I am his worshipper"), then you will easily attain Knowledge.

799*. Brahman Itself sheds tears of grief, being caught in the trap of the five elements. You may close your eyes and convince yourself saying again and again, "There is no thorn, there is no thorn." But the moment you touch it, you feel the prick, and you draw your hand away in pain. Likewise, however much you may reason within yourself that you are beyond birth and death, virtue and vice, joy and sorrow, hunger and thirst—that you are the immutable Atman, the Existence-Knowledge-Bliss Absolute—nevertheless, the moment the body is subjected to ailments, or the mind encounters the temptations of the world and is overwhelmed by the transient pleasures of wealth and sex, and in consequence you happen to commit any sin, you become subject to delusion, pain and misery—become deprived of discrimination and good conduct, and get overwhelmed by utter perplexity. Know therefore that none can have Self-realisation and liberation from all miseries unless God Himself shows mercy to him, and Maya unbars the door. Have you not heard it stated in the Chandi, "This same Goddess, the bestower of boons, when propitiated, removes the bondage of human beings." Nothing can be achieved unless the Divine Mother removes the obstacles from the path. The aspirant can never realise God unless Maya takes pity on him, and moves aside from his path. The moment She bestows Her mercy on the aspirant, he becomes blessed with the vision of God and escapes from all miseries. Otherwise, however much you may go on with your discrimination and other spiritual practices, they will be of little use. They say each grain of Ajowan (Ptychotis) helps one to digest a hundred grains of rice. But when the digestive organ goes out of order, even a hundred grains of Ajowan cannot make one assimilate a single grain of rice.

800.* The Jnana Yogi longs to realise Brahman—God the Impersonal, the Absolute and the Unconditioned. But, as a general rule, such a soul would do better, in this present age, to love, pray, and surrender himself entirely to God. The Lord saves His devotee and will vouchsafe to him even Brahma-jnana if the devotee hungers and thirsts after it. Thus the Jnana Yogi will attain Jnana as well as Bhakti. It will be given to him to realise Brahman. The Lord willing, he will also, realise the Personal God of the Bhakta. The Bhakta, on the other hand, will generally be content to see and realise the Personal God, the Saguna Brahman of the Upanishads. Yet the Lord makes him heir to His infinite glory and grants him Bhakti as well as Jnana, and the realisation of God, Personal as well as Impersonal. For if one can manage to reach Calcutta, will he not succeed in finding his way to the Maidan, the Ochterlony Monument, the Museum and other objects of interest, and know which is which?

801. *Q.* Does a devotee ever attain the state of absolute union with God? If so, how?

A. It is possible for human soul to attain the condition of absolute union with God; and it is then only that one can feel and say, "He is the same as myself." An old servant of the house in course of time, may come to be counted as one of the family, and the master of the house, being extremely pleased with his work, may one day seat him in his own seat of honour, saying to all around him that from that day forward there is no difference between him and the servant. The master may say, "He and I are one; obey his commands as you do mine. Whosoever will not do so will be punished." Though the servant may hesitate through modesty to be thus honoured, the master will by force raise him to the seat of honour. Such is the condition of those souls who realise the state of oneness with God by serving Him for a long time. He graciously endows them with all His glory and attributes, and raises them to His own seat of universal sovereignty.

802.* The Bhakta, as a rule, does not long for Brahma-jnana (the realisation of the Impersonal); but remains content with realising the Divine Person alone—my Divine Mother, or any of Her infinite forms of glory, such as the Divine Incarnations like Sri Krishna and Chaitanya Deva, the visible revelations of God. He is anxious that the whole of his ego shall not be effaced in Samadhi. He would fain have sufficient individuality left to enjoy the vision Divine as a Person. He would fain taste sugar, instead of becoming sugar!

803.* My Divine Mother (the personal phase of Brahman) has declared that She is the Brahman of the Vedanta. It is within Her power to give Brahma-jnana, which she does by causing the effacement of the lower self. Thus, in the first place, you may, my Mother willing, come to Brahman through right discrimination (Vichara). Again you may come through Bhakti. The essence of Bhakti consists in unceasing prayer for light and love and self-surrender to Her. First, come to my Divine Mother (the Personal God) through these. Take my word for it that, if your prayer is really heartfelt, my Mother will respond to it, if you will only wait. Pray to Her again if you want to realise Her Impersonal Self. Should she deign to grant your prayer—for She is omnipotent—you will be in a position to realise Her Impersonal Self in Samadhi. This is precisely the same thing as Brahma-jnana.

DIFFERENCE IN THE TEMPERAMENTS OF THE JNANI AND THE BHAKTA

804. One meets with to classes of spiritual aspirants. One of them resembles the young of a monkey and the other may be likened to a kitten. The young one of the monkey strongly clasps its mother, while the young one

of the cat cannot do so, but mews piteously, staying wherever it is placed by her. If the young monkey lets go the hold on its mother, it falls down and gets hurt. This is because it has to depend upon its own strength. But the kitten runs no such risk, for the mother herself carries it about from place to place. Similarly, the aspirant who follows the path of Knowledge or selfless work depends upon his own effort to attain salvation. On the other hand, the aspirant who follows the path of Love knows that the Lord is the disposer of everything; so with perfect confidence he resigns himself entirely to His mercy. The former is like the young of a monkey and the latter like the kitten.

805. The Jnani says, "I am He, I am that pure Atman;" but the Bhakta declares, "Ah, all these are His glory!"

806. God is attained only when man gets established in one or other of these three attitudes: (1) All this am I; (2) All this art Thou; (3) Thou art the Master and I am the servant.

807. When one is born of the spirit of Siva, he becomes a Jnani. His constant tendency is towards the consciousness that Brahman alone is true and this world is false. But when one is born of the spirit of Vishnu, in him faith and devotion never fail. Even if, for a time, these virtues shrink by the strong influx of reason or dialectic knowledge, in the fulness of time they increase copiously like the Musala (a pestle) that brought ruin to the Yadava dynasty.

808. The Ganges of Knowledge, flowing in the heart of a Jnani, runs only in one direction. To him the whole

universe is a dream. He always lives in his own Self. But the Ganges of Love in a devotee's heart does not always run in the same direction; it has its ebb and flow. The devotee laughs, weeps, dances and sings. He loves to live in and enjoy God's presence; in that ocean of bliss he loves to cast himself, sometimes swimming, sometimes sinking, and again floating, as a block of ice dances in water, tossing up and down.

809. According to the Puranas, the devotee is separate from God. Man is one entity and He is another. This body is like a vessel; the mind, the intellect and the ego are, as it were, the water in it; and Brahman is like the sun. He is being reflected in that water. So the devotees witness the various Divine manifestations. But according to the Vedanta, Brahman alone is the reality, the substance; and every thing else is Maya, unreal like dreams. There is this stick of 'I' lying on the surface of the sea of Brahman. If you take away the stick, there is one undivided sheet of water; but when the stick is there, it divides the water into two parts, one on each side. One falls into Samadhi and then the knowledge of Brahman dawns. Then the ego is blotted out. According to the Vedanta the awakened state also is not real.

810. Narada and other teachers took to Bhakti for the good of the world, even after gaining Knowledge.

811. The Master: Bhakti is the moon, while Jnana is the sun. I have heard that there are oceans in the extreme north and south, and that it is so cold there that the water in them freeze in part, forming masses of ice in which ships are caught and held fast.

A devotee: Are men likewise caught half-way in the path of Bhakti?

The Master: Yes, they are, indeed. But it matters nothing; for the ice in which one is held is the solidified water of the ocean of Existence-Knowledge-Bliss. If you reason, "Brahman alone is real, the universe is false," the ice will thaw in the sun of Jnana, and what will remain? Only the formless water of that ocean of Existence-Knowledge-Bliss.

812. Jnana is like a man and Bhakti is like a woman. Knowledge has entry only up to the drawingroom of God, but Love can enter His inner apartments.

813. A Jnani and a Bhakta were once passing through a forest. On the way they saw a tiger. The Jnani said: "There is no reason why we should flee; the Almighty God will certainly protect us." The Bhakta said: "No, brother, no, let us run away. Why should we trouble the Lord when we can accomplish a thing by our own exertion?"

IV

Path of Work

WHAT IS KARMA YOGA?

814.* Karma Yoga is communion with God by means of Work. Ashtanga Yoga or Raja Yoga is Karma Yoga, if practised without attachment. It leads to communion through meditation and concentration. The performance of the duties of householders (*i.e.*, self-regarding or altruistic work, social and political)—doing them without attachment, to the end that God may be glorified—is Karma Yoga. Again, worship according to the scriptures, silent repetition of the 'name' of God and other pious duties of this kind, is Karma Yoga if done without attachment, for the glorification of God. The end of Karma Yoga is the same (as of other Yogas), namely, the realisation of God, impersonal or personal or both.

815.* In the case of a person endowed with the quality of Sattva (purity of being), action naturally falls off. Even if he tries, he cannot engage himself in action. God would not allow him to act. For example, the daughter-in-law who is with child is gradually relieved of her household work, and when the child is actually born, she is given nothing to do and is left exclusively to attend to the child. Those who are not endowed with the quality of Sattva have to attend to all worldly duties. With complete dedication to the Lord, they should behave like the servants in the house of a rich man. This is what is called Karma Yoga. Its secret consists in repeating the 'name' of the Lord and meditating on Him as much as one can, and at the same time attending to one's duties in the spirit of dedication described before.

816. Whatever you offer to God would return to you a thousandfold. So at the end of all Karma (sacrifice), one has to pour a handful of water, dedicating the fruit of the Karma to Krishna.

817. When Yudhishthira was about to offer even his sins to Krishna, Bhima warned him saying, "No, no, you should not do so; whatever you would offer to Krishna will come back to you a thousandfold."

DEVOTION AS A SAFEGUARD IN THE PATH OF WORK

818.* Work without attachment, however, is exceedingly difficult, especially in this age. Hence communion by prayer, devotion and Love has been enjoined as better adapted to this age than communion by Work or Knowledge and philosophy. No one, however, can avoid work. Every mental operation is work. The consciousness, 'I feel', or 'I think', involves work. What is meant by the path of devotion in its relation to Work is that work is simplified by devotion to, or love of, God. In the first place, this love of God reduces the quantity of one's work by fixing one's mind upon one's own ideal, that is, God. Secondly it helps one to work unattached. One cannot love God and at the same time love riches, pleasure, fame, or power. He who has once tasted the drink prepared with the Ola sugar candy does not care for that made with molasses.

819.* In this age Work without devotion to God has no legs to stand upon. It is like a foundation of sand. First cultivate devotion. All the other things—schools, dispensaries, etc.—will, if you like, be added to you. First devotion, then work. Work, apart from devotion or love of God, is helpless and cannot stand.

820. For this Kali Yuga, Naradiya-Bhakti, or communion with God by love, devotion and self-surrender as practised and preached by the Rishi Narada, is enjoined. There is hardly time for Karma Yoga, *i.e.*, for doing the various ritualistic duties laid on man by the scriptures. Don't you see that the well-known decoction of the ten medicinal roots known as Dashamulapachana, is not the

remedy for fevers of the present day? The patient runs the risk of being carried off before the medicine has had time to take effect. 'Fever mixture' is therefore the order of the day.

821.* A disciple: The pressure of work stands in the way of giving one's mind to God, does it not?

The Master: O yes, no doubt, that is so; but a Jnani may work unattached, and then work will not harm him. If you sincerely desire, the Lord will help you, so that the bondage of work will gradually fall away.

822.* Sri Ramakrishna once said addressing Iswar Chandra Vidyasagar, the great philanthropist of India: "Your nature is made of the Sattva *i.e.*, the pure element which leads to illumination or true Knowledge. Only your Sattva is in that phase which makes you active and devoted to the doing of good works. Charity, compassion, kindness towards others, etc., are good if practised without attachment. If they are so practised, and are accompanied with Bhakti (devotion to the Supreme), they will lead to God.

823.* Should you think of God only at the time of meditation and remain forgetful of Him at all other times? Have you not noticed how during Durga Puja a lamp is kept constantly burning near the image? It should never be allowed to go out. If ever it is extinguished, the householder meets with some mishap. Similarly, after installing the Deity on the lotus of your heart, you must keep the lamp of remembering Him ever burning. While engaged in the affairs of the world, you should constantly turn your gaze inwards and see whether the lamp is burning or not.

WORK AS SERVICE EQUAL TO WORSHIP

824.* Sri Ramakrishna was one day expounding the gist of Sri Gauranga's cult in the following words: "This faith insists that man should at all times try to cultivate three things—delight in the 'name' of the Lord, loving sympathy for all living beings, and service to devotees. God and His 'name' are identical. Knowing this, one should take the 'name' of the Lord with great Love and fervour. The devotees of God should be respected and adored in the conviction that there is no difference between the Lord and his worshippers, between Krishna and the Vaishnava. With the knowledge that the whole universe is the household of the Lord, one should show pity to all creatures. . ." Uttering the last words 'pity to all creatures' in a rather abrupt fashion, the Master went into Samadhi. Sometime after—returning to a semi-conscious state—the Master exclaimed, "Pity to creatures! Pity to creatures! Sirrah! you who are lower than even a worm, how dare you speak of showing pity to creatures! Who are you to show pity to them? No, no, it is not pity to creatures, but service to them in the consciousness that they are verily God Himself."

WORK, A MEANS AND NOT AN END

825.* Addressing a group of enthusiastic social reformers, the Master said: "You talk glibly of doing good to the world. The world to which you desire to do good—is it so small a thing? In the next place, pray, who are you to do good to the world? First, go through devotional practices and see God. Then it is that inspiration and power will come to you, and you may talk of doing good. Not till then."

A devotee: Sir, do you mean to say that we are to give up all work until we have seen God?

The Master: No, my dear sir. Why should you give up all work? Meditation, chanting of hymns, repetition of His holy 'names', and other devotional exercises—these you must go through.

The devotee: I mean work connected with the world. Should we give up all worldly affairs?

The Master: You may attend to them too, just as much as you cannot do without, in order to live in this world. But you should, at the same time, pray to the Lord with tears in your eyes for His grace, and for strength to do your duties without the expectation of any reward or fear of punishment in this world or the next.

826.* You cannot get rid of work, because Nature will lead you on to it. That being so, let all work be done as it ought to be. If work is done unattached, it will lead to God. To work without any attachment is to work without the expectation of any reward or fear of any punishment in this world or the next. Work so done is a means to the end, and God is the end.

827.* Work is a means, if done unattached; but the end of life is to see God. Let me repeat that the means should not be confounded with the end—that the first stage on a road should not be taken for the goal. No, do not regard work as the be-all and the end-all, the ideal of human existence. Pray for devotion to God. Suppose you are fortunate enough to see God. Then what would you pray for? Would you pray for dispensaries and hospitals, tanks and wells, roads and alms-houses? No, these are realities to us so long as we do not see God. But once brought face to face with the Divine vision, we see them as they are—transitory things no better than dreams. And then we would pray for more light—more knowledge in the highest sense, more Divine love—the love which lifts us up from man to God, the love which makes us realise that we are really sons of the Supreme Being of Whom all that can be said is that He exists, that He is Knowledge itself in the highest sense, and that He is the eternal fountain of love and bliss.

828.* Referring to a devotee of his, the Master once said: "Sambhu Mallick once talked of founding hospitals and dispensaries, schools and colleges—of laying roads, sinking wells and digging tanks for the good of all. I said to him: 'Yes, but you must be unattached while doing good to others, and you must be careful to take up only such works as come in your way—such works, again, as appear to be of pressing need. Do not seek them—do not seek more work than you can well manage. If you do, you will lose sight of the Lord."

WORK AND WORKLESSNESS

829. When the pure Sattva arises in a man, he only meditates on God, and does not find pleasure in any other work. Some are born with this pure Sattva on account of their past actions. But one can develop this pure quality if one continues to perform unselfish work in a

spirit of devotion and dedication to God. If there be Sattva with an admixture of Rajas, the mind slowly gets distracted in several directions and brings in its wake the egoistic feeling, "I shall do good to the world." It is highly hazardous for ordinary Jivas to attempt to do good to the world. But it is good if a man works without motive for the benefit of others; there is no danger in it. This kind of work is called Nishkama Karma. It is quite desirable to do such works. But all cannot do it! Very difficult!

830. All have to do work; only a few can renounce it. That kind of pure Sattva is found only in a very few persons. If a person continues to perform his work with devotion and non-attachment, Sattva becomes purged of its Rajas element. And by virtue of this attainment of pure Sattva, he realises God. Ordinary persons cannot understand this state of pure Sattva.

831. Renunciation of work comes of itself when intense love of God swells up in the heart. Let them work who are made to do so by God. When the time is ripe, one must renounce every thing and say, "Come, O my mind, let us watch together the Divinity installed in the heart."

832. Sandhya loses herself in Gayatri; Gayatri loses herself in Pranava; Pranava in the end loses itself in Samadhi. So every Karma (Sandhya and the like) ultimately loses itself in Samadhi.[1]

[1] The idea is this: Sandhya consists of the rituals and prayers performed by high-caste Hindus at sun-rise and sun-set. The most important part of it is the meditation on Gayatri (Rig Veda, III. 62. 10), the greatest Mantra of the Vedas. Pranava or Om, the mystic sound symbol of God, is prefixed to this magnificent Mantra. True meditation on 'Om' leads to

833.* As long as the mind is not absorbed in Sachchidananda, man has to do both—call upon the Lord and attend to work in the world. But when the mind is absorbed in Him, there is no more need of any work. For example, let us take the illustration of the Kirtan. A man sings: "Nitai amar mata hati (My Nityananda is an elephant in rut)." When this is sung first, the singer pays attention to all details—the tune, time, melody, etc. But when his mind is a little absorbed in the song, he says simply "Mata hati, mata hati." At a further stage of absorption he says only, "Hati, hati." At a still further stage, he says simply "Ha, ha," and no further.

834.* So I say, in the beginning there is much fuss of Karma. But the more you will proceed towards God, the less will it grow. Finally comes the complete renunciation of work and the attainment of Samadhi. Generally the body does not remain long after the attainment of Samadhi. But in the case of some it remains for the work of teaching the world. Sages like Narada and Divine Incarnations like Sri Chitanya are examples of this. After a well is dug some throw away all the spades and baskets, but others preserve them with the idea that they may be of some use to any of their neighbours. Such great souls are moved with pity at the sight of the sufferings of the world. They are not so selfish as to care only for the attainment of Jnana for themselves.

Samadhi and realisation of God. Thus Karmas, or pious duties of the type of Sandhya, have their ultimate end in God-realisation.

CHAPTER XVII

THE DIVINE

[Brahman (The Impersonal or Supra-personal Absolute)—Brahman and the reality of relative experiences—Personal Deity, known also as Isvara, Maya and Sakti—God in everything—The Divine both with and without form—Some Divine forms—Divine immanence—The Divine and man's moral responsibility]

BRAHMAN (THE IMPERSONAL OR SUPRA-PERSONAL ABSOLUTE)

835. What is the conception of Brahman? It cannot be explained in words. If a man is called upon to give an idea of the ocean to one who has never seen it, he can only say, "It is a vast sheet of water, a big expanse of water; it is water, water all around."

836. The Vedas, the Tantras, the Puranas and all the sacred scriptures of the world have become Uchchhishta as it were (*i.e.*, defiled like the food thrown out of the mouth), because they have come out of, and have so often been repeated by, human mouths. But Brahman or the Absolute has never been so defiled, for no one has yet been able to express It by speech.

837. What is the nature of Brahman? It is without attributes, without motion, immovable, unshakable, firm as the mount Meru.

838. Brahman is unattached to good or evil. It is like the flame of a lamp. You may read the Bhagavata (a holy scripture), or forge a document—you can do both with the help of the same light. Again, Brahman is like a serpent. What does it matter if it has poison in its fangs? It is none the worse for it; the poison does not cause its death. It is poison only to other creatures whom it may happen to bite. Much in the same way, misery, sin and whatever other evil we find in this world, are just so only in relation to us. Brahman is above and beyond all these. Good and evil in creation are not so to Brahman. He is not to be judged by any human standard of good and evil.

839. Brahman is above and beyond both knowledge and ignorance, good and evil, Dharma and Adharma. It is indeed beyond all dual throngs.

840.* Brahman is beyond mind and speech, beyond concentration and meditation (Dharana and Dhyana), beyond the knower, the known and knowledge, beyond even the conception of the real and the unreal. In short, It is beyond all relativity.

841. The Absolute is like the air which carries odours, be they good or bad, but remains ever untainted by them.

842. The Absolute is beyond all attributes—beyond whatever is connected with Maya.

BRAHMAN AND THE REALITY OF RELATIVE EXPERIENCE

843. God alone is true; His manifestations as living beings and the world (Jiva and Jagat) are untrue, *i.e.*, non-eternal.

844. It is an easy thing to say that the world is an illusion, but do you know what that really means? It is like the burning of camphor, which leaves no risidue. It is not even like the burning of wood, which leaves ashes behind. Only when discrimination ends, and the highest Samadhi is attained, there is absolutely no recognition of 'I', 'thou' and the universe.

845. In the course of his instructions to his disciple, the Guru raised two fingers, by which he meant the duality of Brahman and Maya. Then, lowering one finger, he taught him that, when Maya vanishes, nothing of the universe remains. Only the Absolute Brahman is.

846. Brahman, the absolute and the unconditioned, is realised in Samadhi alone. Then it is all silence—all talk of reality and unreality, of Jiva and Jagat, of knowledge and ignorance, is hushed. There remains, then, only 'Is-ness' (Being), and nothing else. For verily the salt doll tells no tale when it has become one with the infinite sea. This is Brahma-jnana.

847. Q. How has the delusion arisen of the undifferentiated Atman having differentiated into the individual soul?

A. The dialectical Advaitin, as long as he relies on the unaided powers of his reason, answers this question by saying, "I do not know." The answer which realisation gives alone is conclusive. As long as you say, "I know" or "I do not know", you look upon yourself as a person. And as such, you must take these differentiations as facts, not as delusion. When all personality is effaced, one realises the knowledge of the Absolute in Samadhi.

Then alone are set at rest for ever all such questions of delusion and no delusion, fact and fiction.

848. As long as you are a person, your Absolute must imply a 'relative', your Nitya (the Changeless), must imply a Lila (change), your Substance must imply qualities, your Impersonal must imply a 'personal being', your One must imply 'many'.

849. As long as you are in the plane of relativity, you must admit both 'butter' and 'buttermilk',—you must admit both Personal God and the universe. To explain the analogy, the original milk is Brahman realised in Samadhi, the 'butter' the Impersonal-personal God, and the 'buttermilk' the universe made up of the twenty-four categories.

850. Let not the Advaitin say, "My position is the only correct, rational and tenable one; those that believe in a Personal God are wrong." The personal manifestations of God are by no means less real, but infinitely more so, than the body, the mind or the external world.

851. No sooner do you talk of Advaita (monism) than you postulate the Dvaita (pluralism). Talking of the the Absolute, you take for granted the 'relative'. For your absolute, until realised in Samadhi, is at best the correlative of the 'relative', if not indeed a mere empty word. You cannot possibly put It as It is; for in doing so you cannot but enamel It with a foreign element, that is, with your own personality.

852. So long as there is the 'I' in me, there is the Personal God also before me, revealing Himself through various forms of glory, and as the world and living beings.

PERSONAL DEITY KNOWN ALSO AS ISVARA, MAYA AND SAKTI

853. When the Supreme Being is thought of as actionless—neither creating, sustaining nor destroying—I call Him by the name of Brahman or Purusha. But when I think of Him as active—creating, sustaining and destroying—I call him by the name of Sakti or Maya or Prakriti.

854.* While speaking of the Sankhya theory that the world has come out of Purusha and Prakriti, the Master said one day: "The Sankhya philosophy says that the Purusha is actionless and Prakriti is doing all works. The Purusha is only a witness of all these activities. Prakriti too cannot do any work of itself without the Purusha. Have you seen how things take place in a house during a marriage? The Master of the house sits in one place, puffing away at his Hookah and giving commands. But the mistress of the house always moves about here and there in the house, dressed in a cloth marked with turmeric. She is busy supervising the arrangements and cordially receiving women and children. Now and then she goes to the master of the house, and reports about all happenings and seeks advice with the help of gestures and movement of lips. Understanding all that she wants to convey, the master only nods his head or expresses his assent. The case of Prakriti and Purusha is just like this.

855. The actionless Brahman and the active Sakti are in fact one and the same. He who is the Absolute Existence-Intelligence-Bliss, is also the All-knowing, the All-intelligent and All-blissful Mother of the universe. A

precious stone and its luminosity are one and the same, for you cannot imagine a stone without it, and *vice versa*.

856. God the absolute and God the personal are one and the same. A belief in the one implies a belief in the other. Fire cannot be thought of apart from its burning power; nor can its burning power be thought of apart from it. Again the sun's rays cannot be thought of apart from the sun, nor the sun, apart from its rays. You cannot think of the whiteness of milk, apart from milk nor milk apart from its milky whiteness. Thus God the absolute cannot be thought of apart from the idea of God with attributes, *i.e.*, Personal God, and *vice versa*.

857. The distinction between Brahman and Sakti is really a distinction without a difference. Brahman and Sakti are one (Abheda), just as fire and its burning power are one. Brahman and Sakti are one, just as milk and the whiteness of milk are one. Brahman and Sakti are one, just as a gem and its brightness are one. You cannot conceive of one without the other, or make a difference between them.

858. Wherever there is action—creation, preservation and destruction—there is Sakti. Water is water whether it is calm or disturbed. That one Absolute Existence-Intelligence-Bliss is the eternal intelligent Energy that creates, preserves and destroys the universe, just as 'Captain'[1] is the same whether he remains inactive at times or whether he engages himself at other times in performing worship or visiting the Governor-General. He

[1] Visvanath Upadhyaya, the Agent of the Nepal Government in Calcutta. Sri Ramakrishna used to call him 'Captain'.

is the same 'Captain', only these are his different Upadhis or states.

859. As sometimes I am in dress and at other times naked, so Brahman is sometimes with attributes, and at other times without. The Saguna Brahman (God with attributes) is Brahman in combination with Energy (Sakti); He is then called Isvara or Personal God.

860. Be it known that my Divine Mother is both one and many, and also beyond one and many.

861. My Divine Mother is the one Being manifested as many. Of infinite power Herself, She has differentiated Herself into Jiva and Jagat (living beings and the universe) of manifold powers,—physical, intellectual, moral and spiritual. And my Divine Mother is no other than the Brahman of the Vedanta. She is the Personal aspect of the Impersonal Brahman.

GOD IN EVERYTHING

862. Right discrimination is of two kinds—analytical and synthetical. The first leads one from the phenomena to the Absolute Brahman, while by the second one knows how the Absolute Brahman appears as the universe.

863. Even those that have realise the Absolute in Samadhi come down to the lower plane of sense-consciousness, and have just sufficient ego left to hold communion with the Personal God. It is very difficult to raise the voice incessantly to 'Ni' (Si), the highest note of the gamut. Hence the necessity of devotion to Personal God.

864. To him alone who comes down from Samadhi to the plane of sense-consciousness is left a thin ego like a line (Rekha)—a length without breadth—just sufficient individuality to retain only the spiritual vision (Divya-chakshus). This enables him to see Jiva and Jagat, including his own self, as the One manifesting Himself in different forms. This vision of glory comes to the Vijnani who has realised the Nirakara Nirguna Brahman (formless and attributeless Godhead) in Jada or Nirvikalpa Samadhi (ecstasy without objective content), and also the Sakara Saguna Brahman (Godhead with form and attributes) in Chetana or Savikalpa Samadhi, (ecstasy with objective content). You cannot conceive, think of, perceive, God otherwise than as a person, so long as you are a person with an ego of your own; the Unconditioned cannot but manifest Itself to you—both within and without—as a conditioned being, as Personal God. These personal manifestations of the Deity are by no means less real than the body, the mind, and the external world; rather are they infinitely more real than these.

865. It is a case of involution and evolution. You go backward to the Supreme Being and your personality becomes lost in that of His—this is Samadhi. Then, with this higher personality, you retrace your steps and come back to the point whence you started, only to see that the universe and your ego, are evolved from the same Supreme Being, and that God, man and Nature are identities, so that if you hold on to one of them you realise the others.

866. Whose is this Lila (this universe of change, the manifestations of which can be called a play of

God), His is that Nitya (the absolute state). And again, He who is in that Nitya state, His is this Lila. It is through the Lila that you must feel your way up to the Nitya. It is again from the Nitya that you must feel your way back to the Lila—now no longer unreal but the manifestation of the Nitya on the sense plane.

867. As the shell, the pith and the kernel of a fruit are all produced from one parent seed of the tree, so from the one Lord is produced the whole of creation, animate and inanimate, spiritual and material.

868. The Master used to say: "I accept everything: the superconscious state, waking state, dream, deep sleep, Brahman, Jiva, the creation—I do accept all these (different states or manifestations of the Being). Otherwise the full weight will suffer diminution; so I accept both the Absolute and the manifestation."

869.* If God alone exists, how has this world come to be, with its diversities and inequalities caused by individual egos? Referring to this mystery the Master said: "It is His play, His Lila! A king has four sons. They are all princes, but when they play, one becomes the minister, another policeman, and so on. A prince, yet playing as a policeman!"

THE DIVINE BOTH WITH AND WITHOUT FORM

870.* A certain person asked the Master: "Sir, which aspect of God is higher? That with form or without form?" The Master replied: "Formless aspect is of two kinds—mature and immature. The mature one is very high indeed. It has to be reached through God with form. The immature one, as professed by the Brahmos, is like darkness perceived merely by closing the eyes."

871. God is formless, and God is possessed of form too. And He is also that which transcends both form and formlessness. He alone knows what all He is.

872.* Do you know what the form aspect of God is like? It is like the rising of bubbles on a sheet of water. It can be actually seen that the different forms are rising from the Chidakasa (sky of Pure Consciousness). The Divine Incarnation is one of the forms.

873. Unless one sees God one is not able to realise all this. For the sake of those that love the Lord, He manifests Himself in various ways and in various forms.

A dyer had his own way of dying clothes. He would ask the customer, "In what colour do you want your cloths to be dyed?" If he said red, the dyer dipped the cloth in his tub and brought it out saying, "Here is your cloth dyed red." Another wanted his cloth dyed yellow. The dyer dipped it in the same tub, and when he brought it up, it was dyed yellow. In the same way, when some other colour was wanted—blue or orange or violet or green—the same tub was used with the like result.

A customer who was watching all this came up to the dyer and said, "My friend, I am not fond of any one colour. I desire to consult your taste and should like to have my cloth dyed just as you please. I want the colour in which you have dyed yourself." The Lord manifests Himself, with form or without form, just according to the need of the devotee. Manifested vision is relatively true, that is, true in relation to different men placed in different conditions and environments. The Divine Dyer alone knows in what colour He has dyed Himself. Verily He is not bound by any limitation as to the forms of manifestation, or their negation.

874. A certain monk went to the temple of Jagannath at Puri. He had doubts as to whether God is with form or without form. When he saw the holy image, he desired to examine it and settle his doubt. He passed his staff from the left to the right in order to feel if it touched the image. For a time he could not see anything or feel anything with the staff. So he decided that God was without form. When he was about to pass the staff from the right to the left, it touched the image. So the monk decided that God is both with form and without form.

875. When a bell is rung, the repeated ding-dongs may be distinguished, one from the other, as if each sound has a form; but when we stop ringing, the indistinguishable sound, which is audible for a while and gradually dies away, appears formless. Like the sounds of the bell, God is both with and without form.

876. God with form is visible. Yes, we can touch Him and talk to Him face to face as with our own dearest friend.

877. To think of Him as formless is quite right. But take care that you do not run away with the idea that that view alone is true and that all else is false. Meditating upon Him as a being with forms is equally right. But you

must hold on to your particular view until you realise God; and then everything would be clear.

878. God is the absolute and eternal Brahman as well as the Father of the universe. But the indivisible Brahman, who is pure Existence, Intelligence and Bliss, is incomprehensible like a vast shoreless ocean without bounds and limits, in which we only struggle and sink. But when we enter into the spirit of the sportive Personal God, we easily obtain peace like the sinking man on being gently carried ashore.

879. At a certain stage in the path of devotion, the devotee finds satisfaction in God with form, and at another stage, in God without it.

880. To a Bhakta the Lord manifests Himself in various forms. But to a person who reaches the height of Brahmajnana in Samadhi, He is the attributeless Brahman once more, formless and unconditioned. Herein is the reconciliation between Jnana and Bhakti.

881. As water, when congealed, becomes ice, the visible form of the Almighty is the materialised manifestation of the all-pervading formless Brahman. It may be called in fact Sachchidananda solidified. As the ice, which is part and parcel of water, remains in water and afterwards melts into it, so the Personal God, Who is part and parcel of the Impersonal, rises from the Impersonal, remains there, and ultimately merges into It and disappears.

882. Fire itself has no definite shape, but as glowing embers it assumes different forms. Thus the formless fire is seen endowed with forms. Similarly, the formless God sometimes invests Himself with definite forms.

SOME DIVINE FORMS

883. God appears in various ways—sometimes in human form, sometimes as a spiritual expression (Chinmaya-rupa). But one should have belief in Divine forms.

884.* No one can say what Sachchidananda is like. That is why He first took the form of Ardhanarisvara (half man and half woman). Do you know why He has done so? It is to show that both Prakriti and Purusha are Himself. At a step still lower, Sachchidananda became several Purushas and Prakritis.

885. Sea-water appears dark-blue from a distance, but when you take a little of it in your hand, it is all pure and limpid. So Lord Krishna appears azure from a distance, but He is not really so. He is the Absolute, taintless and colourless.

886. Sri Krishna is called Tribhanga, *i.e.*, bent in three different directions. It is only a soft thing that is capable of being twisted. So this form of Sri Krishna implies that He must have been softened in some way or other. The softening in this case is accounted for by Prema, ecstatic Love.

887. A devotee: Why is the Divine Mother called Yogamaya?

The Master: Yogamaya means the union of Purusha and Prakriti. Whatever you see is nothing but that union of the two. Haven't you seen the Siva-Kali image—Kali standing on Siva? Siva is lying prostrate like a corpse and Kali is standing with a fixed gaze upon Siva. All this means the same Purusha-Prakriti union. Purusha is inactive, hence Siva is lying down inert like a corpse. But by virtue of the union with Him, Prakriti is doing everything—creation, preservation and destruction. The same is the significance of the coupled image of Radha and Krishna.

888.* The more you advance towards God, the more you will find his attributive grandeur falling off. The first vision an aspirant gets is of the ten-handed form (Durga) —the form of the Supreme Mistress of the universe. In that form there is a great expression of power and grandeur. Next She appears in a twohanded form; no more are there the ten arms with all their respective weapons. Next comes the vision of the Gopala form. Here there is absolutely no expression of power and grandeur—it is simply the form of a tender child. There is a vision even superior to this—the vision of the effulgent Light.

DIVINE IMMANENCE

889. God is in all men, but all men are not in God: that is why they suffer.

890. Every object is Narayana (*i.e.*, God). Man is Narayana, the animal is Narayana, the sage is Narayana, the knave also is Narayana. All that exists is Narayana. The Deity (Narayana) sports in various aspects. All things are His diverse forms and the manifestations of His glory.

891. Says God, "I am the snake that bites and the charmer that heals; I am the judge that condemns and the servant that inflicts the punishment."

892. The manifestation of Sakti (the Divine power) varies in varying centres of activity; for variety is the

law, not sameness. God is immanent in all creatures; He is even in the ant. The difference is in manifestation only.

893. Divine power is greater in those who are honoured, respected and obeyed by a large following than in those who have no such influence.

894. *Q.* How does the Lord dwell in a physical body?

A. He dwells in the body, as a piston-rod in a syringe; He is in the body, and yet apart from it.

THE DIVINE AND MAN'S MORAL RESPONSIBILITY

895. *Q.* If God has become all, is there no sin and virtue?

A. Yes, there is, and at the same time there is not. As long as He preserves the ego in us, He retains in us also the apprehension of duality, and the consciousness of sin and virtue. But at times, in some, He completely wipes away the ego; then they go beyond all good and bad. So long as one does not Realise God, the perception of duality, and the idea of good and bad, are sure to exist. You may say in words that good and bad have all become equal to you, that you do just what He makes you do. But in your heart of hearts you know that all these are mere words. The moment you do some evil actions, your conscience will begin to prick you.

896.* *Q.* If it is He who is actuating me to all actions, then I am not responsible for my sins. Am I?

A. Duryodhana also said like that. He said "O Lord, Thou abidest in my heart, and I do as Thou makest me do." But he who really believes that God alone is the doer and that he himself is only an instrument, cannot commit any sin. A perfect dancer never takes a wrong step. Indeed, till the heart becomes pure one cannot even believe in the existence of God.

897. A devotee: Sir, I have a doubt. They say that our will is free; that is, we can do whatever we like—good, bad or otherwise. Is it true?

The Master: Everything depends upon the Lord's will! This is all His play. He is making us do various things in various ways, good and bad, great and small, weak and strong—all these are ultimately from Him. Good men, bad men—all these are His Maya, His play. For instance, all the trees of a garden are not equal in height, beauty or grandeur.

So long as one does not realise God, one thinks that his will is free. But it is He who maintains this delusion in man. Otherwise there would have been a mighty increase of sins; people would not have feared to do evil, nor would there have been any punishment for crime or sin.

But do you know the attitude of him who has realised God? He says and feels: "I am the machine, Thou art the mechanic; I am the house, Thou art the dweller; I am the chariot, Thou art the charioteer; I move as Thou makest me move; I speak what Thou makest me speak!"

898. God impels the thief to go and steal, and at the same time warns the householder against the thief. He does everything.

CHAPTER XVIII

REALISATION OF THE DIVINE

[Psychology of man with reference to God-realisation—Kundalini and spiritual awakening—Spurious ecstasy—Perception of Divine forms and sounds—Samadhi and Brahma-jnana—The Psychology of Samadhi—Vijnana which comes after Samadhi]

PSYCHOLOGY OF MAN WITH REFERENCE TO GOD-REALISATION

899. This body which is made of the 'five elements' is called the gross body. The subtle body consists of Manas, Buddhi, Chitta and Ahamkara. The body by which one realises the bliss of God-vision and continues to enjoy His union, is the causal body. In the Tantras it is called Bhagavati-tanu. Beyond all is the Mahakarana—the First Cause.

900. When the mind is attached to the consciousness of the external world, it sees gross objects and abides in the Annamaya-kosa, the physical sheath of the soul, which depends on food. When the mind turns itself inward, it is like shutting the door of a house and entering its inner apartments; that is to say, it goes from the gross into the subtle, thence into the causal, till it reaches the final causal state. In that state the

mind is merged in the Absolute and nothing can be said of it.

901. Lord Chaitanya used to have three sorts of 'states': (1) the conscious state in which the mind dwelt on the gross and the subtle bodies. (2) The semi-conscious state in which the mind soared to the causal body and felt the 'causal bliss' and (3) the state of in-turned consciousness (superconscious state) in which the mind used to merge completely in the Mahakarana—the great First Cause.

There is a great similarity between this and the 'five sheaths' or Kosas of the Vedanta—the Annamaya and Pranamaya Kosas (together forming the gross body), the Manomaya and Vijnanamaya Kosas (together forming the subtle body) and Anandamayakosa (forming the causal body). The First Cause is beyond all these Kosas. When the mind used to merge in this First Cause, he (Sri Chaitanya) used to fall into Samadhi; this is known as the Nirvikalpa or Jada Samadhi.

KUNDALINI AND SPIRITUAL AWAKENING

902. Unless the Kundalini is roused, spiritual awakening never takes place. The Kundalini[1] lies dormant in the

[1] Kundalini, sometimes translated as 'Serpent Power' is the dormant spiritual potentiality of man, located in the root Chakra (force-centre) known as Muladhara. This power is the Divine Sakti in man. Spiritual progress is sometimes described in terms of the rousing up of this latent energy and elevating it along the spinal channel called Sushumna, through the six centres, Svadhishthana, Manipura, Anahata, Visuddha and Ajna, until it reaches the crown centre known as Sahasrara. As the Kundalini ascends, man gains higher and higher spiritual experiences.

Muladhara. When She is roused, She enters into the Sushumna and passes through Svadhishthana, Manipura, and other centres, and finally reaches the cerebral centre, and then comes Samadhi. I actually saw all these.

903. One of the signs of God-realisation is that the Great Energy (Maha-vayu) wakes up with a sudden start and goes to the 'head'. Then one falls into Samadhi and gets God-vision.

904.* Describing his experience of the rise of Kundalini, the Master once said: "Something rises with a tingling sensation from the feet to the head. So long as it does not reach the brain, I remain conscious, but the moment it does so I am dead to the outside world. Even the functions of seeing and hearing come to a standstill, and talking then is out of the question. Who is to speak? The very distinction between 'I' and 'you' vanishes. Sometimes I think I would tell you everything about what I see and feel when that mysterious power rises up to this, or even this (pointing to the heart and the throat). At that stage it is possible to speak, which I do. But the moment it has gone above this (pointing to the throat), somebody stops my mouth, as it were, and I am off my moorings. I make up my mind to relate to you what I feel when the Kundalini goes beyond the throat, but as I think over it, up goes the mind at a bound, and there is an end of the matter!" Many a time did the Master attempt to describe this state, but every time he failed. One day he was determined to tell those present about these experiences and went on with his description of them up to the stage when the energy rises to the level of the throat. Then pointing to the sixth centre, opposite the junction of the eyebrows, he said, "When the mind reaches this point, one catches a vision of the Paramatman and falls into Samadhi. Only a thin, transparent veil intervenes between the Jiva and the Paramatman. He then sees like this . . ." And as he attempted to explain it in detail, he fell into Samadhi! When his mind came down a little, he tried it again, and again he was immersed in Samadhi! After several fruitless attempts like this, he said with tears in his eyes, "Well, I sincerely wish to tell you everything without concealing a bit, but Mother won't let me do so on any account. She gagged me!"

905.* Again referring to the different ways in which the Kundalini rises to the brain, the Master would often say, "Well, that which rises to the brain with a tingling sensation does not always follow the same kind of movement. The scriptures speak of its having five kinds of motion. First, the ant-like motion: one feels a slow creeping sensation from the feet upwards, like a row of ants creeping on with food in their mouths. When it reaches the head, the Sadhaka (spiritual aspirant) falls into Samadhi. Second, the frog-like motion: just as frogs make two or three short jumps in quick succession and then stop for a while to proceed again, in the same way something is felt advancing from the legs to the brain. When this reaches the brain, the man gets Samadhi. Third, the serpentine motion: as snakes lie quietly, straight or coiled up, but as soon as they find a victim in front, or get frightened, they run in a zigzag course, in like manner the 'coiled up power' rushes to the head, and this produces Samadhi. Fourth, the bird-like motion: just as birds in their flight from one place to another take to their wings and fly sometimes a little high and sometimes low without however stopping till they reach their destination, so that power progresses and reaches the brain, and Samadhi ensues. Fifth and last, the monkey-like motion: as monkeys going from one tree to another take a leap from one branch to another and thus clear the distance in two or three bounds, so the Yogi feels the Kundalini going to the brain, and Samadhi ensues."

906.* These experiences he would detail at other times from the Vedantic standpoint, as follows: "The Vedanta speaks of seven planes, in each of which the Sadhaka has a particular kind of vision. The human mind has a natural tendency to confine its activities to the three lower centres—the highest of these being opposite the navel—and therefore is content with the satisfaction of the common physical appetites, such as eating and so forth. But when it reaches the fourth centre, that is, the one opposite the heart, the man sees a divine effulgence. From this state, however, he often lapses into the three lower centres. When the mind comes to the fifth centre opposite the throat, the Sadhaka cannot talk of anything but God. While I was in this state I would feel violently struck on the head if anyboy raised worldly topics before me. I would hide myself in the seclusion of the Panchavati where I was safe from these inflictions. I would flee at the sight of worldly-minded people, and relatives appeared to me like a yawning chasm, from which there was no escape if I once fell into it. I would feel suffocated in their presence,—

almost to the point of death, and I would feel relieved only when I left the spot. Even from this position a man may slip down to the three lower centres. So he has to be on his guard. But he is above all fear when his mind reaches the sixth centre opposite the junction of the eye-brows. He gets the vision of the Paramatman and remains always in Samadhi. There is only a thin transparent veil between this place and the Sahasrara or the highest centre. He is then so near the Paramatman that he imagines he has merged in Him. But really he has not. From this state the mind can come down to the fifth, or at the most, to the fourth centre, but not below that. The ordinary Sadhakas, classed as 'Jivas' cannot come down from this state. After remaining constantly in Samadhi for twenty-one days they break that thin veil and become one with the Lord for ever. This eternal union of the Jiva and the Paramatman in the Sahasrara is known as getting into the seventh plane."

SPURIOUS ECSTASY

907.* Referring to a man who used to have a kind of emotional excitement that looked like Samadhi externally, the Master said: "In real ecstasy one dives into the deeper realms of one's being and becomes perfectly still. But what do we find here! Be quiet; compose yourself. (To the others present). Do you know the nature of this ecstasy? It is like boiling one ounce of milk in a big pan. The pan seems to be full of milk, but remove it from the stove and you would not find a single drop. Even the little quantity that was there would have all stuck to the pan."

PERCEPTION OF DIVINE FORMS AND SOUNDS

908. The realisation of God is of two kinds—one consists in the unification of the Jivatman and the Paramatman and the other in seeing Him in His personal manifestation. The former is called Jnana, and the latter Bhakti.

909.* Really God can be seen, my boys. As we are sitting and talking together, in the very same way God can be seen and conversed with. Truly and sincerely I say so.

910. The manifestation of Personal God is often a Spiritual Form, which is seen only by a purified human soul. In other words, these forms of God are realised by the organs of spiritual vision belonging to the spiritual body (Bhagavati-tanu) which is derived from the Lord. So the perfect man alone can see these Divine Forms.

911.* On being questioned whether those who see God see Him with the ordinary fleshly eyes, the Master replied: "No, He cannot be seen with the physical eye. In the course of Sadhana a 'Love-body' is created in you, with eyes and ears of Love, and with them you see and hear Him."

912. The Anahata sound is always going on of itself. This is the sound of Pranava (Om). It comes from the Supreme Brahman and is audible to the Yogis. The ordinary worldly men cannot hear it. The Yogis can understand that the sound rises on one side, from the 'region of the navel', and on the other, from Supreme Brahman.

SAMADHI AND REALISATION OF BRAHMAN

913. What is the state of one's mind in Samadhi? It is like the state of bliss that is experienced by a live fish

which, after being kept out of water for some time, is again put into it.

914. Mysterious is that sacred state which recognises neither teacher, nor pupil. Brahma-jnana is so mysterious that when one attains it there remains no distinction between the Guru and the disciple.

915. As a lamp brought into a room that has been dark for a thousand years illumines it immediately, the light of Jnana illumines the Jiva, and dispels his age-long ignorance.

916. On being questioned as to whether he was conscious of the gross world in the state of Samadhi, the Master replied, "There are hills and mountains, dales and valleys under the sea, but they are not visible from the surface. So in the state of Samadhi one sees the broad expanse of the Sachchidananda only, and the individual consciousness lies in a latent condition."

917.* In true Jnana not the least trace of egotism is left. Without Samadhi, Jnana never comes. Jnana is like the midday sun, in which one looks around but finds no shadow of oneself. So when one attains Jnana or Samadhi, one retains no shadow of egotism. But even if there be some ego left, know for certain that it is now composed of Vidya (purely divine elements) and not of ignorance or Avidya.

918.* When the question was raised whether the Buddha was an atheist, the Master said: "He was no atheist; only he could not speak out his realisations. Do you know what 'Buddha' means?—To become one with 'Bodha', the Supreme Intelligence—through deep meditation, to become Pure Intelligence Itself. The state of self-realisation is something between 'Asti' and 'Nasti' —' being' and 'non-being'. These 'being' and 'non-being' are modifications of Prakriti. The Reality transcends them both."

919.* Get to the other side of both knowledge and ignorance. Ignorance is the consciousness of the many, *i.e.*, the knowledge of diversity without knowing the Unity, without knowing the one God. The egotism due to erudition proceeds from ignorance. The conviction that God is in all objects—that there is unity in variety—is called knowledge of Oneness. Knowing Him intimately is realisation (Vijnana).

Suppose your foot is pricked with a thorn. Well, you want a second thorn to take it out. When the first thorn is taken out, you throw away both. So, in order to get rid of the thorn of ignorance, you bring in the thorn of knowledge. Then you throw away both ignorance and knowledge with a view to the complete realisation of the Absolute. For the Absolute is beyond knowledge as well as ignorance.

Lakshmana once said to his Divine brother Rama: "O Rama, is it not strange that a God-knowing man like Vasishtha Deva should have wept for the loss of his sons, and would not be comforted?" Thereupon Rama replied: "Brother, bear in mind that whoever possesses relative knowledge of Unity (God) must at the same time have relative ignorance also."

Such a person is not in the nature of things free from ignorance as to God, for knowledge and ignorance in this case are as correlatives. For a knowledge of Unity in the universe presupposes a concurrent knowledge of diversity. One who feels the existence of light has also an awareness of the existence of darkness.

The Absolute is beyond knowledge and ignorance, beyond sin and virtue, good works and bad works, cleanliness and uncleanliness—as understood by the limited faculties of man.

An enquirer: Sir, may I ask what remains after you have thrown away both the thorns as you call them—knowledge and ignorance.

The Master: Well, what remains is the eternally pure and absolute Consciousness (Nitya-suddha-buddha-rupa). But how can I make it clear to you? Suppose some one asks you what is the taste of clarified butter? Is it possible to make the matter perfectly clear to him? The utmost one may say in reply to such a question is, "The taste of butter is precisely like the taste of butter." A girl who was unmarried once asked a friend, "Your husband is come. Do tell me what sort of joy you feel whenever you meet him." Thereupon the married girl said in reply, "My dear, you will know everything when you have got a husband of your own. How can I make it clear to you now?"

PSYCHOLOGY OF SAMADHI

920. When the nest of a bird is destroyed, it betakes itself to the sky. Similarly, when the consciousness of the body and the outer world is effaced from the mind, the Jivatman (individual Spirit) soars into the sky of the Paramatman (Supreme Spirit) and merges itself in Samadhi.

921. Humanity must die before divinity manifests itself. But this divinity must, in turn, die before the higher manifestation of the Blissful Mother (Brahmamayi) takes place. It is on the bosom of the dead divinity (Siva) that the Blissful Mother dances Her celestial dance.

922. When camphor is burnt, no residue is left. When discrimination ends and the highest Samadhi is attained, there is neither 'I' nor 'thou' nor the universe; for the mind and the ego are merged in the Absolute Brahman.

923. When the ego is effaced, the Jiva dies and there follows the realisation of Brahman in Samadhi. Then it is Brahman, not the Jiva, that realises Brahman.

924. When it was contended by a devotee that God is beyond the comprehension of words, thoughts and senses, and that the mind cannot reach Him, the Master remarked, "That is not quite so. It is true enough that the conditioned mind cannot realise God. But He can be realised by the pure mind (Suddha-manas), which is the same thing as the pure reason (Suddha-buddhi), which again is the same thing as the pure unconditioned Spirit. He cannot indeed be realised by the finite reason, or by the finite, relative and conditioned mind that has a sensuous nature due to its attachment to 'woman and gold'. The mind may however be rid of its sensuous nature and may be purified by culture. When freed from all worldly tendencies, desires and attachments, it becomes one with the unconditioned Spirit. Was it not thus that the sages of old saw God? God, the unconditioned Spirit, they saw by means of the purified mind, which they found to be the same as the Atman or the unconditioned Spirit within.

925. God is beyond both mind and intellect as long as they are bound within relativity; but He manifests Himself to them when they are purified. It is lust and greed which make the mind impure. So long as Avidya (ignorance) reigns in the heart, the mind and the intellect can never be pure. Ordinarily, mind and intellect are known to be different from each other; but in their purified state they become one, and are resolved into Chaitanya (Pure Consciousness). Then God, the Chaitanya, becomes manifest to the Chaitanya.

VIJNANA WHICH COMES AFTER SAMADHI

926.* Jnana is the realisation of the Atman by the elimination of all phenomena. By eliminating the phenomena through the process of discrimination, one attains Samadhi and realises the Atman.

And Vijnana means knowing with greater fulness. Some have only heard of milk, some have but seen it, while others have tasted it. He who has only heard of it is an ignorant man. He who has seen it is the Jnani. But only he who has tasted it has attained Vijnana, that is, has known it in its entirety. To see God and have intimate relation with Him as with a near kinsman, is what is called Vijnana.

First you have to follow the process of 'Neti, Neti'—'not this, not this'. He is not the five elements. He is not the senses, nor the mind, nor the intelligence, nor the ego—He is beyond all categories. To get up to the roof you have to leave below all the steps of the staircase one by one. Of course the steps are not the roof. But when you reach the roof, you find that the roof is made of the same brick, lime, mortar and sand as the staircase. That which is the Supreme Brahman, the same has become the Jiva and Jagat—the twenty-four categories of thc philosophers. That which is the Atman has become the five elements. You may ask why the earth is so hard if it has come out of the Atman. Through His will everything is possible. Are not flesh and bone made out of blood and semen. How hard becomes the foam of the ocean?

After attaining Vijnana a man can live in the world as well. For then he clearly perceives that He Himself has become the world of living and non-living substances, that He is not outside the world. When Ramachandra attained Jnana and refused to remain in the world, Dasaratha sent Vasishtha to instruct him. Vasishtha said to Ramachandra: "Rama, if the world is outside God, you may give it up." Ramachandra remained silent, for he well knew that nothing exists without God.

927.* In music the notes gradually rise from the lowest to the highest pitch and again come down in the reverse order; similarly, after experiencing non-duality in Samadhi one descends to a lower plane and lives with the ego-consciousness. After divesting the banana plant of all its sheaths one after another, one reaches its pith and takes that alone to be the essential part. But later he considers that the sheaths also are of the plant itself. Both of them are necessary to make the stem a complete whole.

928.* While examining a Bel fruit one analyses it into its constituent parts, the shell, the seed and the pulp.

Now, which of these is the Bel? First one rejects the shell as non-essential, then the seeds, and lastly takes the pulp separately and considers that alone as the real fruit. But then the after-thought comes that the same fruit which has the pulp, has the shell and the seeds as well. All these together make the whole fruit. Similarly, after having directly perceived God in His attributeless aspect, one realises that the same Deity Who is eternal by nature has assumed the form of the world in a playful mood.

929.* Once Sri Ramakrishna asked Narendra (Swami Vivekananda) what his ideal in life was. "To remain absorbed in Samadhi," replied Narendra. "Can you be so small-minded as that?" the Master said, "Go beyond Samadhi. Samadhi is a trifling thing for you!"

To another he said, "Bhava (divine ecstasy) and Bhakti—these are not final."

930. On another occasion Sri Ramakrishna asked the same question to Narendra, and received the same reply as before. To which the Master remarked: "Why! I thought you were made of better stuff. How can you be satisfied with such a one-sided ideal? My strength is all-sidedness. I would like to enjoy fish, for instance, in a variety of ways—fried and boiled, made into soup, pickled, etc. I enjoy the Lord not only in His unconditioned state of Oneness, as unqualified Brahman, in Samadhi, but also in His various blessed manifestations through sweet human relationship. So do you likewise. Be a Jnani and a Bhakta in one."

CHAPTER XIX

THE MAN OF DIVINE REALISATION

[*Varieties of perfect men—At the advent of the Divine in the heart—Some characteristics of spiritual perfection —Non-attachment of the perfect man—Perfect man transcends good and evil, but never does evil—Perfect man and work*]

VARIETIES OF PERFECT MEN

931. People do not see that science deals only with conditioned knowledge. It brings no message from the land of the Unconditioned. Such message has been brought by holy men who have seen and realised God, like the Rishis of old. It is they alone that are competent to say, "God is of this nature."

932. There are five kinds of Siddhas (perfect men) found in the world. They are: (1) The Svapna-siddhas, or those who attain perfection by means of dream-inspiration. (2) The Mantra-siddhas, or those who attain perfection by means of a Mantra or sacred 'name' of God. (3) The Hathat-siddhas, or those who attain perfection suddenly, like a poor man who at once becomes rich by finding a hidden treasure or by marrying a rich wife. Similarly, many who are sinful somehow become pure all of a sudden and enter the Kingdom of Heaven. (4) The

Kripa-siddhas, or those who attain perfection through the grace of God. As a man in clearing a forest may discover some ancient tank or house and himself need not construct one with pain and trouble, so some fortunately become perfect with very little effort on their own part. (5) The Nitya-siddhas, or those who are ever perfect. As the vine of a gourd or pumpkin brings forth first its fruit and then its flower, so the ever perfect soul is born a Siddha, and all his seeming exertions after perfection are merely for the sake of setting an example to humanity.

933. The perfect man among the Saktas is called Kaula; among the Vedantins, Paramahamsa; among the Vaishnavas of the Baul sect, Sayin.

934. There are some who would wipe their lips clean after eating a mango lest others should know of it; but there are also those who, if they get a mango, would call others and share it with them. So there are some who, having realised the Divine bliss themselves, cannot rest without helping others also realise it.

AT THE ADVENT OF THE DIVINE IN THE HEART

935.* He who has seen the Lord is a changed being.

936.* Some are already awake. These have certain marks. They do not care to hear or speak of anything but what relates to God, just as the bird called Chataka cries only for rain-water, though there are the seven seas and the Ganges and the Yamuna and all the other rivers, full of water. Though its throat might be parched with thirst, it would drink no other water than rain-water.

937. What are the indications of God's advent into the human heart? As the glow of dawn heralds the rising sun, so unselfishness, purity and righteousness announce the advent of the Lord.

938. Before visiting a servant's house to receive his hospitality, a king will send there the necessary articles like seats, ornaments and food from his own stores so that the servant may be enabled to receive his master properly and show due honour. In the same manner the Lord sends love, reverence and faith into the yearning heart of the devotee before He makes His advent.

939. Ananda, or perfect bliss within, is one of the signs of God-vision. The waves roll on the surface of the ocean but the deep expanse of water lies unruffled beneath.

940. When Divine bliss is attained, a person becomes quite intoxicated with it; even without drinking wine, he looks like one fully drunk. When I see the feet of my Divine Mother, I feel as intoxicated as if I have drunk five bottles of wine. In this state one cannot take food indiscriminately.

941. What is the state which a Siddha (perfect man) attains? As a potato or brinjal becomes soft and pulpy when it gets Siddha,[1] so a man, when he becomes a Siddha, is seen to be all humility and tenderness.

SOME CHARACTERISTICS OF SPIRITUAL PERFECTION

942. He is truly an Atma-jnani, knower of the Self, who is dead even in this life; that is, whose passions and desires have been destroyed as in a dead body.

[1] There is a pun on the word Siddha, which means both 'a perfect man, and 'well-cooked'.

943.* Sri Ramakrishna once said to Keshab Chandra Sen: "If you advance further, and preach higher and higher things, your 'sect' will fall to pieces. In the state of Jnana, forming sects becomes meaningless—false as a dream."

944. When man attains true Jnana, he does not perceive God as a far-off being. He is no more felt thereafter as 'He', but as 'This,' 'here within'—as within one's own soul. He is within all; whoever seeks Him, meets Him there.

945. A jar kept in water is full of water inside and outside. Thus the soul immersed in God sees the all-pervading Spirit within and without.

946. After the attainment of God-realisation, one sees Him everywhere, in everything. But greater is His manifestation in man; and greatest of all, is He manifest in devotees full of Sattva-guna—in those who have not the slightest passion for 'woman and gold'.

947.* It is true, however, that when the devotee has realised God, he wishes to witness His sport (Lila). When Ramachandra entered the city of the Rakshasas (demons) after the destruction of Ravana, the old Nikasha began to run away. Lakshmana said, "How is this, Rama? This Nikasha is so aged and has suffered so much from the loss of her sons, and yet she is afraid of losing her life, and is running away!" Rama bade her have no fear, and called her near him to learn why she was flying. Nikasha replied, "O Rama, it is because I have lived so long that I could witness so much of your 'sport'. I, therefore, desire to live longer so that I shall see more of your 'sport'."

948. Can there be Maya in the emancipated soul? Ornaments cannot be made of pure gold; some alloy must be mixed with it. As long as man has a body he must have some Maya, at least to carry on the functions of the body; a man totally devoid of Maya will not survive more than twenty-one days.

949.* When the head of a goat is severed from its body, the trunk struggles for some time, still showing signs of life. Similarly, though Ahamkara (egotism) is slain in the perfect man, yet enough of its vitality is left to make him carry on the functions of physical life; but it is not sufficient to bind him again to the world.

950. The body is born, and it will have to die. But there is no death to the soul. When the betel-nut is ripe, the nut separates from the outer case, but it is very difficult to separate it while the nut is green. When God is attained, there dawns the consciousness that the soul is separate from the body.

951. When the Jews nailed Jesus to the cross, how was it that he could, in spite of so much pain and suffering, pray that they should be forgiven? When an ordinary cocoanut is pierced through the shell, the nail enters the kernel of the nut. But in the case of the dry nut the kernel becomes separate from the shell; and when the shell is pierced, the kernel is not touched. Jesus was like the dry nut; his inner soul was separate from his physical shell. Consequently the sufferings of the body did not affect him. Though the nails were driven through and through, he could pray with calm tranquillity for the good of his enemies.

NON-ATTACHMENT OF THE PERFECT MAN

952. When a leaf of the cocoanut tree drops off, it leaves a mark on the trunk. This helps us to understand that there was once a leaf there. In the same way he who has attained God keeps only the marks, the withered scars, of anger and passion. His nature is just like that of a child. Having none of the consistency of Sattva, Rajas and Tamas, it is as quick to attach itself to a thing as to leave it. You can persuade a little boy to hand over to you clothing worth several rupees in exchange for a toy worth a single pie, though at first he will tell you, "No, I won't give it to you; my father bought it for me." To the child every one is equal; he has no discrimination between the high and the low, and consequently no distinction of caste. If his mother says, "So and so is your brother," he will take rice from the same plate with him even if the other is a carpenter's son (*i.e.*, of low caste). Nor has he any hatred, nor any idea of cleanliness and pollution (Suchi and Asuchi).

953.* How does the emancipated soul live in the world? He lives in the world like the diver-bird. It dives into water, but the water does not wet its plumage; the few drops of water which may possibly stick to its body are easily shaken off when it once flaps its wings.

954. The snake is very venomous; it bites when any one tries to catch it. But the person who has learnt the art of snake-charming can not only catch snakes but also carry several of them hanging about his neck and arms like so many ornaments. Similarly he who has acquired spiritual

Knowledge can never be poisoned by the venom of lust and greed.

955. When the tail of the tadpole drops off, it can live both in water and on land. When the tail of delusive ignorance drops off from man, he becomes free. He can then live both in God and in the world equally well.

956. The wind carries both the fragrance of the sandal wood and the smell of the rotten carcase equally, but it does not mix with any of these. In the same way the emancipated soul lives in the world but does not get itself mixed with it.

957. Iron, after it is converted into gold by the touch of the 'philosopher's stone', may be kept under the earth or thrown into a rubbish heap. It will always remain gold and will not return to its former condition. Similar is the state of the man whose soul has touched, even once, the feet of the Almighty Lord. Whether he dwells in the bustle of the world, or in the solitude of the forest, nothing ever contaminates him.

958. Milk poured into water mixes readily with it; when converted into butter, it no longer gets mixed with water but floats in it. So having attained to the state of God, one may live in constant contact with innumerable unregenerate souls; one will not at all be affected then by such evil association.

959. Good and evil cannot bind him who has realised the oneness of the Nature and his own self with Brahman.

PERFECT MAN TRANSCENDS GOOD AND EVIL, BUT NEVER DOES EVIL

960. When a man is on the plains, he sees the lowly grass and the mighty pine tree and says, "How big is the

tree and how small is the grass!" But when he ascends the mountain and looks down from its high peak the grass and the tree blend into one indistinguishable mass of verdure. So, in the sight of worldly men, there are differences of rank and position—one is a king and another is a cobbler; one is a father and another is a son; and so on. But when the divine vision is opened, all appear equal; and there remains no distinction of good and bad, or of high and low.

961. Once a God-intoxicated Sadhu came to Rani Rasmani's Kali temple where the Master was living. One day he did not get any food; and even though feeling hungry, he did not ask anybody for it; but seeing a dog eating the remnants of food thrown away in a corner after a feast, he went there and embracing the dog, said, "Brother, how is it that you eat alone without giving me a share?" So saying, he began to eat along with the dog. Having finished his meal in this strange company, the sage entered the temple of Mother Kali, and prayed with such earnestness of devotion as sent a thrill through the temple. When, after finishing his prayers, he was going away, the Master asked his cousin, Hriday, to follow that man, and talk with him. When Hriday followed him for some distance, the sage turned round and said, "Why do you follow me?" Hriday replied, "Sir, give me some instruction." The sage said, "When the water of this dirty ditch and the holy Ganges yonder will appear as one in your sight, and when the sound of the flageolet and the noise of the crowd will have no distinction to your ear, then you will reach the state of true Knowledge." When Hriday returned and told this to the Master, he said, "That man

has reached the true state of ecstasy and of Knowledge. A Siddha roams about in various disguises—as a child, as an unclean spirit, or even as a mad man."

962. The state of a Paramahamsa (a perfect man) is just like that of a child. Like a child of five years, he feels no difference between man and woman. Yet, to set an example to the world, he should be on his guard against the other sex.

963.* Once a Sannyasini (a nun) came to the royal court of Janaka. To her the king bowed, without looking at her face. Seeing this, the Sannyasini said: "How strange it is, O Janaka, that you have still so much fear of woman!" When one attains to full Jnana, one's nature becomes like that of a little child,—one sees no distinction between male and female.

964. But these slight spots that cling to the Jnani in this world do not matter much. The moon has spots but that never interferes with her giving light.

965. The steel sword turns into a gold one at the touch of the 'philosopher's stone': and though it retains its former shape, it is incapable of causing injury like the steel sword. Similarly, the outward form of the man who succeeds in touching the feet of God is not changed, but he can no loger do any evil.

966. With the divine Knowledge of Advaita (non-duality) in you, do whatever you wish; for then no evil can ever come out of you.

967. Once a holy man, while passing through a crowded street, accidentally trod upon the toe of a wicked person. The latter, furious with rage, mercilessly beat the Sadhu

until he fell down unconscious. At great pains to themselves, his disciples tried various measures to revive him. When they saw that he was regaining consciousness a little, one of them asked, "Sir, do you recognise who is now serving you?" The Sadhu replied, "Assuredly he who beat me!" A true Sadhu finds no distinction between a friend and a foe.

PERFECT MAN AND WORK

968.* He who has seen God roams about, sometimes like a mad man, sometimes like an unclean spirit, feeling no distinction between cleanliness and its opposite. Sometimes he remains like an inanimate object, being struck dumb by seeing God within and without. Sometimes, like a child, he attaches his mind to nothing, and goes about with his clothes bundled in his arms. But when he works for the good of others, he is as brave as a lion.

969. After the attainment of Samadhi, all Karma drops away—Karma such as external worship, the telling of beads, and worldly activities. In the beginning there is a great fuss of work. But the more one proceeds towards God, the less becomes the bustle until even prayer and the singing of the Lord's glorious 'name' are eventually given up. (Addressing Sivanath Sastri of the Sadharan Brahmo Samaj): So long as you do not come to the meeting, much talk about your name, attainments, qualities, etc., passes round; but the moment you come in, all that talk ceases. Everybody feels joy at your sight, and they simply cry out, "Here comes Sivanath Babu,"—and there ceases all further talk about you.

970. A newly married young woman remains deeply absorbed in the performance of domestic duties so long as no child is born to her. But as soon as she has a child, she begins to neglect the minor details of household work, and does not find much pleasure in them. Instead, she fondles the new-born baby all the day and kisses it with intense joy. Thus a man in his state of ignorance is ever busy in the performance of all sorts of work; but as soon as he sees in his heart the presence of God, he finds no pleasure in them. On the contrary, his happiness consists now only in serving God and doing His will. He no longer finds happiness in any other occupation, and he cannot withdraw himself from the ecstasy of that holy communion.

971. When God is realised, the world never appears empty. He who has attained Him sees that the Lord Himself has become all these—the universe and its creatures. When he feeds his children, he feels as if he is feeding Gopala Himself; he looks upon his parents as God, and serves them in the same manner. If one happens to be in the world, and leads a family life after the realisation of God, it is sure that he cannot keep any physical connection with his wife. Both become devotees of God and spend their lives in prayer and devotion. They serve all creatures. As God is in all beings, they worship Him in all.

CHAPTER XX

GLIMPSES OF THE MASTER'S EXPERIENCES IN HIS OWN WORDS

[*Experiences of early days—Tantric and other Sadhanas—Experience of the Nirvikalpa state—The Master's perpetual God-consciousness—How the Master prayed—The Divine in good and evil alike—The Master on his illness—The Master a combination of humanity and Divinity.*]

EXPERIENCES OF EARLY DAYS

972.* In his younger days, when taken to task by his elder brother for neglecting his studies, the Master said in reply: "Brother, what shall I do with a mere bread-winning education? I would rather acquire that wisdom which would illumine my heart—that wisdom gaining which one felt satisfied for ever."

973.* In the early days of his spiritual life, the Master's nephew, Hriday, noticed him meditating at night in the seclusion of a jungle, quite naked, and without even the sacred thread. On being asked how nudeness was connected with meditation, the Master replied: "One should meditate free from all bondages and fetters. From his very birth man has been fettered by the eightfold shackle of hatred, shame, family pride, social conventionalities, fear, prestige, pride of caste and egotism. Even the sacred thread is a fetter—it is a token of egotism and makes one feel that one is a Brahmin and is superior to all. So, when one meditates on the Divine Mother, one should make oneself free by throwing aside all these shackles."

974.* When the great yearning for God had developed in him, the Master found life unbearable without His vision. He was therefore about to put an end to his life, when the blessed vision dawned on him suddenly. Describing it the Master said: "The room with all its doors and windows, the temple and everything around me, vanished from sight. I felt as if nothing existed, and in their stead I perceived a boundless effulgent ocean of intelligence. Whichever side I turned my eyes, I saw from all quarters huge waves of that shining ocean rushing towards me, and in a short while, they all came, and falling upon me, engulfed me completely. Thus getting suffocated under them, I lost my ordinary consciousness and fell down." Referring to the same experience he said on another occasion: "I fell down on the floor of the room, completely lost in the ecstasy of the vision. I was perfectly unconscious as to what happenened outside, and also how that day and the next passed. The one thing which I was internally conscious of was that through my soul was rolling an ocean of ineffable joy, the like of which I had no experience before. At the same time I was also conscious, to the inner core of my being, of the hallowed presence of the Divine Mother."

975.* But this experience of God did not bring on the Master a state of perpetual God-consciousness. He had to pass through periods of dryness, and a yearning for the constant vision of the Divine therefore goaded him on to pray unceasingly to the Divine Mother with bitter tears of grief and loud cries. Describing the state of his mind in that period, the Master said: "If a concourse of people happened to gather round me (attracted by loud cries and prayers) they appeared to me like shadows or so many figures drawn in a picture—so unreal and shadowy they appeared—and therefore I never used to feel any kind of shame or shyness before them. But whenever I used to lose my external consciousness through an unbearable pang of the heart, the next moment I always used to behold the radiant spiritual form of the Mother. I used to see the form sometimes laughing, sometimes talking with me, and sometimes advising and consoling me.

976. Describing the days he passed in intense yearning for God, the Master said: "As I was perfectly unmindful of cleaning the body at that time, the hairs grew long and got matted of themselves, being smeared with dirt and dust. When I used to sit in meditation, the body used to become stiff and motionless like a stock through intense concentration of mind, and birds, taking it to be an inert substance, came freely, perched on the head, and pecked into the matted hair in search of food. Sometimes I used to feel so intensely the pangs of separation from God, that in great bitterness I rubbed my face on earth; often it used to get lacerated and bleed. And in meditation, prayer and other devotional practices, the

day used to fly away so quickly that I was not conscious of it. At dusk, when the approach of night was announced by the ringing of bells and the blowing of conchs from the temple, I used to be reminded that the day had passed and the night had set in. With this consciousness a frenzy of despair would seize my soul, and I would throw myself on the ground and rub my face on it, crying loudly, 'Mother, a day has passed; still Thou hast not appeared before me!' A gnawing anguish used to torment my soul, and those who saw me like that, writhing in agony, thought that I was suffering from colic pain."

977.* Soon after the Master's return to Dakshineswar after his marriage, his old divine madness seized him again. About the state of his mind in those days he said: "The ordinary man would have died, if he were to experience even a fourth of the spiritual metamorphosis that my body and mind underwent. And of this body too (meaning himself) the same would have been the fate; but fortunately the major portion of my days was passed in ecstatic oblivion of the Mother's divine vision. Henceforth for six long years not a wink of sleep ever visited my eyes, and the eyelids would never close, try though I might. All sense of time vanished from me, and the body idea was totally obliterated. A terrible fear would seize me at the slightest reversion of the mind from the Mother to the body. Often the fear came whether I had really run mad. I would stand before my image in a mirror, and when on poking my eyes I would find them insensitive, I would burst into tears in terror, and pray to the Mother: 'O Mother, is it that as a result of all my prayers and absolute reliance on Thee, Thou hast brought on me an incurable disease?' But next, the alternating thought would come: 'O Mother, whatever fate may overtake my body, do Thou never forsake me! Vouchsafe unto me Thy vision and Thy mercy! O Mother, have I not taken complete shelter at Thy hallowed feet? Except Thee, O Mother, I have no other refuge!' And thus praying tearfully, my mind would be filled with a strange enthusiasm, creating an unbounded disgust for the body, and would lose itself in the comfort of the Mother's Divine vision and consoling words."

978.* The Master's pure mind was itself his first and most important teacher. About this the Master said: "Whenever necessity arose, a young Sannyasin from inside my body, in appearance exactly like myself, would come out and teach me everything. When he came out in this way, sometimes I would retain a little consciousness of external objects and at other times, I would lose all consciousness of the outside world except for the awareness of his presence and doings. When he re-entered the body, I would again become aware of the external world. What I had heard from him before, the same teachings I heard from Brahmani, Totapuri, and others. What I learnt from him before, the same I learnt from these teachers later."

TANTRIC AND OTHER SADHANAS

979.* Referring to his Tantrik Sadhana under the guidance of Bhairavi Brahmani the Master said: "The Brahmani would go during the day to places far away from Dakshineswar and collect the various rare things mentioned in the Tantric scriptures as requisites of Sadhana. At nightfall she would ask me to go to one of the seats. I would go, and after performing the worship of the Mother Kali, I would begin to meditate according to her directions. I could hardly tell my beads, for as soon as I began to do so I was always overwhelmed with divine fervour and fell into deep Samadhi. I cannot now relate the varieties of wonderful visions I used to have. They followed each other in quick succession, and the effects of those practices I could feel most tangibly. The Brahmani guided me through all the exercises mentioned in the sixty-four principal Tantric works. Most of these are extremely difficult Sadhanas, which generally cause many a devotee to slip his foot and sink into moral degradation. But the infinite grace of the Mother carried me through them unscathed."

980.* Describing his experience of the awakening of Kundalini, the Master said: "When I realised this state (the state of God-consciousness), one looking exactly like me came and thoroughly shook my Ida, Pingala and Sushumna nerves. He licked the 'lotuses' of the six 'centres' with his tongue, and the drooping lotuses at once turned their faces upwards. And at last the Sahasrara 'lotus' became full-bloomed."

981.* The Master used to describe his mentality when he practised Islamic Sadhanas, as follows: "Then I used to repeat the name of Allah, wear my cloth in the fashion of the Mohammedans, and recite the Namaz regularly. All Hindu ideas being wholly banished from the mind, not only did I not salute the Hindu Gods, but I had no inclination even for visiting them. After passing three days in that way, I realised the goal of that form of devotion."

982.* I had to practise the various religions once, Hinduism, Islam and Christianity, and I have walked the paths of the different sects of Hinduism again—the Sakta, the Vaishnava, the Vedantic and others. And I have found that it is the same God towards Whom all are travelling, only they are coming through diverse ways.

983.* The Master experienced how a man died when he witnessed the death of his beloved nephew, Akshay. Describing his experience, the Master said: "Akshay died before my very eyes. But it did not affect me in the least. I stood by and watched how a man died. It was like a sword taken out from the scabbard. The sword remained as it was, only the scabbard was left behind. I enjoyed the scene, and laughed and danced and sang over it. They removed the body and cremated it. But next day as I stood there (pointing to the south-eastern verandah of his room), I felt a racking pain for the loss of Akshay, as if somebody was squeezing my heart like a wet towel. I wondered and thought that Mother was teaching me a lesson. I was not much concerned with the body even—much less with a nephew. But if such was my pain at his bereavement, how much more must be the grief of the householders at the loss of their near and dear ones."

EXPERIENCE OF NIRVIKALPA STATE

984.* Describing his experience of Nirvikalpa Samadhi, the Master said: "After the initiation, 'the naked one'[1] began to teach me the various conclusions of the Advaita Vedanta and asked me to withdraw the mind completely from all objects and dive into the Atman. But in spite of all my attempts I could not cross the realm of name and form and bring my mind to the unconditioned state. I had no difficulty in withdrawing the mind from all objects except one, and this was the all-too-familiar form of the Blissful Mother—radiant and of the essence of Pure Consciousness—which appeared before me as a living reality and would not allow me to pass beyond the realm of name and form. Again and again I tried to concentrate my mind upon the Advaita teaching but every time the Mother's form stood in my way. In despair I said to 'the naked one', 'It is hopeless. I cannot raise my mind to the unconditioned state and come face to face with the Atman.' He grew excited and sharply said, 'What! You can't do it! But you have to.' He cast his eyes around for something, and finding a piece of glass, took it up, and pressing its point between my eyebrows, said, 'Concentrate your mind on this point.' Then with a stern determination I again sat to meditate, and as soon as the gracious form of the Divine Mother appeared before me, I used my discrimination as a sword and with it severed it into two. There remained no more obstruction to my mind, which at once soared beyond the relative plane, and I lost myself in Samadhi."

985.* I was for six months in that state of Nirvikalpa from which ordinary mortals cannot return. For after

[1] This was the appellation which Sri Ramakrishna, out of respect, invariably used for his Guru, who, being a Naga Sannyasin, generally went about naked.

twenty-one days the body drops off like a withered leaf. Days and nights succeeded one another perfectly unnoticed. Flies would enter the mouth and nostrils just as in the case of a corpse without producing any sensation. Hairs became all matted with dust. Sometimes even Nature's calls were answered unawares. Hardly would the body have survived this state but for a Sadhu who happened to come at this time. He at once recognised my condition, and also understood that the Mother had yet to do many things through this body—that many persons would be benefited if it were preserved. So at meal time he used to fetch some food and try to bring me to external consciousness by administering a good beating to the body. As soon as traces of consciousness were perceived, he would thrust the food into the mouth. In this way a few morsels would be swallowed on some days; on other days, not even that. Full six months were thus passed. Later, after some days, stay in this state, I came to hear the Mother's command, "Remain on the threshold of relative consciousness (Bhavamukha) for the instruction of mankind." Then appeared blood dysentery. There was acute writhing pain in the intestines. Through this suffering for six months the normal body consciousness slowly reappeared. Or else, every now and then the mind would, of its own accord, soar to the Nirvikalpa state.

986.* The natural tendency of this (my) mind is upwards (towards the Nirvikalpa state). Once that state is reached, it does not like to come down. For your sake I drag it down perforce. Downward pull is not strong enough without a lower desire. So I create some trifling desires, such as, for instance, for smoking, for drinking water, for tasting a particular dish, or for seeing a particular person, and repeatedly suggest them to my mind. Then alone the mind slowly comes down (to the body). Again, while coming down, it may run back upward. Again it has to be dragged down through such desires.

987.* The Master would go into the highest state of Nirvikalpa Samadhi by uttering the word Tat (That) only, out of the formula, Om Tat Sat. Sat (existence) might bring a remote suggestion of its opposite, 'Asat', and even the most sacred symbol 'Om' seemed to fall short of the mark. But when he uttered 'Tat' (That), all ideas of relativity would be completely effaced from his consciousness; all discrimination between existence and non-existence would cease; he would become merged in the realisation of the One that transcends all limitations.

988. *Q.* Do you have, Sir, the slightest idea of ego when you are merged in Samadhi?

A. Yes, usually a little ego remains. It is like the particle of gold leaf, which, if rubbed on a lump of gold, does not wear itself off completely. All outward consciousness disappears, but the Lord keeps a little ego to let me enjoy Him.

Sometimes, however, He drives away even that little. This is the highest Samadhi. No one can say what that state is—it is the absolute transformation of one's own self into His. The doll made of salt plunged into the ocean to measure its depth. But no sooner did it touch the water than it was dissolved. Then who could come up to give information as to how deep the ocean was!"

THE MASTER'S PERPETUAL GOD-CONSCIOUSNESS

989.* The Master was questioned: "Do you believe in God, Sir?"

"Yes," the Master replied.

"Can you prove it, Sir?"—"Yes."

"How?"—"Because I see Him just as I see you here, only very much more intensely."

990. A logician once asked the Master, "What are subject, object and knowledge?"

The Master replied, "Good man, I do not know all these niceties of scholastic learning; I know only the Self in me and my Divine Mother."

991. Hriday used to say after seeing the condition of my body: "I have never seen so much spirituality and illumination in such a frail state of body!" But although my body was weak, still I never stopped talking of God with others. At one time, I remember, I was reduced to a skeleton, yet I would hold conversations on spiritual subjects for hours, without feeling that I had a body.

HOW THE MASTER PRAYED

992.* I used to pray to the Divine Mother in this way: "O Mother, Who art the embodiment of bliss, Thou must reveal Thyself to me." And sometimes I would pray: "O Lord of the meek! O Lord of the humble! Am I outside Thy universe? I have neither knowledge, nor devotion, nor the merit of austerities. I know nothing. O Lord, in Thy infinite mercy Thou must vouchsafe Thy vision to me."

993. O Mother Divine! I want no honour from men, I want no pleasures of the flesh, only let my soul flow into Thee as the permanent confluence of the Ganges and the Jumna. Mother, I am without Bhakti, without Yoga, I am poor and friendless, and I want no one's praise; only let my mind always dwell at Thy lotus feet.

994. Mother, I am the Yantra (the instrument), Thou art the Yantri (the mover); I am the room, Thou art the tenant; I am the sheath, Thou art the sword; I am the chariot, Thou art the charioteer. I do as Thou makest me do; I speak as Thou makest me speak; I behave as Thou within me behavest; not 'I', not 'I', but 'Thou'.

995. One is sure to realise God, if only one has great devotion to truth. On the contrary, if one has no regard for truth, everything of his will be destroyed gradually. After attaining to this state (of God-realisation), I told Mother, taking flowers in my hand, "O Mother, here take back Thy[1] knowledge and Thy ignorance, Thy purity and Thy impurity, Thy good and also Thy bad, Thy virtue and Thy sin; give me only pure Bhakti, Mother." But when I said all these to Mother, I could not say, "Take back Thy truth and untruth." All I could return back to Mother, but not truth.

THE DIVINE IN GOOD AND EVIL ALIKE

996.* With God-realisation all Karma drops off. It was thus that my ceremonial worship came to an end. I used to perform worship in the Kali temple. One day

[1] Here 'Thy' means 'of Thy creation'.

it was suddenly revealed that everything was Chinmaya—Pure Spirit. The utensils of worship, altar, door-way—all was Spirit. Men, beasts, birds, everyone was Chinmaya. And like one mad, I began to rain flowers all around. Whatever I saw I worshipped.

One day, in course of Siva-worship, I was putting the Vajra on the Siva-lingam, when came the revelation that the universe itself is Siva. I did not reason it out, but it came to me in a flash. That day ended my worship of Siva in His images. I was once plucking flowers when suddenly it was revealed that each flower plant was a nosegay adorning the universal form of God. That was my last flower-gathering.

997. I had once a vision: I felt that One Substance had taken the form of the cosmos with all living creatures, which resembled a house of wax with men, animals, gardens, roads and the rest, all made of wax and nothing but wax.

998. Do you know what I see? I see Him as All! Men and other creatures appear as veritable skin-bound figures, shaking the head and moving the hands and feet, but the Lord is within.

999.* She has placed me in the state of a Bhakta—of a Vijnani. Hence it is that I can joke and make fun with Rakhal and others. Had I been in the condition of a Jnani, that would not have been possible. In this condition I see that Mother Herself has become all this. I see Her everywhere. In the Kali temple I found that Mother has become even the wicked—even the brother of the Bhagavat Pandit. Try though I might, I failed to rebuke Ramlal's mother. I found she was Mother in another form. It is because I find the Mother in the maidens that I worship them. My wife strokes my feet, but I salute her afterwards. Because I am placed in such a condition, I have to return your salutes. You see, I cannot ignore even a wicked man. A Tulsi leaf, however dry or small, can be offered to the Deity.

1000.* Do you know how I see? Trees, plants, men, animals, grass—these and all other things I see as different coverings like pillow cases, some made of fine cotton and others of coarser stuff, some round in shape and others square. But within all these pillow cases there is one and the same substance, cotton. In the same way all the objects of the world are stuffed with the unconditioned Sachchidananda. I feel as if the Mother has wrapped Herself in different clothes, and is peeping out from them. I was once in a state in which I used to perceive this every instant. Without understanding this state of mine, people came to pacify me. The mother of Ramlal wept. Looking at her, I felt that the Mother Who is in the temple has Herself come dressed as she. I rolled with laughter and said: "How beautifully you have dressed." One day I was meditating on the Divine Mother within the Kali temple. I found it impossible to visualise Her form. Sometime after I saw Her looking up from the side of the pot used for worship. She was in appearance like a prostitute named Ramani who comes to the Ghat for her bath. I laughed in wonder and said: "Very good! You like to be Ramani to-day. Accept then to-day's worship in that form." In this way the Mother taught me, "Even the prostitute is I Myself. There is nothing except

Myself." Another day while going in a carriage through Mechua Bazaar, I saw the Mother as a woman out to tempt people, dressed fashionably, with vermilion mark on the forhead and wig on head, and smoking from a Hookah. Wondering I asked whether the Mother had chosen to take this form also, and prostrated before Her.

1001. I do see the Supreme Being as the veritable Reality with my very eyes! Why then should I reason? I do actually see that it is the Absolute Who has become all things around us; it is He who appears as the finite soul and the phenomenal world! One must have an awakening of the spirit within to see this reality. As long as one is unable to see Him as the one reality, one must reason or discriminate, saying, "Not this; Not this." Of course, it would not do for one merely to say, "I have seen beyond the possibility of a doubt that it is He Who has become all!" Mere saying is not enough. By the Lord's grace the spirit must be quickened. Spiritual awakening is followed by Samadhi. In this state one forgets that one has a body; one loses all attachment to the things of the world, *i.e.*, 'woman and gold'; one likes no other words than those relating to God; one is sorely troubled if called upon to listen to worldly matters. The spirit within being awakened, the next step is the realisation of the Universal Spirit. It is the spirit that can realise the Spirit.

1002.* Many years ago Vaishnavacharan told me that one attains perfect Knowledge only when one sees God in man. Now I see that it is He Who is moving about in different forms, now as an honest man, now as a cheat and again as a villain. So I say, "Narayana in the form of an honest man, Narayana in the form of a swindler, Narayana in the form of a villain, Narayana in the form of a lewd person." Now the problem is how I can entertain all. I wish to feed everyone. Therefore I keep one at a time with me and entertain him.

1003. When I look on a woman of character belonging to a respectable family, I see in her the Divine Mother arrayed in the modest garb of a chaste lady; and again when I look upon the public women of the city, sitting in their open verandahs arrayed in the garb of immodesty and shamelessness, I see in them the same Divine Mother sporting in a different way.

1004. In God there are both Vidya and Avidya. The Vidya Maya takes man towards God, whereas the Avidya Maya entices him away from the path of the Lord. Knowledge, devotion, dispassion, compassion—all these are the expressions of the Vidya Maya; only with their help can one reach God.

But if you ascend one step higher, you attain Brahmajnana. In this state I feel—I actually see—that He has become all. There is nothing to reject or to accept! It becomes impossible for me to get angry with anybody.

Once while going in a carriage, I happened to see two courtesans standing on a balcony. But I actually saw in them the Divine Mother, and made salutations.

When this state (of consciousness) dawned in me, I could not worship or offer anything to the Mother Kali (at the Dakshineswar Temple). At that, the temple manager began to abuse me. But I only laughed at his abuse without feeling offended in the least.

1005.* Describing a vision, which revealed to him, the real nature of the world, the Master said: "Do you know what I saw now? A Divine vision—the vision of the Divine Mother! She appeared with a child in the womb, which She brought forth and swallowed up the next instant. And as much of it as went into Her mouth became void! She showed me that all is Void. And She said as it were, 'Come confusion! come confusion!'"

THE MASTER ON HIS ILLNESS

1006. Pandit Sasadhar, seeing the Master ill,[1] asked him: "Why do you not concentrate your mind upon the diseased part and thus cure yourself?"

The Master: How can I fix my mind, which I have dedicated to God, upon this wretched cage of flesh and blood?

Sasadhar: Why do you not pray to the Divine Mother for the cure of your illness?

The Master: When I think of my Mother, the physical body vanishes, and I am entirely out of it. So it is impossible for me to pray for anything concerning the body.

1007. When the Master was badly ill, and could even hardly speak or swallow any food, he exclaimed: "I am now speaking and eating through so many mouths. I am the Soul of all the souls, I have infinite mouths. I am the

[1] In his last days he was suffering from the cancer of the throat.

Infinite Spirit covered by a human skin which has a wound somewhere in the throat: When the body is ill, that illness reacts upon the mind. When one is scalded by hot water one says, 'This water has injured me,' but in truth what injures is the heat, and not the water. All pain is in the body, all disease is in the body, but the Spirit is above pain and is beyond the reach of disease."

1008.* I told the Mother that on account of this (pointing to his diseased throat) I could not swallow anything, and prayed to Her that I might be enabled to eat a little food. But the Mother, pointing to you all, said, "Why? Here you are eating with so many mouths!" I was utterly abashed and I could not speak a word more.

1009. The Mother has brought this illness on me in order to teach man how to think of the Spirit and how to live in God-consciousness, even when there is extreme pain in the body. When the body is suffering from excruciating pain and starvation, and when it is beyond all human power to give any relief, even then the Mother shows me that Spirit is the master of the body. My Divine Mother has brought this illness upon this body to convince the sceptics that the Atman is divine, that God-consciousness is true, that when one reaches perfection, freedom from all bondages is attained.

1010.* When, during his last illness, the Master was earnestly requested by his disciples to pray to the Lord to cure his illness and retain his body in the world for sometime more, at least for their sake he said: "Well, nothing comes of my speaking to the Lord about it. His will be done. I now see that my Divine Mother and I have become one, once for all. Radha said to Krishna, 'O beloved, abide Thou within my heart, and appear not any longer in Thy human form.' But She soon yearned to see Krishna in human form. Her heart struggled and panted for the Beloved. But the Lord's will must be done, and Krishna did not appear in human form for a long time."

THE MASTER, A COMBINATION OF HUMANITY AND DIVINITY

1011.* Indeed, there are three words which prick me to the core: (1) Guru (spiritual preceptor), (2) Karta (doer of action), and (3) Baba (father). God is the only Guru. My Divine Mother is the sole doer of actions, I am only an instrument in Her hands. I feel myself always to be Her child.

1012.* About his meeting with a celebrated Pandit, the Master said: "When I heard that the Pandit was coming to see me, I got frightened. For I am not even conscious of the cloth I am wearing. I had no idea of what I should reply when he talked with me. To the Mother I said: 'Apart from Thee I do not know anything—these scriptures and other matters.' So I told the people here: 'You all sit here. I shall feel encouraged by your presence.' When the Pandit actually came, I still continued to have a little fear. I sat quiet, gazing at him and listening to him. Just then I saw the Mother revealing to me the whole of the Pandit's mind. What is the good of reading the scriptures if one has no discrimination and dispassion? There (pointing to his own body) I felt something creeping up to the head. All my fear was gone and I ceased to be conscious of myself. I raised my face, and words began to flow from my mouth. I felt as if somebody was replenishing my thoughts as they were spoken out. At Kamarpukur when people measured grain, one person would be pushing the grain forward as another measured it. It was like that. I myself did not know what all I spoke. When I regained my external consciousness a little, I saw the Pandit weeping and his body wet with tears. I experienced such states now and then. Keshab sent me word that he would take me on a cruise along the Ganges, and that a European missionary and tourist named Mr. Cook would be accompanying us. Hearing this, I began to go to the casuarina tree again and again (*i.e*, answer the calls of Nature out of nervousness). Afterwards they came, and I got into the steamer. Soon a change came over me. What all did I say then! All these people (pointing to the devotees) said that I gave excellent instructions. But I knew nothing about that."

1013.* The one who is within me is doing all this through me. At times I used to get the mood of Godhood —I would never be pacified unless worshipped. I am the instrument and He is the wielder. I do as He makes me do, I speak as He makes me speak.

1014.* Girish Chandra Ghosh, even after having given his 'power-of-attorney'[1] to the Master, felt restless thinking over the power of the evil tendencies acquired by him in his past life. At this the Master said: "You fellow, is it a water snake that has caught you? No, it is a poisonous

[1] This is a term which the Master was wont to use to express complete self-surrender.

one. Even if you go home running, you will have to die. Don't you see that? When a water snake catches a frog, it dies only after croaking many times. Sometimes it may escape, too. But if it is a poisonous snake, the frog dies with one or two croaks. Even if it escapes, it hops a short distance and dies in its hole. The same is the case with one who has come here."

1015.* One day, while a disciple was shampooing his feet, the Master said referring to this act of service, "This has a deep significance." Then placing his hand on his own heart, he said, "If there is anything (Divine) in it, then (by this act of service) ignorance and Avidya will vanish once for all." And then he added with a serious look: "There is no outsider here. That day I had a vision. Harish was near me then. I saw Sachchidananda coming out of the sheath (*i.e.*, his body). Having come out He said: 'I incarnate in every age.' I thought I was delirious. So I kept quiet. Then I heard that He was even saying: 'Even Chaitanya worshipped Sakti.'"

1016.* During his illness the Master said to his devotees one day: "Here (*i.e.*, within himself) there are two persons. One is the Divine Mother—the other person is Her devotee. It is the latter who is now taken ill . . . The Lord comes with His disciples as a Divine Incarnation. He takes a human body. His disciples go back with Him to the Divine Mother. A band of Bauls (singing mendicants) comes into a house all on a sudden. They chant the 'name' of the Lord and dance with joy. That done, they leave the house at once. As abrupt in going as in coming! And the people know them not!"

1017. I realise that the three are of the same substance—the block for sacrifice, the victim to be sacrificed, and he who immolates the victim of the sacrifice.

1018.* In his last days, while lying seriously ill, the Master asked Narendra: "Well, what do you think is the nature of my feelings?"

Narendra: Why, Sir, you are everything! A hero who has cut his way to the Reality with the sword of discrimination and with a strength which the world cannot give! You have the feeling of a Sakhi (lady friend) too—Love unspeakable, the ecstasy of Divine love which is called up by the Divine Lover alone. You are a hero, Sakhi and everything else in your yearning for the Lord.

The Master had all his feelings stirred up. He laid his hands upon the heart and said, addressing Narendra and other disciples: "I see—I realise—that all things, every conceivable thing—comes out of this!"

1019.* A couple of days before the Master's passing away, when six months of suffering from the dreadful disease of cancer in the throat had already reduced him to a mere skeleton, Narendra, the disciple (the future Swami Vivekananda), felt a curious inclination to test the Master's oft-repeated assertion of his being an Incarnation. So he said to himself: "If in the midst of this dreadful physical pain he can declare his Godhead, then I shall believe him to be true." Strange to say, the moment this thought flashed in his mind, the Master summoned all his energy and said distinctly: "He who was Rama and Krishna is now Ramakrishna in this body—but not in your Vedantic sense."

BOOK IV

MAXIMS AND PARABLES

He Who is our protector, Who is the generator and sustainer of ourselves and of all things existing, Who knows all forms in this universe as His abode, Who created the Gods and allotted to them their respective duties—it is of Him, the One, that all other beings go about enquiring, "Who is the Supreme Lord?"

O men, you do not know Him Who has brought into existence all this. He dwells hidden within you, transcending even your sense of selfhood. Not knowing Him due to ignorance, which covers your insight like a mist, you spend your lives in false notions of your real self, pursuing physical satisfactions and performing rituals that bestow enjoyments in heavens hereafter.

Rig Veda

CHAPTER XXI

SOME MAXIMS

[*Maxims of ethical significance—Maxims of spiritual significance*]

MAXIMS OF ETHICAL SIGNIFICANCE

1020. The washerman keeps a large store of unwashed clothes in his house, but these are not his. As soon as the clothes are washed, his room becomes empty. Men having no original thoughts of their own are like the washerman. Be not a washerman in your thoughts.

1021. Do yourself what you wish others to do.

1022. Man becomes small by begging. Even the Lord Himself had to assume the form of a dwarf (Vamana) when he went to Bali for begging. By this example we learn that we demean ourselves, the moment we beg something from anybody.

1023. Men are quick to praise and quick to blame; so pay no heed to what others speak of you.

1024. In living your life of peace and virtue, be indifferent alike to the praise and censure of mankind.

1025. There are certain beings with whom one should be careful. First, rich men. They have money, men and great influence. They can injure you if they like. You will have to deal with them very carefully; perhaps you will have to nod to all that they say. Secondly, the dog. When it attacks or barks, you must stop and pacify it by whistling. Thirdly, the bull. When it attempts to gore you, it should be calmed by making some sounds. Fourthly, the drunkard. If you excite him, he will abuse you in all sorts of filthy language. But if you accost him endearingly, "Well, uncle, how are you getting on?"—he will be immensely pleased with you and he will come and smoke with you.

1026. The man who has eaten radish has eructations with the smell of radish, and he who eats cucumber emits its smell in his belching; in the same way the mouth speaks out sometimes what the heart conceives within.

1027. One develops various propensities according to the company one moves in; and again one seeks the company congenial to one's propensities.

1028. There are some who have the nature of a serpent. You never know when they will bite you. You have to struggle hard to counteract their poison. Otherwise you will be so enraged as to feel the passion of revenge (against them).

1029. Anger is a sign of Tamas. In anger man loses all discrimination. Hanuman set fire to Lanka, but he had not the sense then to apprehend that it might burn even the place where Sita was staying.

1030. "Gurus can be had by hundreds and thousands, but of Chelas (disciples) there is not one" is an ancient saying. It means that many are the persons who can give good advice, but those who follow it are few.

1031. Why do religions degenerate? Rain water is pure, but by the time it reaches earth it gets dirty owing to the medium it passes through. If the roofs and the pipes and the channels are all dirty, the water discharged through them must also be dirty. (So religion gets defiled by the medium through which it manifests.)

1032. Sin and mercury are hard to digest.

1033. When visiting a sage or going to a temple, you should never go empty-handed. You have to take something, however trifling, in your hand as an offering.

1034. As thieves cannot enter a house if its inmates are wide awake, so if you are always on your guard, no evil thought will enter your mind to rob it of its goodness.

1035. Maya is the attachment towards one's own relatives such as father, mother, brother, sister, wife, children and cousin. And the love that flows for all creatures equally is called Daya.

1036. As long as I live, so long do I learn.

1037. As long as you live, learn every day of the mysteries of Love and devotion. It will be always to your advantage.

1038. Bow your head where others are bowing. Veneration never goes unrewarded.

1039.* Remain always strong and steadfast in your own faith, but eschew all bigotry and intolerance.

1040. Bharata, Prahlada, Sukadeva, Vibhishana, Parasurama, Bali, and the Gopis of Brindavan—these persons disobeyed their superiors for the sake of God.

1041.* The best course for you is to renounce desire and to work unattached.

MAXIMS OF SPIRITUAL SIGNIFICANCE

1042. Heaven sometimes speaks through the mouths of lunatics, drunkards and children.

1043. The devil never enters the house wherein songs in praise of Hari are always sung.

1044. Hallowed are they who live on the banks of the Ganges.

1045. The Ganges-water is not to be regarded as water; nor the dust of Sri Brindavana as dust! nor the Mahaprasada of Sri Sri Jagannatha Deva as rice. These three are objective manifestations of the Supreme Being.

1046. If it pleases the Lord, He can even pass an elephant through the eye of a needle. He can do whatever He likes.

1047. His steps falter not, who has taken refuge in Him.

1048. Hari means He who steals (Harati) our hearts; and Haribal means Hari is our strength.

1049. Unless the spirit in man gets awakened, he cannot know God.

1050.* Take refuge in God and forsake shame and fear. "If I were to dance in the name of God, what would people say?"—cast off all such ideas.

1051.* To someone the Master said: "Well, you have come to seek God now, after spending the greater part of your life in the world. Had you entered the world after realising God, what peace and joy you would have found!"

1052.* If you have faith, you will attain to that for which you long.

1053. First, the realisation of God, and then His creation. Valmiki was given the Mantra 'Rama' to meditate upon, but was instructed to begin repeating it reversely 'Mara' 'Mara'—that is, Ma, or Isvara, and Ra, or Jagat,—first God and then the universe.

1054. It is absurd to speak of harm from excessive absorption in God. The rays of a diamond illumine and soothe but never burn.

1055. Try to know the Nitya through the Lila.

1056. Betake yourself to Chit (Pure Consciousness) to realise the Sat (Pure Existence).

1057. The Eternal is to be reached by means of the non-eternal, the Real through the help of the unreal, and the noumenon through the help of the phenomenon.

1058. His name is Intelligence (Chinmaya): His abode is Intelligence; and He, the Lord, is All-Intelligence.

CHAPTER XXII

PARABLES

[*The bane of worldliness—Sex and its bondage—Spiritual progress depends on mind—Dangers of misunderstood philosophy—The foolishness of fanaticism—Faith, devotion and resignation—Yoga and Vairagya—Nature of Maya—Realisation of the Divine*]

THE BANE OF WORLDLINESS

1059.* God is like the wish-yielding tree of the celestial world (Kalpataru), which gives whatever one asks of it. So one should be careful to give up all worldly desires when one's mind has been purified by religious exercises. Just hear a story. A certain traveller came to a large plain in the course of his travels. As he had been walking in the sun for many hours, he was thoroughly exhausted and heavily perspiring; so he sat down in the shade of a tree to rest a little. Presently he began to think what a comfort it would be if he could but get a soft bed there to sleep on. He was not aware that he was sitting under the celestial tree. As soon as the above thought rose in his mind, he found a nice bed by his side. He felt much astonished, but all the same stretched himself on it. Now he thought to himself how pleasant it would be were a young damsel to come there and gently stroke his legs. No sooner did the thought arise in his mind than he found a young damsel sitting at his feet and stroking his legs. The traveller felt supremely happy. Presently he felt hungry and thought: "I have got whatever I have wished for; could I not then get some food?" Instantly he found various kinds of delicious food spread before him. He at once fell to eating, and having helped himself to his heart's content, stretched himself again on his bed. He now began to revolve in his mind the events of the day. While thus occupied, he thought, "If a tiger should attack me all of a sudden!" In an instant a large tiger jumped upon him and broke his neck and began to drink his blood. In this way the traveller lost his life. Such is the fate of men in general. If during your meditation you pray for men or money or worldly honours, your desires will no doubt be satisfied to some extent; but, mind you, there is the dread of the tiger behind the gifts you get. Those tigers—disease, bereavements, loss of honour and wealth, etc.,—are a thousand times more terrible than the live tiger.

1060. A group of fisher-women, who were on their way home from a distant market held on an afternoon, were overtaken by a heavy hail-storm at nightfall, and were compelled to take shelter in a florist's cottage near by. Their kindly host allowed them to sleep that night in a room where he had kept some baskets of sweet-smelling flowers for supplying his customers on the morrow. The atmosphere of the room, filled with the fragrance of flowers, was too good for the fisher-women, and they could not, therefore, get even a wink of sleep. At last one of them suggested a remedy. "Let us sprinkle," she said, "a little water on our empty fish-baskets and place them close to us. That would keep this troublesome smell of flowers from spoiling our sleep." Every one gladly agreed to the proposal and did accordingly; and soon all began to snore. Such, indeed, is the power and influence of habit! The worldly soul, brought up in, and accustomed to materialistic thoughts and surroundings, cannot breathe long in an atmosphere of purity and renunciation without feeling restlessness and discomfort.

1061. Once a sage was lying by the roadside deeply immersed in Samadhi. A thief, while passing by that way, saw him and thought: "This fellow here must be a thief. He must have broken into some houses last night, and is now sleeping through exhaustion. The police will be very soon here to catch him. So let me escape in time." Thus cogitating, he ran away. Soon after a drunkard came there, and seeing the sage, said, "Halloa! you have fallen into the ditch by drinking too much. Eh! I am steadier than yourself and am not going to tumble down." Last of all there came a sage, and realising that a great saint was lying in the state of Samadhi, sat down by his side and began to press his holy feet gently. (Thus do our worldly tendencies prevent us from recognising true holiness and piety.)

1062. With regard to the priestly class, Sri Ramakrishna used to tell an incident from the life of Gauranga. When Sri Gauranga, being wholly self-absorbed in Bhava Samadhi, fell into the ocean, he was hauled up in a net by the fishermen; but as they came into contact with his sacred person through the net, they too were thrown into a trance. Abandoning all their work, they roamed about like maniacs simply chanting the sacred name of Hari. Their relatives could not cure the malady by any means, and finding no other remedy, they came at last to Sri Gauranga and told him about their sorrow. Sri Gauranga then said to them, "Get some rice from a priest's house and put it into their mouth, and you will see them cured." They did accordingly, and the fishermen lost their blissful ecstasy. (Such is the contaminating influence of worldliness, and impurity on spiritual growth.)

1063. The steward of a certain rich man was left in charge of his master's property. When asked by someone as to whose property it was, he used to say: "Sir, this is all my property; these houses and these gardens are all mine." He would speak in this strain and go about with an air of vanity. One day he happened to catch fish in a pond of his master's garden-house in contravention of his strict prohibition. As ill-luck would have it, the master came upon the scene just then, and saw what his dishonest steward was doing. Finding out the faithlessness of his servant, the master at once drove him away from his estate, disgraced and dishonoured, and confiscated all his past earnings. The poor fellow could not take with him even his rickety box of utensils which was his sole private property. Such is the punishment that overtakes false pride.

1064. A barber, who was passing under a haunted tree, heard a voice say, "Will you accept seven jars full of gold?" The barber looked around, but could see no one.

The offer of seven jars of gold, however, roused his cupidity, and he cried aloud, "Yes, I shall accept the seven jars." At once came the reply. "Go home, I have carried the jars to your house." The barber ran home in hot haste to verify the truth of this strange announcement. And when he entered the house, he saw the jars before him. He opened them and found them all full of gold, except the last one which was only half-full. A strong desire now arose in the mind of the barber to the seventh jar also; for without it his happiness was incomplete. He therefore converted all his ornaments into gold coins and put them into the jar; but the mysterious vessel was as before, unfilled. This exasperated the barber. Starving himself and his family, he saved some amount more and tried to fill the jar; but the jar remained as before. So one day he humbly requested the king to increase his pay, as his income was not sufficient to maintain himself. Now the barber was a favourite of the king, and as soon as the request was made the king doubled his pay. All this pay he saved and put into the jar, but the greedy jar showed no signs of filling. At last he began to live by begging from door to door, and his professional income and the income from begging all went into the insatiable cavity of the mysterious jar. Months passed, and the condition of the miserable and miserly barber grew worse every day. Seeing his sad plight, the king asked him one day, "Halloa! When your pay was half of what you now get, you were happy, cheerful and contended; but with double that pay, I see you morose, care-worn and dejected. What is the matter with you? Have you got 'the seven jars'?"

The barber was taken aback by this question and replied, "Your Majesty, who has informed you of this?" The king said, "Don't you know that these are the signs of the person to whom the Yaksha consigns the seven jars. He offered me also the same jars, but I asked him whether this money might be spent or was merely to be hoarded. No sooner had I asked this question than the Yaksha ran away without any reply. Don't you know that no one can spend that money? It only brings with it the desire of hoarding. Go at once and return the money." The barber was brought to his senses by this advice, and he went to the haunted tree and said, "Take back your gold, O Yaksha." The Yaksha replied, "All right." When the barber returned home, he found that the seven jars had vanished as mysteriously as they were brought in, and with it also had vanished his life-long savings. Such is the state of some men in the Kingdom of Heaven. Those who do not understand the difference between what is real expenditure and what is real income, lose all they have.

1065. Once in the month of June a kid was playing near its mother. With a merry frisk it told her that it intended to make a good feast of Ras-flowers (a species of flowers budding abundantly during the festival of Rasa-lila in November). "Well, my darling," replied the dam, "it is not such an easy thing as you seem to think. You will have to pass through many a danger before you can hope to feast on Ras-flowers. The ensuing months of September and October are not very auspicious to you? For someone may take you to be sacrificed to the Goddess

Durga. Then there is the terrible time of Kali-puja; and if you are fortunate enough to survive that period also, there is still the Jagaddhatri-puja when almost all that remain of the male members of our species are sacrificed. If your good luck carries you safely through all these crises, then you can hope to make a feast of Ras-flowers in the beginning of November." Like the dam in the fable, we should not hastily approve of all the aspirations which our youthful fancies may entertain, considering the manifold crises which we may have to pass through in our lives.

SEX AND ITS BONDAGE

1066. A gentleman of modern education was once arguing with the master that it was possible for family men to remain uncontaminated by worldliness. To him the Master said, "Do you know of what sort is your so-called 'uncontaminated family man' of the present day? Being uncontaminated by the world, and therefore having no concern in money matters, his finances and all his household affairs are managed by his wife. So if a poor Brahmin comes to beg of this 'master of the house', he tells him, "Sir, I never touch money. Why do you waste your time in begging of me?" If the Brahmin, however, be an importunate fellow, your uncontaminated family man, being tired of his entreaties, thinks that the man must be paid something, and tells him "Well, sir, come to-morrow. I shall see what I can do for you." Then going in, this exemplary family man tells his wife, "Look here, my dear, a poor Brahmin is in great distress. Let us give him a rupee." Hearing the word 'rupee', the wife flares up with anger and says tauntingly, "Ah, what a generous man you are! Rupees are to you like leaves and stones to be thrown away without the least thought." "Well, my dear," replies the master of the house in an apologetic tone, "the Brahmin is very poor, and we should not give him less." "No," says the wife, "I cannot spare that much. Here is a two-anna bit; you may give him that, if you like." But as the Babu is a family man quite uncontaminated by worldliness, he takes, of course, what his wife gives him, and next day the beggar gets only the two-anna piece. So you see, your so-called uncontaminated family men are not really masters of themselves. Because they themselves do not look after the family affairs, they think that they are very good and holy men, while, as a matter of fact, they are hen-pecked husbands guided entirely by their wives, and so are but very poor specimens even of common humanity."

1067. In former days, the priests of the temple of Govindaji in Jaypur never married. Then they were supremely puissant with the strength of the Self. Once the king sent for them, but they did not go. They said, "Ask the king to come to us." But afterwards they began to marry and then there was no necessity for the king to send for them! They of their own accord would go to the king and say, "Maharaj, Maharaj, we have come to bless you. Here we have brought the offered flowers from the shrine for you. Please accept them." For they were now compelled to do so. What could the poor fellows do? One day they had to build their houses; another day they had to perform the Annaprasana ceremony (giving the first morsel of cooked rice to a child) of their sons, still another day they had to marry their daughters, and so on. All these kept them in constant need of money !

You can see for yourself what you have become by serving under others. Those of you young men who are quite learned in English and educated after the Western model, silently put up with the kicks of their masters ! Do you know what is at the back of all these humiliations and pangs of thraldom ? It is 'woman'—subjection to the attractions of sex.

1068. A poor man was in great distress for want of employment. He went several times to an office and danced attendance on the Bara Babu (head-clerk or manager) of the place, but was always sent back with such evasive answers as, "Not to-day, come tomorrow," "Come and see me now and then," and so on. The poor man spent much time in this way. One day he spoke about his lot to one of his friends. The friend at once said, "How thoughtless you are Why have you worn away the soles of your feet by going to that fellow ? Go to Golap and supplicate her, and believe me, you will get an appointment to-morrow." In great surprise the poor man exclaimed, "Is it so ! Just now I shall run up to her." Golap was the mistress of the manager of the office. The poor man went to her and said, "Mother, I am in great distress, and none but you can save me from it. I am a Brahmin and have no other means. I have been without any employment for a long time, and my wife and children are starving. I can get a job if you say only a word."

Then Golap said, "Yes, but on saying to whom can it be managed?" And she thought compassionately, "Ah, what a pity that the Brahmin is in such a plight!" The poor man at once said, "If you say one word to the Bara Babu on my behalf, I am sure to get a job." Then Golap promised to ask the Bara Babu that very night to give him a job, and lo! the next morning a peon came to the poor man from the Bara Babu requesting him to attend his office from that day. The Bara Babu recommended the man to the chief officer with the words, "Sir, this gentleman has very high qualifications, and thinking that it would greatly benefit our office to have his services, I have given him a place here." Such is the charm that woman weaves upon man. The whole world is mad after 'woman and gold.'

1069. A poor Brahmin had a rich cloth merchant as his disciple. The merchant was very miserly by nature. One day the Brahmin was in need of a small piece of cloth for covering his sacred book. He went to his disciple and asked for the required piece of cloth; but the merchant replied, "I am very sorry, Sir. Had you told me of this a few hours earlier, I would have given you the thing wanted. Unfortunately, now I have no small piece of cloth which will answer your purpose. However, I shall remember your requirement, but please remind me of it now and then." The Brahmin had to go away disappointed. This conversation between the Guru and his worthy disciple was overheard by the wife of the latter from behind a screen. She at once sent a man after the Brahmin, and calling him inside the house, said, "Revered Father, what is it that you were asking from the master of the house?" The Brahmin related all that had happened. The wife said, "Please go home, Sir. You will get the cloth to-morrow morning." When the merchant returned home at night, the wife asked him, "Have you closed the shop?" The merchant said, "Yes, what is the matter?" She said, "Go at once and bring two clothes of the best quality in the shop." He said, "Why this hurry? I shall give you the very best clothes to-morrow morning." The wife, however, insisted, "No, I must have them just now, or not at all." What could the poor merchant do? The person whom he had now to deal with was not the spiritual Guru whom he could send away with vague and indefinite promises, but the 'curtain Guru' whose behests must be instantaneously obeyed, or else there would be no peace for him at home. At last the merchant, willingly enough, opened the shop, at that late hour of the night, and brought the cloths for her. Early next morning, the good lady sent the article to the Guru with the message, "If in future you want anything from us, ask me, and you will get it. (Therefore those who pray to the merciful Divine Mother and ask for Her blessings have better chances of having their prayers heard than those who worship God in the sterner paternal aspect).

1070. When asked why he did not lead the life of a householder with his wife, the Master replied: "Kartikeya (son of Siva) one day happened to scratch a cat with his nail. On going home, he saw that there was a mark of the scratch on the cheek of his divine mother, Parvati. Seeing this he asked her, 'Mother, how did you get this ugly scar on your cheek? The Mother of the universe replied, 'This is the work of your hand; it is the scratch of your nail.' Kartikeya asked in wonder, 'How is it, Mother? I do not remember to have scratched you at any time.' The Mother replied, 'Darling, have you forgotten the fact of your having scratched a cat, this morning?' Kartikeya said, 'Yes, I did scratch a cat, but how did your cheek get the scar?' The Mother replied, 'Dear child, nothing exists in this world but myself. The whole creation is myself; whomsoever you may hurt, you only hurt me.' Kartikeya was greatly surprised to hear this; and then he determined never to marry. For whom could he marry? Every woman was mother to him. Realising thus the motherhood of woman, he gave up marriage. I am like Kartiyeka. I consider every woman as my Divine Mother."

SPIRITUAL PROGRESS DEPENDS ON MIND

1071. The spiritual gain of a person depends upon his mental condition and thought—life. It proceeds from his heart, and not from any of his external actions. Two friends, while strolling about, happened to pass by a place where the Bhagavata was being expounded. One of them said, "Well, let us go there for a while and hear the holy scripture." The other replied, "No, my dear friend, what is the use of hearing the Bhagavata? Let us spend the time in yonder brothel in amusement and pleasure." The first one did not consent to this proposal. He went to the place where the Bhagavata was being read and sat down to hear it. The other went to the brothel but did not find the pleasure which he had anticipated there. So he was thinking within himself, "Ah me! Why have I come here? How happy must my friend be to be hearing all the while an account of the sacred deeds of Lord Hari." Thus he meditated on Hari even though he was in an unholy place. The other man also, who was hearing the exposition of the Bhagavata, did not find pleasure in it. Sitting there he began to blame himself, saying, 'Ah! What a fool I was to have not accompanied my friend to the brothel! What great pleasure he must be having at this time there!" The result was that he was merely sitting where the Bhagavata was being read, while all the time his mind was dreaming of the pleasures he might have enjoyed in the bawdy-house. Now as his mind was blackened with these thoughts, he got all the sin of visiting the brothel, although he did not go there in person. And the man who had gone to the brothel acquired all the merit of hearing the Bhagavata, because his mind was meditating on the sacred book even though he was in that bad place.

1072. A Sannyasin dwelt by the side of a temple. There was the house of a harlot in front. Seeing the constant concourse of men in the prostitute's house, the Sannyasin one day called her and censured her saying, "You are a great sinner. You sin day and night. Oh, how miserable will be your lot hereafter!" The poor prostitute became extremely sorry for her misdeeds, and with genuine inward repentance she prayed to God beseeching forgiveness. But as prostitution was her profession, she could not easily adopt any other means of gaining her livelihood. And so, whenever her flesh sinned, she always reproached herself with greater contrition of heart and prayed to God more and more for forgiveness. The Sannyasin saw that his advice had apparently produced no effect upon her, and thought, "Let me see how many persons will visit this woman in the course of her life." And from that day forward, whenever any person entered the house of the prostitute, the Sannyasin counted him by putting a pebble for him, and so in course of time there arose a big heap of pebbles. One day the Sannyasin said to the prostitute, pointing to the heap, "Woman, don't you see this heap? Each pebble in it stands for every commission of the deadly sin you have been indulging in since I advised you last to desist from the evil course. Even now I tell you, 'Beware of your evil deeds!'" The poor wretch began to tremble at the sight of the accumulation of her sins, and she prayed to God shedding tears of utter helplessness, and inwardly repeating: "Lord wilt Thou not free me from the miserable life that I am leading?" The prayer was heard, and on that very day the angel of death passed by her house, and she ceased to exist in this world. By the strange will of God, the Sannyasin also died on the same day. The messengers of Vishnu came down from Heaven and carried the spirit body of the contrite prostitute to the heavenly regions, while the messengers of Yama bound the spirit of the Sannyasin and carried him down to the nether world. The Sannyasin, seeing the good-luck of the prostitute, cried aloud, "Is this the subtle justice of God? I passed all my life in asceticism and poverty, and I am carried to hell, while that prostitute, whose life was a whole record of sin, is going to Heaven!" Hearing this, the messengers of

Vishnu said, "The decrees of God are always just; as you think, so you reap. You passed your life in external show and vanity, trying to get honour and fame; and God has given you this. Your heart never sincerely yearned after Him. This prostitute earnestly prayed to God day and night, though her body sinned all the while. Look at the treatment which your body and her body are receiving from those below. As you never sinned with your body, they have decorated it with flowers and garlands, and are carrying it with music in a procession to consign it to the sacred river. But this prostitute's body, which had sinned, is being torn to pieces at this moment by vultures and jackals. Nevertheless, she was pure in heart and is therefore going to the regions of the pure. Your heart was always absorbed in contemplating her sins and thus became impure. You are therefore going to the regions of the impure. You were the real prostitute, and not she."

DANGERS OF MISUNDERSTOOD PHILOSOPHY

1073. A Rajah was once taught by his Guru the sacred doctrine of Advaita, which declares that the whole universe is Brahman. The king was very much pleased with this doctrine. Going in, he said to his queen, "There is no distinction between the queen and the queen's maid-servant. So the maid-servant shall be my queen henceforth." The queen was thunderstruck at this mad proposal of her lord. She sent for the Guru and complained to him in a piteous tone, "Sir, look at the pernicious result of your teachings," and told him what had occurred. The Guru consoled the queen and said, "When you serve dinner to the king today, have a potful of cow-dung also served along with the dish of rice." At dinner-time the Guru and the king sat down together to eat. Who could imagine the rage of the king when he saw a dish of cow-dung served for his meal! The Guru, seeing this, calmly interrogated, "Your Highness, you are well-versed in the knowledge of Advaita. Why do you then see any distinction between the dung and the rice?" The king became exasperated and exclaimed, "You who pride yourself to be such a great Advaitin, eat this dung if you can." The Guru said, "Very well," and at once changed himself into a swine and devoured the cow-dung with great gusto and afterwards again assumed his human shape. The king became so ashamed that he never made again his mad proposal to the queen.

1074. A Brahmin was laying out a garden. He looked after it day and night. One day a cow strayed into the garden and browsed on a mango sapling of which the Brahmin used to take special care. When he saw the cow destroying his favourite plant, the Brahmin became wild with rage, and gave such a severe beating to the animal that it died of the injuries received. The news soon spread like wild-fire that the Brahmin had killed the sacred animal. When any one attributed the sin of that act to him, the Brahmin, who professed himself to be a Vedantin, denied the charge, saying, "No, I have not killed the cow; it is my hand that has done it; and as God Indra is the presiding deity of the hand, it is he who has incurred the sin of killing the cow, not I." Indra in his heaven heard of this. He assumed the shape of an old Brahmin, and coming to the owner of the garden, said, "Sir, whose Garden is this?

Brahmin: Mine.

Indra: It is a beautiful garden. You have got a skilful gardener; for see how neatly and artistically he has planted the trees.

Brahmin: Well, sir, that is also my work. The trees were planted under my personal supervision and direction.

Indra: Very nicely done, indeed! Who has laid out this path? It is very well-planned and neatly executed.

Brahmin: All that has been done by me.

Then Indra said with folded hands, "When all these things are yours, and when you take credit for all the work done in this garden, it is not proper that poor Indra should be made responsible for killing the cow."

1075. A serpent dwelt in a certain locality. No one dared to pass by that way; for whoever did so was instantaneously bitten to death by that serpent. Once a holy man passed by. As usual the serpent pursued the sage with a view to bite him, but when it approached the holy man, it lost all its ferocity and was over-powered by his gentleness. Seeing the snake, the holy man said, "Well, friend, do you want to bite me?" The snake was abashed and made no reply. At this the sage said again, "Hearken, friend, do not injure any one in future." The snake bowed and nodded assent. After the sage had gone his own way, the snake entered its hole, and thenceforth began to live a life of innocence and purity without even wishing to harm anyone. In a few days it became a common belief in the neighbourhood that the snake had lost all its venom and was no more dangerous, and so people began to tease it. Some pelted stones at it, and others dragged it mercilessly by the tail. Thus there was no end to its troubles. Fortunately, sometime after, the sage again passed that way, and seeing the bruised and battered condition of the poor snake, was very much moved to pity and inquired the cause of its distress. At this the snake replied, "Sir, I have been reduced to this state, because I have not been injuring anyone since I received your instruction. But alas! they are so merciless!" The sage smilingly said, "Dear friend, I simply advised you not to bite anyone, but I never asked you not to hiss and frighten others. Although you should not bite any creature, still you should keep every one at a considerable distance from you by hissing." Similarly, if you live in the world, make yourself feared and respected. Do not injure anyone, but do not at the same time let others injure you.

1076. A teacher once instructed his disciple, "Everything that exists is God." The disciple understood this instruction literally and not in its true spirit. One day, while he was passing through a street, he came across an elephant. The driver (Mahut) shouted aloud from the back of the animal "Move away, move away!" The disciple however, argued within himself, "Why should I move away? I am God and so also is the elephant. What fear has God from Himself." Reflecting thus, he did not move. So the elephant caught hold of him by his trunk and dashed him aside. He was hurt severely, and going back to his teacher, related the whole story. The teacher then said, "All right. You are God, and the elephant too is God; but God in the shape of the elephant-driver was warning you from above. Why did you not pay heed to his warning?"

THE FOOLISHNESS OF FANATICISM

1077. Be not a bigot like Ghantakarna. There was a man who worshipped Siva but hated all the other deities. One day Siva appeared to him and said, "I shall never be pleased with you so long as you hate other Gods." But the man was inexorable. After a few days Siva again appeared to him. This time He appeared as Hari-Hara—a form, of which one half was Siva and the other Vishnu. At this the man was half-pleased and half-displeased. He laid his offerings on the side representing Siva, but nothing on that representing Vishnu. When he offered the burning incense to Siva, his beloved form of the Deity, he was audacious enough to press the nostrils of Vishnu lest he should inhale the fragrance. Then Siva said, "Your bigotry is ineradicable. By assuming this dual aspect, I tried to convince you that all Gods and Goddesses are but the various aspects of the one Being. You have not taken the lesson in good part, and you will have to suffer for your bigotry. Long must you suffer for this." The man went away and retired to a village. He soon developed into a great hater of Vishnu. On coming to know this peculiarity of his, the children of the village began to tease him by uttering the name of Vishnu within his hearing. Vexed by this, the man hung two bells on his ears, and when the boys cried out, "Vishnu, Vishnu," he would ring the bells and make those names inaudible to his ears. And thus he came to be kown by the name of Ghantakarna or the Bell-eared.

1078. Four blind men went out to see an elephant. One touched the leg of the elephant and said, "The elephant is like a pillar." The second touched the trunk and said, "The elephant is like a thick club." The third touched the belly and said, "The elephant is like a big jar." The fourth touched the ears and said, "The elephant is like a big winnowing basket." Thus they began to dispute hotly amongst themselves as to the shape of the elephant. A passer-by, seeing them thus quarrelling, said, "What is it you are disputing about?" They told him everything and asked him to arbitrate. The man said, "None of you has seen the elephant. The elephant is not like a pillar, its legs are like pillars. It is not like a winnowing basket, its ears are like winnowing baskets. It is not like a stout club, its trunk is like a club. The elephant is the combination of all these—legs, ears, belly, trunk and so on." In the same manner, those who quarrel (about the nature of God) have each seen only some one aspect of the Deity.

1079. A frog lived in a well. It had lived there for a long time. It was born and brought up there. And it was a small little frog. One day another frog that had lived in the sea came and fell into that well. The frog of the well asked the new-comer, "Whence are you?" The frog of the sea replied, "I am from the sea." The frog of the well questioned, "The sea! How big is that?" The frog of the sea said, "It is very big." The frog of the well stretched its legs and questioned, "Ah! is your sea so big?" The frog of the sea, "It is much bigger." The frog of the well then took a leap from one side of the well to other, and asked, "Is it as big as this, my well?" "My friend," said the frog of the sea, "how can you compare the sea with your well?" The frog of the well asserted, "No, there can never be anything bigger than my well. Indeed, nothing can be bigger than this! This fellow is a liar, he must be turned out." Such is the case with every narrow-minded man. Sitting in his own little well, he thinks that the whole world is no bigger than his well.

FAITH, DEVOTION AND RESIGNATION

1080. Once a washerman was beating a devotee, severely, and the devotee was crying, "Narayana! Narayana!" Lord Narayana was in Sri Vaikuntha, sitting near Lakshmi. As soon as He heard the cry of the devotee, He got up and proceeded to protect the man. But he returned to His seat after going only a few steps. Seeing this, Lakshmi asked the Lord why He had returned so quickly. Lord Narayana replied, "Because I found no need of my going there. That fellow too has become a Dhobi (washerman). He has begun to protect himself; he is now giving blows in return to the man who has been beating him before. So where is the necessity of my going there?" The Lord saves one, only if one surrenders oneself completely to Him.

1081. Having received no news of her Gopal (Krishna, God incarnate), Yasoda once came to Radha and asked her if she had any news from him. At that time Radha was in a deep trance, and so did not hear Yasoda. Subsequently, when her trance was over, she saw Yasoda, the queen of Nanda, sitting before her. Bowing down to her at once, Radha asked Yasoda the reason of her visit, and when Yasoda stated the reason, she said, "Mother, shut your eyes and meditate upon the form of Gopala, and you will be able to see him." And as soon as Yasoda shut her eyes, Radha, who was herself the very essence of spiritual feelings (Bhava), overwhelmed her with her power, and in that superconscious mood, Yasoda saw her Gopala. Then Yasoda asked this boon of Radha, "Mother, grant me that I may see my beloved Gopala whenever I close my eyes."

1082. Sri Ramachandra, in the course of His travels through the forest, descended into the lake called Pampa for drinking water, leaving His bow and arrow fixed on the ground. Coming up, he found that a frog was lying covered all over with blood, having been run through by His bow. He was very sorry and said to the frog, "Why did you not make some kind of sound? Then I could have known that you were here, and you would not have come to this plight." The frog replied, "O Rama, when I fall into danger, I call on Thee, saying, 'O Rama, save me.' Now that Thou Thyself art killing me, to whom else shall I turn and pray?"

1083. Once a servant of a rich man came to his master's house, and stood in a corner with great reverence and humility. He held in his hand something covered with a cloth. The master enquired, "What is there in your hand?" The servant brought out a small custard-apple from the cloth and kept it humbly before the master, feeling that he would be much gratified if the master would take it. The master was much pleased to see the loving devotion of the servant and accepted the offering, though a trifle. With great delight he exclaimed, "Ah, what a fine fruit is this!

Where did you get it from?" In the same way God looks into the heart of the devotee. He is infinite in his grandeur, yet He is responsive to the influence of love and devotion.

1084. The Master (to Pratap Ch. Mazumdar): You are an educated and intelligent man, and you are a deep thinker too. Keshab and yourself were like the two brothers, Gour and Nitai. You have had enough of this world—enough of lectures, controversies, schisms and the rest. Do you still care for them? Now it is high time for you to collect your scattered mind and turn it towards God. Plunge into the ocean of Divinity.

Mazumdar: Yes, revered Sir, that I ought to do; there is no doubt about it. But all this I do simply to preserve Keshab's name and reputation.

Sri Ramakrishna (smiling): Let me tell you a story. A man built a cottage on a mountain top. It cost him hard labour and much money. After a few days there came a cyclone and the cottage began to rock to and fro. The man, being very anxious to save it, prayed to the Wind-god, saying, "Lord, I beseech Thee, do not destroy this cottage." But the Wind-god did not listen. He prayed again, but the cottage kept on rocking. Then he thought of another plan to save it. He remembered that according to mythology, Hanuman was the son of the Wind-god. So he cried out, "Lord, I beg of Thee, spare this cottage; for it belongs to Hanuman, Thy son." But the Wind-god did not listen. Then he said, "Lord, I pray Thee, spare this cottage, for it belongs to Hanuman's Lord, Rama." Still the Wind-god did not listen. Then, as the cottage began to topple over, the man ran out of it to save his life, and he began to swear saying, "Let this miserable cottage be destroyed. What is it to me?"

You may now be anxious to preserve Keshab's name; but console yourself with the thought that it was after all owing to God's will that the religious movement connected with his name was set on foot, and that if the movement has had its day, it is also due to that same Divine will. Therefore dive deep into the sea of Immortality.

1085. A man went to a Sadhu and said with a great show of humility, "Sir, I am a very low person. Tell me O Master, how I am to be saved." The Sadhu, reading the heart of the man, told him, "Well, go and bring me that which is meaner than yourself." The man went out and looked all round but found nothing whatsoever meaner than himself. At last he saw his own excrement and said, "Well, here is something which is certainly worse than myself." He stretched forth his hand to take it up and carry it to the Sadhu when suddenly he heard a voice say from within the ordure, "Touch me not, O sinner. I was a sweet and delicious cake, fit to be offered to the Gods and in appearance so pleasing to all the spectators. But my ill-fortune brought me to you, and by your evil contact I have been reduced to such a detestable condition that men run away from me with faces turned and with handkerchiefs covering their noses. Once only did I come in contact with you and this has been my fate. What deeper degradation may I not be thrown into if you touch me again?" The man was thus taught true humility, and became the humblest of the humble. As a result he attained the highest perfection.

1086. Once upon a time conceit entered into the heart of Narada, and he thought there was no greater devotee than himself. Reading his heart, the Lord said, "Narada, go to such and such a place. A great devotee of mine is living there. Cultivate his acquaintance; for he is truly devoted to me." Narada went there and found an agriculturist who rose early in the morning, pronounced the name of Hari (God) only once, and taking his plough, went out and tilled the ground all day long. At night, he went to bed after pronouncing the name of Hari once more. Narada said to himself, "How can this rustic be a lover of God? I see him busily engaged in worldly duties, and he has no signs of a pious man about him." Then Narada went back to the Lord and spoke what he thought of his new acquaintance. Thereupon the Lord said, "Narada, take this cup of oil and go round this city and come back with it. But take care that you do not spill even a single drop of it. Narada did as he was told, and on his return the Lord asked him, "Well, Narada, how many times did you remember me in the course of your walk round the city?" "Not once, my Lord," said Narada, "and how could I, when I had to watch this cup brimming over with oil?" The Lord then said, "This one cup of oil did so divert your attention that even you did forget me altogether. But look at that rustic, who, though carrying the heavy burden of a family, still remembers me twice every day."

1087. Once there lived two Yogis who were practising austerities with a view to realise the Lord. One day Narada, the divine sage, was passing by their hermitage, when one of them asked him, "Are you coming from

Heaven?" Narada replied, "Yes, that is so." The Yogi said, "Do tell me what you saw the Lord doing in Heaven." Narada replied, "I saw the Lord playing by making camels and elephants pass through the eye of a needle." At this the Yogi observed, "There is nothing in it to marvel at. Nothing is impossible with God!" But the other man exclaimed, "O nonsense! That is impossible! It only shows that you have never been to the Lord's abode."

The first man was a Bhakta and had the faith of a child. Nothing is impossible to the Lord, nor can any one know His nature fully. Everything can be predicted of Him.

1088. Once the son of a certain man lay at the point of death, and it seemed that none could save his life. A Sadhu, however, said to the father of the dying son, "There is but one hope. If you can get in a human skull the venom of a cobra mixed with a few drops of rain-water under the constellation of the Svati star, your son's life can be saved." The father looked up the almanac and found that the constellation of the Svati would be in the ascendant on the morrow. So he prayed, saying, 'O Lord, do Thou make possible all these conditions, and spare the life of my son." With extreme earnestness and longing in his heart, he set out on the following evening and diligently searched in a deserted spot for a human skull. At last he found one under a tree, and holding it in hand, waited for the rain, praying. Suddenly a shower came, and a few drops of rain were deposited in the upturned skull. The man said to himself, "Now I have the water in the skull under the right constellation." Then he prayed earnestly: "Grant, O Lord, that the rest may also be obtained." In a short time he discovered, not far from there, a toad, and a cobra springing to catch it. In a moment the toad jumped over the skull, followed by the cobra whose venom fell into the skull. With overwhelming gratitude the anxious father cried out, "Lord, by Thy grace even impossible things are made possible. Now I know that my son's life will be saved." Therefore I say, if you have true faith and earnest longing, you will get everything by the grace of the Lord.

1089. Spiritual practices (Sadhanas) are absolutely necessary for Self-realisation, but if there be perfect faith, then a little practice is enough. The sage Vyasa was about to cross the river Jumna. Just then the Gopis arrived at the place where the sage was. They also wanted to cross the river, but there was no ferry-boat. So they asked Vyasa, "Sir, what shall we do?" Vyasa replied, "Do not worry. I will take you across the river. But before that, can you give me something to eat? For I am very hungry. The Gopis had with them a quantity of milk, cream and fresh butter, which they offered him, and he consumed them all. The Gopis then asked, "What about crossing the river?" Vyasa stood near the bank of the water and prayed: "O Jumna, if I have not eaten anything to-day, by that virtue I ask you to part your waters, so that we may walk across your bed and reach the other side." No sooner did he utter these words than the waters parted, and the dry river-bed was laid bare. The Gopis were amazed. They thought: "How could he say, 'If I have not eaten anything to-day,' when he ate so much just now?" They did not understand that this was the proof of Vyasa's firm faith—that he did not eat anything, but the Lord who dwelt within him was the real eater.

1090. There was a certain Brahmin priest who served in a household chapel. Once he went away leaving the charge of the service in the chapel to his little son. He asked the boy to place the daily offering of food before the Deity and see that He ate it. The boy, following the injunctions of his father, placed the offering before the image and silently waited. But the image neither spoke nor ate. The boy watched for a long time. He had the firm faith that the Deity would come down from the altar, take the seat before the offering and eat it. So he prayed, "O Lord, come and eat. It is getting very late, I cannot wait any longer." But the Lord did not speak. Then the boy began to cry saying, "Lord, my father asked me to see that you didst eat the offering. Why dost Thou not come? Thou comest to my father and eatest his offering. What have I done that Thou dost not come to me and partake of my offering?" He cried bitterly for a long time. Then, as he looked up at the seat, he saw the Deity in a human form eating the offering! When the service was ended, and the boy came out, the people in the house said to him, "If the service is over, bring out the offering." The boy replied, "Yes, but the Lord has eaten everything." In amazement they asked, "What do you say?" In absolute innocence the boy repeated, "Why, the Lord has eaten all that I offered." Then they entered the chapel and dumbfounded at the sight of the empty dishes. Such is the power of true faith and true yearning!

1091. Extreme longing is the surest way to God-vision. One should have faith like an innocent child, and a child's longing for its mother.

There was a boy named Jatila. He used to go to school alone through the woods. Often he felt lonely and afraid. He told his mother about it, and she said to him, "Why are you afraid, my child? You call aloud for Krishna when you get frightened." "Who is Krishna, mother?" the boy asked. The mother answered, "Krishna is your brother." After that, when Jatila was passing through the woods alone, and felt frightened, he called aloud, "Brother Krishna!" When no one came, he called again, "O brother Krishna, where are you? Come to me and protect me. I am frightened." Hearing the call of the child, so full of faith, Krishna could no longer remain away. He appeared in the form of a young boy and said, "Here am I, your brother! Why are you frightened? Come, I will take you to school." Then having escorted him to school, Lord Krishna said to him, "I will come to you whenever you call me. Do not be afraid." Such is the power of true faith in the Lord and of real longing for Him.

1092. A milk-maid used to supply milk to a Brahmin priest living on the other side of a river. Owing to the irregularities of the boat service, she could not supply him milk punctually every day. Once, being rebuked for her going late, the poor woman said, "What can I do? I start early from my house, but have to wait for a long time at the river bank for the boatman and the passengers." The priest said, "Woman! they cross the ocean of life by uttering the 'name' of God, and can't you cross this little river?" The simple-hearted woman became very glad at heart on learning this easy means of crossing the river. From the next day the milk was being supplied early in the morning. One day the priest said to the woman, "How is it that you are no longer late now-a-days?" She said, "I cross the river by uttering the name of the Lord as you told me to do, and don't stand now in need of a boatman." The Priest could not believe this and said, "Can you show me how you cross the river?" The woman took him with her and began to walk over the water. Looking behind, the woman saw the priest in a sad plight and said, "How is it, Sir, that you are uttering the name of God with your mouth, but at the same time with your hands you are trying to keep your cloth untouched by water? You do not fully rely on Him." Entire resignation and absolute faith in God are at the root of all miraculous deeds.

1093. Once, finding it difficult to reconcile the contradictory doctrines of man's free will and God's grace, two disciples of the Master went to him for a solution of the same. The Master said, "Why do you talk of free will? Everything is dependent upon the Lord's will. Our will is tied to the Lord's, like the cow to its tether. No doubt we have a certain amount of freedom even as the cow has, within a prescribed circle. So man thinks that his will is free. But know that his will is dependent on the Lord's."

Disciples: Is there then no necessity of practising penance, meditation and the rest? For one can as well sit quiet and say, 'It is all God's will; whatever is done, is done at His will.'

Sri Ramakrishna: Oh! to what effect, if you simply say that in so many words? Any amount of your verbal denial of thorns can never save you from their painful prick when you place your hand on them. Had it been entirely with man to do spiritual practices according to his will, everybody would have done so. But no; everyone can't do it, and why? But there is one thing. If you don't utilise properly the amount of strength He has given you, He never gives more. That is why self-exertion is necessary. And so everyone has to struggle hard even to become fit for the grace of God. By such endeavour, and through His grace, the sufferings of many lives can be worked out in one life. But some self-effort is absolutely necessary. Let me tell you a story:

Once Vishnu, the Lord of Goloka, cursed Narada, saying that he would be thrown into hell. At this Narada was greatly disturbed in mind; and he prayed to the Lord, singing songs of devotion, and begging Him to show where hell is and how one can go there. Vishnu then drew the map of the universe on the ground with a piece of chalk, representing the exact position of heaven and hell. Then Narada said, pointing to the part marked 'hell', 'Is it like this? This is hell then!" So saying he rolled himself on the spot and exclaimed he had undergone all the sufferings of hell. Vishnu smilingly asked, "How is that?" and Narada replied, "Why, Lord, are not heaven and hell Thy creation? When Thou didst draw the map of the universe Thyself and point out to me the hell in the plan, then that place became a real hell; and as I rolled myself there, my sufferings were intense. So I do say that I have under-gone the punishments of hell." Narada said all this sincerely and so Vishnu was satisfied with the explanation.

1094. Pride once entered into the heart of Arjuna, the beloved friend of Sri Krishna. Arjuna thought that none equalled him in love and devotion to his Lord and friend. The omniscient Lord, Sri Krishna, reading the heart of His friend, took him one day for a walk. They had not proceeded far when Arjuna saw a strange Brahmin eating dry grass as food, but nevertheless had a sword dangling at his side. Arjuna at once knew him to be a holy and pious devotee of Vishnu, one whose highest religious duty was to injure no being. As even grass has life, he would not eat it green but sustained his life by eating it dry and lifeless. Yet he carried a sword. Arjuna, wondering at the incongruity, turned towards the Lord and said, "How is this? Here is a man who has renounced all ideas of injuring any living being, down to the meanest blade of grass; yet he carries with him a sword, the symbol of death and hatred!" The Lord said, "You better ask the man yourself." Arjuna then went up to the Brahmin and said, "Sir, you injure no living being, and you live upon dry grass. Why then do you carry this sharp sword?"

The Brahmin: It is to punish four persons if I chance to meet them.

Arjuna: Who are they?

The Brahmin: The first is the wretch Narada.

Arjuna: Why, what has he done?

The Brahmin: Why, look at the audacity of that fellow; he is perpetually keeping my Lord awake with his songs and music. He has no consideration whatsoever for the comfort of the Lord. Day and night, in and out of season, he disturbs the peace of the Lord by his prayers and praises.

Arjuna: Who is the second person?

The Brahmin: The imprudent Draupadi.

Arjuna: What is her fault?

The Brahmin: Look at the inconsiderate audacity of the woman; she was so rash as to call my beloved Lord just at the moment He was going to dine. He had to give up His dinner and go to the Kamyaka Vana to save the Pandavas from the curse of Durvasas. And her presumption went so far that she even caused my beloved Lord to eat the impure remnant of her own food.

Arjuna: Who is the third?

The Brahmin: It is the heartless Prahlada. He was so cruel that he did not hesitate for a moment to ask my Lord to enter the boiling cauldron of oil, to be trodden under the heavy feet of elephants, and to break through an adamantine pillar.

Arjuna: Who is the fourth?

The Brahmin: The wretch Arjuna.

Arjuna; Why, what fault has he committed?

The Brahmin: Look at his felony. He made my beloved Lord take the mean office of a charioteer of his car in the great war of Kurukshetra.

Arjuna was amazed at the depth of the poor Brahmin's devotion and love, and from that moment his pride vanished, and he gave up thinking that he was the best devotee of the Lord.

1095. In a certain village there lived a very pious weaver. Every one loved and trusted him. The weaver used to go to the market to sell his cloths. If a customer asked the price of a piece of cloth, he would say: "By the will of Rama, the thread costs one rupee; by the will of Rama, the labour costs four annas; by the will of Rama, the profit is two annas; by the will of Rama the price of the cloth as it stands is one rupee and six annas." People used to have such confidence in him that they would immediately pay the price and take the cloth. The man was a true devotee. At night after supper he would sit for a long time and meditate on God and repeat His holy 'name'.

Once it was late in the night. The weaver had not yet gone to sleep. He was sitting alone in the courtyard near the entrance, smoking. A gang of robbers was passing that way. They wanted a porter, and seeing this man, they dragged him away with them. Then they broke into a house and stole a great many things, some of which they piled on the poor weaver's head. At this moment the watchman came. The robbers at once ran away, but the poor weaver was caught with his load. He had to spend that night in confinement. Next morning he was brought before the magistrate. The people of the village, hearing what had happened, came to see the weaver. They unanimously declared, "Your Honour, this man is incapable of stealing anything." The magistrate then asked the weaver to describe what had occurred. The weaver said: "Your Honour, by the will of Rama, I was sitting in the courtyard. By the will of Rama, it was very late in the night. By the will of Rama, I was meditating upon God and repeating His holy 'name'. By the will of Rama, a band of robbers passed that way. By the will of Rama, they dragged me away with them. By the will of Rama, they broke into a house. By the will of Rama, they piled a load on my head. By the will of Rama, I was caught. Then by the will of Rama, I was kept in prison, and this morning I am brought before your Honour." The magistrate, seeing the innocence and spirituality of the man, ordered him to be acquitted. Coming out, the weaver said to his friends, "By the will of Rama, I have been released."

Whether you live in the world or renounce it, everything depends upon the will of Rama. Throwing your whole responsibility upon God, do your work in the world.

1096. A thief entered the palace of a king at the dead of night and overheard the king saying to the queen, "I shall give my daughter in marriage to one of those Sadhus (holy men) who are dwelling on the bank of the river." The thief thought within himself, "Well, here is good luck for me. I will go and sit among the Sadhus to-morrow in the disguise of a Sadhu, and perchance I may succeed in getting the king's daughter." The next day he did so. When the king's officers came soliciting the Sadhus to marry the king's daughter, none of them consented to it. At last they came to the thief in the guise of a Sadhu, and made the same proposal to him. The thief kept quiet. The officers went back and told the king that there was a young Sadhu who might be influenced to marry the princess, and that there was no other who would consent. The king then went to the Sadhu in person and earnestly entreated him to honour him by accepting the hand of his daughter. But the heart of the thief was changed at the king's visit. He thought within himself, "I have only assumed the garb of a Sadhu, and behold! the king himself comes to me and is all entreaties. Who can say what better things may not be in store for me if I become a real Sadhu!" These thoughts so strongly affected him that, instead of marrying under false pretences, he began to mend his ways from that very day, and exerted himself to become a true Sadhu. He did not marry at all, and ultimately became one of the most pious ascetics of his day. The counterfeiting of a good thing sometimes leads to unexpected good results.

TYAGA AND VAIRAGYA

1097. A man who was out of employment was constantly pressed by his wife to seek some job. One day when his son was dangerously ill and the doctors pronounced the case to be hopeless, he went out in search of employment. In the meantime the son died, and a search was made for the father, but he could not be found anywhere. At last, late in the evening, he returned home and was seriously taken to task by his wife for his callousness in leaving the house at a time when his son lay dying. The husband replied with a smile, "Well, once I dreamt that I had become a king and had seven sons, with whom I passed my time happily. But when I woke up I found none of them. It was all a dream. Well, tell me for whom should I grieve—for those seven sons of mine, or for the one you have lost just now?" He who feels this world to be a dream does not, like ordinary men, feel the pleasure or pain springing from worldly attachments.

1098. Once a young Sannyasin went to a house to beg his meal. He had embraced the monastic life from his very boyhood and so had not much knowledge of the world. A young lady came out from the house to give him alms. Seeing her breast, the young Sannyasin questioned her if she was suffering from boils on her chest. To that her mother replied, "No, my son, she hasn't got any boil. A child will be soon born to her, and so God has provided her with two breasts to suckle the child. The child will suck milk from those breasts after it is born." No sooner did the young Sannyasin heard this than he exclaimed, "No more will I beg my meals. He who created me, will feed me too."

1099. A husband and wife renounced the world and together undertook a pilgrimage to various holy shrines. Once as they were walking along a road, the husband, being a little ahead of the wife, saw a piece of diamond on the road. Immediately he began to scratch the ground to hide the diamond in it, thinking that, if his wife saw it, perchance she might be moved to avarice, and thus lose the merit of her renunciation. While he was thus scratching the ground, the wife came up and asked him what he was doing. He gave her, in an apologetic tone, an evasive reply. She, however, finding out the diamond and reading his thoughts, remarked, "Why did you leave the world, if you still feel the distinction between diamond and dust."

1100. How does a man come to have Vairagya (dispassion)? A wife once said to her husband, "Dear, I am very anxious about my brother. For the past one week he has been thinking of becoming an ascetic, and has been busy preparing for that life. He is trying to reduce gradually all his desires and wants." The husband replied, "Dear, be not at all anxious about your brother. He will never become a Sannyasin. No one can become a Sannyasin in that way." "How does one become a Sannyasin then?" asked the wife. "Thus" exclaimed the husband, so saying, he tore his flowing dress to pieces, took a piece and tied it round his loins, and told his wife that she and all of her sex were thenceforth mothers to him. He left the house, never more to return.

1101. "I shall complete it by and by", "I am about to take it up", "I am going to begin this"—all this is indicative of a procrastinating mood, and can result only in a lukewarm spirit of Vairagya. But he in whose heart the fire of renunciation burns intensely who pants after God as a mother's heart does for her child—he wants nothing except God. To him the world appears like a well without a wall; and he is always cautious lest he should fall into it. He does not think like others, "Let me first settle my family affairs and then I shall meditate on God." He has a fiery determination within him.

Once there was a great draught in a country. and all the husbandmen were busy bringing water into their fields by digging canals. One of them was a man of great determination, and had resolved to go on digging until he could connect his canal with the river. So he went on working, though it was getting late for his bath and meal. His wife sent him oil by their daughter, who came and said, "Papa, it is almost noon; rub this oil and have your bath." The father replied, "Wait, I have work still." It was past two o'clock, and still the peasant gave no thought to his bath or meal. At last his wife came to the field herself and said: "Why have you not taken your bath as yet? The meal has become cold and stale. You always go to extremes. Come away now at least. Do the rest of the work to-morrow, or after you have taken your food." The man at once grew furious, and chased her away with the hoe in hand, calling her names and abusing her. "Foolish and senseless woman!" he exclaimed, "don't you see the crop is drying up, and all of you will have to die of starvation? First I am determined to bring the water into the field to-day, and then shall think of other things." At this the woman went away. After herculean labour till late in the night, the man was at last able to carry out his determination. When he saw the water of the river flowing into the fields with a murmuring noise, his delight knew no bounds. Then coming home, he asked his wife to give some oil and prepare a pipe of tobacco. After his bath and meal, he slept soundly. This sort of determination is the right example of intense Vairagya.

Another peasant was also engaged in the same task. But when his wife came and asked him to come home, he followed her without any protest, laying the hoe on his shoulder and saying, "Well, as you have come, I must go." He was never able to bring the water into his field in time. This illustrates idle and procrastinating Vairagya. Without intense determination the irrigation of the field is not practicable; so without intense longing for Him no one can attain the blessed state of God-vision.

1102. Once a fisherman stealthily entered the garden of a certain gentleman in the night, and was poaching fish in his pond. The gentleman, having come to know of this, ordered his men to surround the place, and came with torches to find out the thief. In the meantime the fisherman, finding no means of escape, sat down underneath a tree like a Sadhu, having smeared his body with some ashes. So when the people came, they found no thief anywhere but only a Sadhu besmeared with holy ashes and deeply absorbed in meditation underneath a tree. Next morning it was made known to the people of the neighbourhood that a great Sadhu had come to such-and-such a person's garden. And so hundreds of people began to pour in with various presents of fruits and sweets to pay their homage to the Sadhu. Coins of silver and gold also began to gather in heaps before him. Then the fisherman thought within himself: "How wonderful! I am not a real Sadhu, still they are showing so much reverence to me! Then assuredly, if I become a real Sadhu, I can realise God." Thus even mere pretension brought about real awakening in the mind of that fisherman.

1103. Once a Sadhu acquired great occult powers, and so became very vain. But he was, on the whole, a good man and had performed many austerities. So to correct him, the Lord appeared before him in the garb of a Sannyasin and said, "Sir, I hear that you have attained great occult powers!" The Sadhu welcomed him with great respect, and asked him to sit down there. Just then an elephant was passing by, and seeing it, the Sannyasin said to the Sadhu, "Well, Sir, can you kill this elephant if you choose?" The Sadhu replied, "Yes, it can be done," and so saying, he took a handful of dust and threw it at the elephant, chanting certain incantations. The elephant at once fell down dead, writhing in agony. Then the Sannyasin observed, "Oh! how wonderful is your power! How easily have you killed the elephant!" The Sadhu smiled at these words of praise. The Sannyasin said again, "Well, can you bring the elephant back to life?" "Yes, that too can be done," he replied, and threw again a handful of dust at the dead elephant, whereupon the animal got up quite revived. At this the Sannyasin remarked, "Wonderful indeed is your power! But I would like to ask you one question. Just now you killed the elephant and then revived it, but what benefit did it bring to you? What improvement has it brought in you? Did it help you to attain God?" So saying, he disappeared.

1104. A wood-cutter led a very miserable life with the slender means he could procure by daily selling the load of wood be brought from a neighbouring forest. Once a Sannyasin, who was wending his way through the forest, saw him at work, and told him that he should go further into the forest so that he would be a gainer thereby. The wood-cutter obeyed the injunction and proceeded onward until he came to a sandalwood tree. He was much pleased, and took away with him as many sandal logs as he could carry and sold them in the market at a great profit. Then he began to consider why the good

Sannyasin did not tell him anything about the sandal trees, but simply advised him to proceed into the interior of the forest. So next day he went even beyond the region of the sandal trees, till at last he came upon a copper mine. He took with him as much copper as he could carry, and by selling it in the market got much money. Next day, without stopping at the copper mine, he proceeded further still, as the Sadhu had advised him to do, and came upon a silver mine. Then he took with him as much silver as he could carry, and sold it all and got even more money. And thus daily proceeding further and further, he reached gold mines and diamond mines, and at last became exceedingly rich. Such is also the case with the man who aspires after true Knowledge. If he does not stop in his progress after attaining a little of any extra-ordinary supernatural power, he at last becomes really rich in the eternal knowledge of the supreme Truth.

1105. During the reign of Akbar there lived a Fakir (a Muslim ascetic) in a certain forest near Delhi. Many used to resort to the cottage of this holy man. But as he had nothing with which to show hospitality to these visitors, he was in need of some money for this purpose and went for help to Akbar Shah, who was well known for his kindness to holy men. Akbar Shah was then saying his prayers, and the Fakir took his seat in the prayer room. In the course of his prayers Akbar was heard to say, "O Lord, do Thou grant me more wealth, more power, more territories!" At once the Fakir rose up and was about to steal out of the room when the Emperor beckoned him to be seated again.

At the end of the prayer, Akbar asked the Fakir, "Sir, you came to see me. How is it then that you wanted to depart without saying anything to me?" The Fakir said, "The object of my visit to Your Majesty . . . well, I need not trouble you with that." When Akbar repeatedly pressed him to say what he wanted, the Fakir at last said, "Your Majesty, many people come to me to be taught, but for want of money I am unable to see to their comforts. So I thought it well to come to Your Majesty for help." Akbar then asked why he was about to go away without having told him the object of his visit. The Fakir replied, "When I saw that you were yourself a beggar, begging of the Lord for fortune and power and territory, I said to myself, 'Why should I go a-begging to a person who is himself a beggar? I had better beg of the Lord Himself, if indeed it is not possible for me to do without begging altogether'."

1106. A Brahmin met a Sannyasin, and both had a long talk on worldly and religious topics. At last the Sannyasin said to the Brahmin: "Behold, child, there is no depending upon anyone in this world. None whom you call your own is yours." The Brahmin would not believe it. How could he think that those for whom he was toiling day and night, that is, the members of his own family, were not his friends on whom he could count for help? So the Brahmin said: "Sir, when I am troubled with even a slight headache, my mother is so much concerned that she is ready to give up even her life gladly if it will only bring relief to me. That such a mother is not a friend whom I can depend upon, is something I cannot conceive." The Sannyasin replied: "If such be the case, then of course she is a friend. But, to tell you the truth, you are greatly mistaken. Never believe for a moment that your mother, wife and son will sacrifice their lives for your sake. You can verify the truth of this if you like; go home and feign excruciating pain in your stomach and groan with it; I will come and show you some fun."

The Brahmin acted accordingly. Physicians were called in, but no one could afford any relief. The mother of the patient was sighing and sorrowing; the wife and children were crying. The Sannyasin turned up at this moment.

"The disease is of a serious nature," said the Sannyasin, "and I do not see any chance of the patient's recovery unless someone comes forward to give up his or her life for the sake of the patient." At this, all of them looked aghast. The Sannyasin, addressing the old mother of the patient, said: "To live or to die will be the same thing to you, if in your old age you lose your son who earns for himself and for you all. If you can give your life in exchange for his, I can save your son. If you, as his mother, cannot make this sacrifice for him, who else in this world will care to do it?"

The old woman blubbered forth through her tears: "Revered father, I am ready to do anything you order for the sake of my son. But the thing is, my own life. . . and what is my life in comparison to that of my son? The thought—what will become of my little ones after my death—makes me a coward. Unfortunate that I am, these little ones are in my way."

While listening to this dialogue between the Sannyasin and the mother-in-law, the wife of the patient wept bitterly and said, addressing her own parents, "For your sake, dear father and mother, I cannot make the sacrifice." The Sannyasin turned to her and asked her whether she would not sacrifice her life for the sake of her husband, now that his mother had fallen back. The wife said: "The wretch that I am! If widowhood is to be my lot, be it so. I cannot make up my mind to cause grief to my father and mother for the loss of their child." In this way every one wriggled out of the difficulty. Then the Sannyasin told the patient: "Look now, no one is ready here to sacrifice a life for you. Do you understand now what I meant by saying that there was no depending upon anybody in this world?" When the Brahmin saw all this, he abandoned his so-called home and followed the Sannyasin.

1107. A disciple said to his Guru that his wife loved him very much and so he could not renounce the world. The disciple used to practise Hathayoga. To convince him of the hollowness of his plea, the Guru taught him some secrets of this branch of Yoga. One day all on a sudden there was great consternation in the disciple's house, and wailings and sobbings were heard all around. The neighbours came running to the house and saw the Hatha Yogi disciple in a room, quite motionless, in a peculiar convoluted posture. They all thought that life was extinct in the body. The wife of the man was crying: "Alas! where have you gone, dear? Why have you forsaken us? Ah! we never knew that such a calamity would befall us!" In the meantime the relatives brought a cot to take the corpse out for cremation. Then they found themselves face to face with a serious difficulty. As the man was in a contorted posture, his body would not come out through the door. Seeing that, one of the neighbours brought an axe and began to cut the wooden frame of the door. Till then the wife was weeping in an uncontrollable fit of sorrow; but no sooner did she hear the sound of the axe than she ran to the spot, and, though still weeping, anxiously enquired what they were about. One of the neighbours told her that they were cutting the door as her husband's body could not otherwise be taken out owing to its peculiar posture. "No, no," cried out the wife, "don't do so now. I have been widowed, and there is none to look after me. I have to bring up my fatherless children. If you now cut the door, it cannot be repaired again. Whatever was to happen has happened to my husband. You had better cut his hands and legs and take him out." Hearing this, the Hatha Yogi at once stood up, the effect of the drug having gone by this time, and bawled out, "Woman, you want to cut my hands and legs?" And so saying, he went away with his Guru renouncing hearth and home.

NATURE OF MAYA

1108. A man was going through the woods. On his way he was caught by a band of three robbers. They robbed him of everything he had. Then the first robber asked, "What is the use of letting this man alive?" And drawing his sword, he was about to kill him, when the second robber stopped him, saying, "What is the good of killing him? Tie his hands and feet, and throw him aside." So they bound him hand and foot, and went away leaving him there. After they had gone some distance, the third robber returned and said to him, "Ah! are you hurt? Come, let me untie the cords and release you?" Then when he had removed the cords, he said, "Now come with me. I will show you the road." After walking a long distance, they found the road, and then the robber said, "Look, there is your home. Follow the road and you will soon reach it." The man thanked him and said, "Sir, you have done me a great service, I am greatly obliged to you. Will you not come with me to my house? The robber answered, "No, I cannot go there, the police will find me out."

This world is the wilderness. The three robbers are the three Gunas (constituents) of Nature—Sattva, Rajas and Tamas. Jiva or the individual soul is the traveller. Self-knowledge is his treasure. Tamas binds him with the fetters of the world, but Sattva protects him from the action of Rajas and Tamas. By taking refuge in Sattva, the Jiva becomes free from lust, anger and delusion which are the effects of Tamas; thus the Sattva quality emancipates the Jiva from the bondage of the world. But the Sattva quality itself is also a robber. It leads one, however, up to the path of the Supreme Abode and then it says, "Behold, there is your home!" Then it disappears. Even the Sattva quality cannot go into the region of the Absolute.

1109. A priest was once going to the village of a disciple of his. He had no servant with him. Seeing a cobbler on the way, he addressed him, saying, "Holloa!

good man, will you accompany me as a servant? You will be fed well and taken good care of if you come with me." The cobbler replied, "Sir, I am of the lowest caste. How can I come as your servant?" The priest said, "Never mind. Do not tell anybody what you are. Do not also speak to anyone, or make anybody's acquaintance." The cobbler agreed. At twilight, while the priest was sitting at prayers in the house of his disciple, another Brahmin came and said to the priest's servant, "Go and bring my shoes from there." True to the behest of his master, he made no response. The Brahmin repeated his order a second time, but even then the servant remained silent. The Brahmin repeated it again and again, but the cobbler did not move an inch. At last, getting annoyed, the Brahmin angrily said, "Sirrah! how dare you disobey a Brahmin's command?" What is your name? Are you indeed a cobbler?" The cobbler, hearing this, began to tremble with fear, and looking piteously at the priest, said, "O venerable Sir! I am found out. I dare not stay here any longer. Let me flee." So saying, he took to his heels. Just so, as soon as Maya is recognised, she flies away.

1110. Maya is unknowable. Once Narada besought the Lord of the universe, "Lord, show me that Maya of Thine which can make the impossible possible." The Lord nodded assent. Subsequently the Lord one day set out on a travel with Narada. After going some distance, He felt very thirsty and fatigued. So He sat down and told Narada, "Narada, I feel much thirsty; please get me a little water from somewhere." Narada at once ran in search of water.

Finding no water near by, he went far from the place and saw a river at a great distance. When he approached the river, he saw a most charming young lady sitting there, and was at once captivated by her beauty. As soon as Narada went near her, she began to address him in sweet words, and ere long, both fell in love with each other. Narada then married her, and settled down as a householder. In course of time he had a number of children by her. And while he was thus living happily with his wife and children, there came a pestilence in the country. Death began to collect its toll from every place. Then Narada proposed to abandon the place and go away somewhere else. His wife acceded to it, and they both came out of their house leading their children by the hand. But no sooner did they come to the bridge to cross the river than there came a terrible flood, and in the rush of water, all their children were swept away one after another, and at last the wife too was drowned. Overwhelmed with grief at his bereavement, Narada sat down on the bank and began to weep piteously. Just then the Lord appeared before him, saying, "O Narada, where is the water? and why are you weeping?" The sight of the Lord startled the sage, and then he understood everything. He exclaimed, "Lord, my obeisance to Thee, and my obeisance also to Thy wonderful Maya!"

1111. Once a tigress attacked a flock of sheep. She was with child, and so when she jumped on the flock, she gave birth to a cub and died. But the cub survived and grew up among the flock of sheep. The sheep grazed in the field and the cub too did accordingly. They bleated and it also tried to imitate them. In course of time it became a full-grown tiger. By chance, one day, another tiger came and attacked the flock, but he was surprised to see the sheep-tiger in the flock. Then he chased it and caught it by the neck. But it began to bleat in fear like the sheep. The old tiger, however, dragged it to a pond and showing it the reflection of both of them in the water, said, "Look, your form is similar to mine. You are also a tiger like myself. Now eat this piece of flesh." And so saying, he forced the flesh into its mouth. But at first the sheep-tiger would eat it by no means. It bleated and said that it was a sheep. But as soon as it got a little taste of blood, its dormant instinct was quickened and it began to eat the flesh. Then the old tiger said, "Now have you understood that you are the same as myself? So come along with me into the forest." In the same way if one has the grace of the Guru, there is no fear. The Guru will open your eyes and tell you who you are and what your real self is.

1112. In the course of self-analysis, when the mind reaches the state of perfect peace, there comes the revelation of Supreme Brahman.

Once a man wanted to see the king. The king lived in the inner apartment of the palace beyond seven gates. The man came to the palace and saw at the first gate a person sitting in a great pomp surrounded by a retinue. Seeing him, the man who was going to the king asked his friend, "Is that the king?" The friend said with a smile, "No." Next he passed through the other gates one after another and in each successive gate he saw persons sitting surrounded with greater and greater pomp and show. The more he advanced into the interior of the palace the more was the grandeur of the people whom he saw. And at every succeeding stage he thought that he beheld the king and so questioned his friend. But when he crossed the seventh gate, and came face to face with the king himself, he felt no necessity of asking his friend whether the man was the king. For he was dumbfounded by the very sight of the immense grandeur of the king, and felt sure that he was standing in the august presence of royalty.

REALISATION OF THE DIVINE

1113. A Certain devout lady, who was also a faithful wife, lived with her husband, serving him and their children with a loving heart, and at the same time keeping her mind fixed on the Lord. At her husband's death, as soon as the cremation was over, she broke her glass bangles and wore a pair of gold bracelets in their place. People wondered at her unnatural conduct, but she explained to them, "Hitherto my husband's body was fragile like the glass bangles. That ephemeral body is now gone, and he is therefore like one unchangeable and whole in every respect. His body is no longer fragile. So I have discarded the fragile glass bangles and put on ornaments of a permanent nature."

1114. Once there came to Dakshineswar two Sadhus who were father and son. The son had attained true Knowledge, but the father had not. Both were sitting in the room where Sri Ramakrishna lived and were talking with him. In the meantime, a young cobra came out of a rat-hole and bit the son. Seeing that, the father was terribly frightened and began to call all the people around. But the son sat quiet, and that puzzled the father still more. When he asked the son why he was sitting quiet, the son laughed and was heard to explain, "Which is the snake and whom has it bitten?" He had realised the Unity, and hence he could not make any distinction between a man and a snake.

1115. An outcaste was carrying baskets of meat from a slaughter-house. On the way he met Sankaracharya who was returning after his bath in the sacred Ganges. It chanced that the outcaste touched the person of the holy man. Sankara was offended and cried out, "You have touched me, sirrah!" The outcaste replied, "Sir, neither have I touched you, nor have you touched me! Please reason with me and say whether your true Self is the body or the mind or the intellect; tell me what you truly are. You know that the true Self is not attached to any of the three Gunas of Nature, Sattva, Rajas and Tamas." Then Sankara was abashed and had the true awakening.

1116. Once a Sadhu placed his disciple in a magnificent garden with the intention of imparting to him the knowledge of the real Self and went away. After a few days he came back and asked the disciple, "Do you feel any want, my boy?" On being answered in the affirmative, he left with him a fair woman named Shyama, and advised him to take fish and meat freely. After a considerable time he came again and asked the same question as before. This time the disciple replied, "No, I have no want, thank you." The Sadhu then called both the disciple and Shyama to him and pointing to Shyama's hands, asked the disciple, "Can you tell me what these are?" "Why, these are Shyama's hands," replied the disciple. He put the same question several times, pointing to Shyama's eyes, nose and other parts of the body, and the disciple gave appropriate answers. Presently the idea struck the disciple, "I am talking of everything as Shyama's 'this' and Shyama's 'that'. What then is this Shyama?" Bewildered, he asked his Guru the question, "But who is this Shyama to whom belong these eyes, ears and the rest?" The Sadhu said, "If you wish to know who this Shyama is, come with me, and I will enlighten you." So saying, he revealed to him the secret.

1117. A certain father had two sons. When they were old enough, they were admitted to the first stage of life (Brahmacharya), and placed under the care of a religious preceptor to study the Vedas. After a long time the boys returned home, having finished their studies. Their father asked them if they had read the Vedanta. On their replying in the affirmative, he asked, "Well, tell me what is Brahman." The elder son, quoting the Vedas and other scriptures, replied: "O Father, It is beyond words and thought. It is so and so. I know it all." And to support what he said, he again quoted Vedantic texts.

"So you have known Brahman!" said the father, "you may go about your business." Then he asked the younger son the same question. But the boy remained silent; not a word came out of his mouth, nor did he make any attempt to speak. At this the father remarked: "Yes, my boy, you are right. Nothing can be predicated of the Absolute and the Unconditioned. No sooner do you talk of It than you state the Infinite in terms of the finite, the Absolute in terms of the relative, the Unconditioned in terms of the conditioned. Your silence is more eloquent than the recitation of a hundred verses and the quoting of a hundred authorities."

1118. A learned Brahmin once went to a wise king and said, "I am well-versed, O king, in the holy scriptures. I intend to teach you the Bhagavata." The king, who was the wiser of the two, knew well that a man who had really studied the Bhagavata would seek to know his own Self rather than go to a king's court for wealth and honour. So the king replied, "I see, O Brahmin, that you yourself have not mastered that book thoroughly. I promise to make you my tutor, but first learn the scripture well." The Brahmin went his way, thinking, "How foolish it is of the king to say that I have not mastered the Bhagavata, seeing that I have been reading the book over and over all these years." However, he went through the book carefully once more and appeared again before the king. The king told him the same thing again and sent him away. The Brahmin was sorely vexed, but thought that there must be some meaning in the behaviour of the king. He went home, shut himself up in his room and applied himself more than ever to the study of the book. By and by hidden meanings began to flash into his mind and the vanity of running after the bubbles of riches and honour, kings and courts, wealth and fame, appeared to his unclouded vision. From that day forward he gave himself up entirely to attaining perfection by the worship of God, and never thought of returning to the king. A few years after, the king thought of the Brahmin and went to his house to see what he was doing. Seeing him, now radiant with Divine light and love, he fell upon his knees and said, "I see that you have now realised the true meaning of the scriptures. I am ready to be your disciple if you will duly condescend to make me one."

1119. There was a Hindu monastery in a certain village. The monks used to go out every day with begging bowls to gather food. One day, a monk, while going on his rounds, saw a Zemindar (landlord) severely beating a poor man. The holy man, being very kindhearted, entreated the Zemindar to stop beating the man. The Zemindar, blind with rage, immediately turned on the monk and vented all his anger upon him. He belaboured him so heavily that the monk fell down unconscious on the ground. Another man, seeing the condition of the monk, went to the monastery and told what had happened. His brethren ran to the spot where he was lying. They carried him to the monastery and laid him in a room; but the holy man still remained unconscious for a long time. Sorrowful and anxious, the Brothers fanned him, bathed his face with cold water, poured milk into his mouth, and did all that was possible to revive him. Gradually he regained consciousness. When he opened his eyes and looked at the monks, one of them, desiring to know whether he could recognise his friends, asked him in a loud voice, "Revered sir, do you recognise him who is feeding you with milk?" The holy man answered in a feeble voice, "Brother, he who beat me is now feeding me." One cannot realise this oneness of Spirit unless one has reached God-consciousness and has gone beyond good and evil, and virtue and vice.

1120. Once in a certain village there lived a young man named Padmalochan, who was nicknamed as Podo by the villagers. In that village there was an old dilapidated temple. There was no sacred image of God inside the temple, and the whole building was overgrown with shrubs and trees, and formed a convenient residence for birds and bats. One evening, all of a sudden, people heard the sounds of song and conch issuing from the deserted temple. Men, women and children all ran eagerly to the place, thinking that some devotee might have newly installed an image of God, and was performing the evening service. With folded hands they all waited outside to see the image listening to the sacred sounds. But one of them, more inquisitive than the rest, had the courage to peep in through the doors. To his surprise he saw that it was Podo who was ringing the bell and blowing the conch inside. The floor of the shrine room was as dirty as before, and there was no image to worship. He then called out saying, "O Podo, you have no image of Madhava in your temple! And behold! you have not even taken the trouble of cleansing and purifying the temple! Day and night the eleven bats screech there. Ah, for nothing you have raised all this clamour by the loud blowing of the conch!" So if you want to install the sacred image of God within the temple of your heart, that is, if you want to realise Him, what is the use of merely blowing your conch for nothing?

First purify your heart. When the mind becomes pure, the Lord Himself comes and makes it His seat. No image of God can be set up in a dirty place. The eleven bats referred to above are the eleven senses (the five organs of knowledge, the five organs of action and the mind). First dive deep within your own self and get the gems lying hidden there. After that you can have everything else. First you have to enshrine Madhava in the heart; then you can have enough of lecturing and preaching.

INDEX

(The outline of the subject-matter of each chapter may also be consulted for reference. The numbers given below are of the sayings, and not of the pages. The sayings indicated by asterisks in the body of the book are new ones incorporated from the enlarged fourth edition onward.)